COMPARATIVE
CULTURAL
ANALYSIS

COMPARATIVE CULTURAL ANALYSIS

AN INTRODUCTION TO ANTHROPOLOGY

Second Edition

KEITH F. OTTERBEIN
State University of New York at Buffalo

HOLT, RINEHART AND WINSTON
New York Chicago San Francisco Atlanta Dallas Montreal Toronto London Sydney

To My Wife

Extracts and photographs from *The Andros Islanders: A Study
of Family Organization in the Bahamas* by Keith F. Otterbein.
© copyright 1966 by the University of Kansas Press. By
permission of the University Press of Kansas.

Extracts and photographs from *The Qemant: A Pagan-Hebraic Peasantry
of Ethiopia* by Frederick C. Gamst. Copyright © 1969 by Holt, Rinehart and
Winston, Inc., and extracts from *Yąnomamö: The Fierce People* by Napoleon
A. Chagnon. Copyright © 1968 by Holt, Rinehart and Winston, Inc.
Reprinted by permission of the publisher.

Yąnomamö photographs courtesy of Napoleon A. Chagnon.

Library of Congress Cataloging in Publication Data

Otterbein, Keith F
      Comparative cultural analysis.

      Bibliography: p. 257
      1. Ethnology.   I. Title.
GN316.085   1977   301.2   76–47694

ISBN 0–03–089991–5

PREFACE

Basically what this book does is to lay out systematically the important topics and key concepts of cultural anthropology. The topics and concepts are discussed in detail in the following chapters, and they are summarized on a data sheet at the end of this book. This set of concepts is fundamental to all research in anthropology. It is the conceptual order that, so to speak, underlies the anthropological subculture. Mastery of this order is a *sine qua non* for becoming a professional anthropologist. Thus it is necessary for students—both those wishing only an introductory knowledge of anthropology and those wishing to become competent professionals—to learn the important concepts of cultural anthropology. This book (and it is the only one of its kind) provides a technique which makes it possible for students in a classroom situation to simultaneously learn many key concepts while becoming familiar with a few of the cultures which have been studied by anthropologists. Students learn to analyze a cultural system, as presented in an ethnography, in the same manner that an ethnographer analyzes the way of life of the particular people among whom he is conducting fieldwork.

This textbook is based upon a teaching technique which I developed ten years ago for use in an introductory cultural anthropology course. The technique consisted of reducing many of the important topics in anthropology to a set of questions which incorporated, as answers to the questions, many of the key concepts of the discipline. A data sheet listed twenty-five questions and the accompanying concepts. The sheet contained no definitions of the concepts, since these were provided through classroom lectures. The first week of the course (it was a six-week summer course) consisted of lectures in which I discussed the topics and defined the concepts. For the remainder of the course the students read four different ethnographies and, using copies of the data sheet, recorded passages which provided information on the twenty-five topics. They also tried to identify the concepts which correctly described the passages which they had recorded. Methodologically the concepts represented the culture traits, processes, or activities which were described in the ethnographies. Throughout most of the course the students and I discussed the reasons for classifying the different ethnographic statements as examples of the various concepts. Then during the last week of the course we recorded on a chart the concepts which pertained to each culture. We were thus able to compare our four cultures in terms of the twenty-five topics and to draw inferences as to what topics might be functionally related. That is, we attempted to make intelligent guesses as to what culture traits and processes are related in the real world. For example, population density might be related to the type of subsistence technology practiced. Specifically, it was found that a low population density was associated with a hunting and gathering technology, and a high population density was associated with agriculture.

This technique was developed in response to what I believe is a major defect in most anthropology textbooks. The ethnographic examples used in the textbooks are drawn from a large number of cultures—seldom do more than several examples come from any one culture. Often the examples are either extreme, rare, or atypical cases. In response, many instructors of anthropology, including myself, have found it easier to teach using ethnographic case studies, such as those published by Holt, Rinehart and Winston, than using a standard textbook. This allows us to illustrate concepts with examples from a limited number of cultures and to devote our time to discussions of functional interrelationships between culture traits and processes within specific cultures. The reading of these case studies shows a student how the different aspects of a cultural system are interrelated in each of a small number of cultures. Thus emphasis is not placed upon atypical examples taken out of context. Nor is the student confused by dozens of exotic examples from dozens of cultures.

In a volume titled *The Teaching of Anthropology* (Mandelbaum, Lasker, and Albert 1963), David Mandelbaum has expressed a similar viewpoint in this way (1963:52–53):

Good ethnographic monographs . . . make fine reading for undergraduates. I have found it effective to have students read one or two brief monographs in the first few weeks of introductory cultural anthropology. Even in a few weeks they can acquire some of the leading concepts which they can apply to the data in the monographs. The analytic, problem-tackling, frontier-exploring qualities of anthropology can be brought in usefully in these early stages, so that the student is not simply reading about quaint customs and discovering that he too has customs and culture, but is also encouraged to set his mind to seeing some order, themes, and linkages within a culture.

Four pedagogical purposes are also served by developing the above technique into an introductory anthropology textbook: (1) The book provides a succinct list of the major topics and concepts in cultural anthropology. Thus it can be used as a reference or as a glossary of terms. (2) The book assists students in learning the fundamental concepts of cultural anthropology by requiring them to find examples in ethnographic case studies which correctly illustrate the concepts. Most instructors and most textbooks do this for the student; however, if the student is asked to do it for himself, the learning process becomes active rather than remaining passive. (3) By reading and rereading portions of the textbook and by applying the concepts, the students develop a "set" which will make ethnographically important facts (that is, the data pertaining to theoretically important topics) readily apparent while the case studies are being read. (4) The book furnishes a systematic outline which can be used to record ethnographic data. Once the descriptions found in a particular case study have been classified as to what concepts they illustrate, the completed outline can be used by students in reviewing for examinations. Once two or more outlines have been completed, the cultures which have been succinctly described can be compared. Such comparisons can be used by the instructor to demonstrate the possible existence of functional relationships between culture traits and processes, and the outlines can be used by students in doing research projects and in writing term papers.

A new edition of *Comparative Cultural Analysis* has been prepared in order to make it easier for students and instructors to analyze nonprimitive cultures with the technique developed in the first edition. While many colleagues and former students seem satisfied in general with the technique, they have in particular felt that its utility could be enhanced if I broadened the scope of the book to explicitly cover such groups of peoples as modern nations and peasant communities. This I believe I have done by adding new sections and a new set of examples from an additional ethnography.

Five new sections have been added, three of which—The People, Language, and History—have formed the nucleus of a new chapter titled "Land and People." The introductory section of this chapter describes the scope of ethnographic research, as it once was and as it is today. The background information provided permits delineation of the kind of group the anthropologist studied, whether it be a state (primitive, preindustrial, or modern), a primitive culture, a dependent native people, a peasant community, or an ethnic group. Two new sections—House Form and Stratification—have been added to the chapter on "Technology and Economy." Nearly all the sections have been revised, the main purpose being to increase clarity. Two sections have been combined—Local Economy and Economy of the Culture are now Economy. The section on Political Communities has been incorporated into the Political System section. One section has been dropped—Subsistence Participation. In some sections the discussion and the question have been simplified (for example, Kindreds); in other sections new material has been added to clarify (for example, Descent Groups). Where appropriate recent empirical studies are reviewed.

The new set of examples is taken from my own ethnography dealing with the family organization of the inhabitants of Andros Island in the Bahamas. The Andros Islanders were chosen primarily because they are an English-speaking people whose culture is similar, in terms of the concepts and culture traits described in this book, to the culture of many Americans. By first presenting an example, for each topic discussed, which is similar to the beliefs and practices of many readers, it is hoped that the student will begin to realize that we are all—not just so-called primitive peoples—participants in cultural systems. In other words, the student will be introduced to the familiar first, rather than to the unfamiliar and exotic, as was the case in the first edition. Furthermore, since the fishing and farming communities of the Andros Islanders are in a modern nation, the student is first introduced to a nonprimitive culture. This will show the applicability of the technique to the kinds of groups of people found frequently in the modern world.

Also new to this edition are the Study Guide Questions at the end of each chapter as well as the Case Study Questions on seven published case studies which are at the end of this text.

Comparative Cultural Analysis has been and can be used in the following kinds of courses. In introductory anthropology courses it can be used in conjunction with two or three ethnographies and two other small books, one dealing with archaeology and the other physical anthropology. In a general cultural anthropology course it can be used with several ethnographies and a collection of articles or reprints which deal in greater depth with the topics covered in the textbook. It can be used in area courses along with a general work on the area, plus several ethnographies. It can be used as a supplementary book in methods courses, whether a course on field methods or comparative methods. And, in graduate level survey courses it can be assigned if a basic reference work is desired.

K. F. O.

Buffalo, N. Y.
December 1976

ACKNOWLEDGMENTS

I am indebted to several individuals who have assisted me at various stages in the preparation of this manuscript. My wife, Charlotte Swanson Otterbein, encouraged me to develop the teaching technique presented here into a book which could be used in introductory cultural anthropology courses. She has spent many hours commenting on and editing the manuscript of both editions of the book. The distinction between economic relationships within the local group and between local groups is the contribution of Terrence A. Tatje. Ralph Bolton, Alan G. LaFlamme, Gay E. Kang, and Donald F. Griffiths critically read the first edition and their thinking influenced various sections of the second edition. George and Louise Spindler reviewed the manuscript in its earliest stages. Roger Basham contributed the Study Guide Questions at the end of each chapter as well as the questions for the seven Case Studies in the Appendix.

CONTENTS

Preface   v

1. Introduction   1

Basic Concepts   2
Anthropological Research   8
How To Use This Book   12
Study Guide Questions   14

2. Land and People   17

The People   18
Language   24
Physical Environment   27
History   32
Study Guide Questions   36

3. Technology and Economy   39

Subsistence Technology   40
Population Density   44
Division of Labor   47
House Form   49
Settlement Pattern   54

Settlement Size   57
Economy   59
Stratification   67
Study Guide Questions   70

4. Family and Kinship   75

Residence   76
Marriage   83
Household Type   88
Descent Groups   95
Kindreds   104
Cousin Marriage   108
Kinship Terminology   112
Study Guide Questions   118

5. Law and Warfare   121

Political System   122
Political Leaders   129
Legal System   133
Military Organizations   137
Feuding   141
Warfare   146
Causes of War   148
Study Guide Questions   151

6. World View and Life Cycle   155

Supernatural Beings   156
Religious Practitioners   163
Magic   166
Sorcery   171
Post-partum Sex Taboo   176
Games   179
Initiation Rites   184
Art   188
Study Guide Questions   193

7. Conclusion   197

Comparison of Cultures and Culture Traits   198
Linkages and Hypotheses   203

Testing of Hypotheses   206
Study Guide Questions   211

Appendix   **215**

1. Data Sheet   215
2. Case Study Questions for Seven Cases   220

      Downs: *The Navajo*, 220; Downs: *The Two Worlds of the Washo*, 223;
      Hart and Pilling: *The Tiwi of North Australia*, 225; Hoebel: *The*
      Cheyenne: Indians of the Great Plains, 228; Lessa: *Ulithi: A*
      Micronesian Design for Living, 230; Keiser: *The Vice Lords: Warriors*
      of the Streets, 233; Kuper: *The Swazi: A South African Kingdom*, 235

Glossary   **241**

References   **257**

Name and Title Index   **265**

Subject Index   **267**

COMPARATIVE CULTURAL ANALYSIS

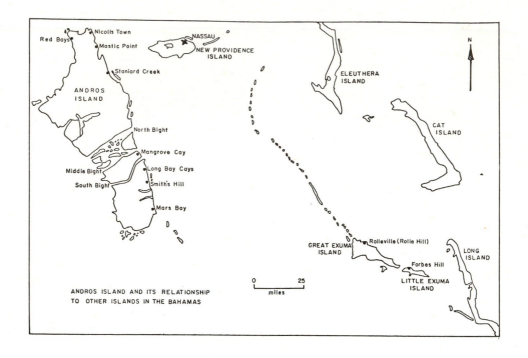

ANDROS ISLAND AND ITS RELATIONSHIP
TO OTHER ISLANDS IN THE BAHAMAS

Aerial view of Long Bay Cays, Andros Island, Bahamas.

1

INTRODUCTION

Basic Concepts
Anthropological Research
How to Use This Book

When I was an undergraduate I told my father that I wanted to become an anthropologist. He asked me what I was going to do with it. I knew that his question meant: How are you going to earn a living? But at that time I did not care if I ever earned a living. I told him that an anthropologist studies people. I then went on to say that I wanted to be a cultural anthropologist and that cultural anthropology is the study of the way different groups of people live. He looked puzzled, so I told him that I wanted to go to a tropical island and study the sex life of the natives. That ended the conversation. Several years later I did go to a tropical island. The study resulting from this trip is a detailed description of the way of life of the people who

1

live on Andros Island in the Bahamas (see map on facing p. 1), and focuses on courtship, marriage, and the family (Otterbein 1966).

This introductory chapter describes, in more precise terms than I told my father, what cultural anthropologists study and how they conduct their research. A few basic concepts are defined, and instructions are provided for using this book.

BASIC CONCEPTS

The primary concept employed by anthropologists is *culture*. It is used in two senses. First, culture refers to the way of life of a particular group of people. It is everything that a group of people thinks, and says, and does, and makes. Culture is learned: it is transmitted from generation to generation. When anthropologists refer to the culture of a people, they are referring to a large and diverse number of topics which include technological pursuits, marriage customs, military practices, and religious beliefs. All the topics discussed in the next five chapters, with the exception of physical environment, are aspects of the culture or way of life of a people. Second, if the article *a* precedes the term culture, it refers to the particular group of people themselves. If the term *culture* is used in the plural, it refers to different groups of people. Anthropologists have no difficulty in shifting from one usage of the term *culture* to the other; in fact, they often speak of the culture of a culture. For example, it is as easy to speak of the culture of the Andros Islanders as it is to say that the Andros Islanders are a Caribbean culture. (The way of life of the Andros Islanders, of the Yanomamö Indians of South America, and of the Qemant of Ethiopia will be used throughout this book to illustrate many aspects of culture.)

Although there is not complete agreement among anthropologists, perhaps the most satisfactory way of distinguishing one group of people—one culture—from another is to use two criteria: language distinctness and geographic separation (Ember 1963: 235–236). Language distinctness is an appropriate criterion because not only is it an important aspect of culture, but it is also the major means by which culture is transmitted or taught to the young. If two groups of people speak different languages, they are different cultures. Languages are different if the speaker of one language cannot understand the speaker of the other language. (The criterion of language distinctness is difficult to apply in those few regions of the world where there are "linguistic continuums" or "language chains." For example, the German-Dutch dialects spoken along the Rhine

River constitute a linguistic continuum. Naroll [1968: 248–249] has proposed a technique for dividing these continuums into "chain links," each link of which can be considered a culture.) Geographic separation, the second criterion, permits the delineation into separate cultures those peoples who, though not living contiguously, speak the same language. For example, the various English-speaking peoples throughout the world who are geographically separate from each other constitute different cultures. On the other hand, English-speaking North Americans whether they live in Canada or the United States are one culture since they speak one language and are geographically contiguous. Using these two criteria, a culture can be defined as "a continuously distributed population whose members speak a common language . . ." (Ember 1963:236).

The use of the term *culture* to refer both to a group of people and to their way of life entered the vocabulary of anthropologists after 1900, due primarily to the efforts of Franz Boas and many of his students. Until his death in 1941, Boas was the major figure in American anthropology. Prior to 1900 the term culture was used in a different sense—it referred to the "progressive accumulation of the characteristic manifestations of human creativity: art, science, knowledge, refinement . . ." (Stocking 1966:870). Different groups of people could have a greater or a lesser amount of culture. Thus Edward B. Tylor, one of the founders of anthropology, could state in 1888 that "among peoples of low culture . . ." (this passage is quoted in its entirety in the section dealing with cousin marriage). Tylor's definition of culture (1958:1; orig. 1871) as "that complex whole which includes knowledge, belief, art, morals, law, custom, and any other capabilities and habits acquired by man as a member of society" is ambiguous since it does not state that culture is acquired by men as members of particular cultures, nor does it make explicit that only creative, rational capacities were considered culture at that time (Stocking 1966).

Since the days of Franz Boas, the concept of culture has undergone modification and elaboration. The major direction in which these changes have occurred is toward a position which views a culture as an entity composed, on one hand, of beliefs, symbols, and values, sets of standards for perceiving, believing, evaluating, and acting, cultural traditions, or jural rules, and, on the other hand, of interactive behavior, social interaction, and social structure, a material-behavioral system of interacting people and things, relationships between human beings, or statistical norms. Thus a culture is viewed as consisting of rules (that is, statements of ideal behavior) and behavior (whether the behavior corresponds to the rules or not).

Some anthropologists speak of the rules as being culture per se and the behavior as forming a social system; then the entity composed of rules and behavior together is termed a society, a sociocultural system, or for short, a cultural system. This distinction is important, for it forces the anthropologist to take cognizance of the ideals which motivate people and at the same time to examine the frequency with which a people conform to the rules. Attention is paid to this distinction in this book, particularly in the chapter titled "Family and Kinship."

For convenience and because most anthropologists—in conversation at least—still employ the term culture in its two senses, the dual usage of Boas will be maintained throughout this book. Thus, the entire way of life of a group of people is referred to as their culture, while at the same time the group of people themselves is referred to as a culture. Moreover, although some anthropologists use the term *society* in referring to a particular culture, cultures such as the Andros Islanders will not be referred to as societies, nor will the term *societies* be used as synonymous with the plural form of culture—cultures.

Cultures can be viewed as systems composed of overlapping subsystems. Four subsystems are usually distinguished (Beals 1967: 250–251): economic, social, political, and belief systems. An economic system consists of the means by which the physical environment is exploited technologically and the means by which the products of this endeavor are differentially allocated to the members of the culture. A social system is composed of the relationships between kinsmen and the groups formed by kinsmen as well as voluntary groups formed from kinsmen and/or nonkinsmen. A political system consists of power-oriented organizational units, their leaders, the relationships which leaders have with members of their units, and relationships between units. And finally, a belief system is composed of the knowledge which people have of the world around them and the practices and customs by which people utilize that knowledge. Each subsystem forms a complete system in the sense that it is not possible to understand any aspect of that subsystem without knowing something about the other aspects of the subsystem. For example, in the economic system it is not possible to understand how products are differentially allocated until one knows how each product is produced, who produces it, how scarce it is, and what materials from the physical environment are utilized in its production. By the same token, each subsystem can only be completely understood when something is known about the other three subsystems, because in reality the four subsystems are interdependent.

Using the above example again, one might ask—are the products (economic subsystem) allocated to kinsmen (social system), political leaders (political subsystem), or supernatural beings (belief subsystem)? For this reason the four subsystems are said to overlap and to form a single cultural system. Various aspects of each of these subsystems are described in the chapters of this book. The economic system is described in a chapter titled "Technology and Economy," the social system in a chapter titled "Family and Kinship," the political system in two chapters titled "Land and People" and "Law and Warfare," and the belief system in a chapter titled "World View and Life Cycle." Each of these subsystems is a network of interrelated culture traits.

The culture of a people is composed of innumerable culture traits. Although the *culture trait* has been defined as the "smallest identifiable unit in a given culture" (Herskovits 1948:170), the term in actual practice is applied to any aspect of a people's way of life. It is used in such an all-encompassing sense that, for example, every house or dwelling in a culture, the most frequently occurring type of house in a culture, and the rules or "blueprint" used to build this typical house can all be considered culture traits (see House Form in Chapter 3). In other words, a culture trait is a catch-all term for any pursuit, custom, practice, or belief characteristic of a particular group of people. Hence, it is a useful term for referring to an aspect of a culture. Sometimes cultures are described or summarized by lists of culture traits. (In the "Conclusion" of this book, a list of thirty-four culture traits is used to summarize Andros Island, Yanomamö, and Qemant culture.) These lists of culture traits may be short, ten or twenty items, or they may be long—one list exceeds 2000 items (Herskovits 1948:169–182).

Some culture traits are considered to be more important than others. The more culture traits a particular culture trait influences or is influenced by, the more important it is deemed to be. Since important culture traits are interrelated, in the sense of having a mutual influence upon each other, they form networks or systems. Four such systems, described above, are the economic, social, political, and belief systems. They can be thought of as subsystems since they overlap—some important culture traits are members of two or more subsystems—and form a single cultural system. For example, American Indians who lived on the Great Plains used the horse economically for hunting, but when it was used in marriage transactions it also fell within the social system; if the horse conferred leadership standing, it entered the political system; and, finally, if the horse was killed at the death of the warrior, it entered the belief system. Important culture traits and the subsystems in which they are usually found are described in the five main chapters of this book. For an anthropologist an adequate description of a people's culture is a report which describes the important culture traits— and their interrelationships—which are present in the culture. A major purpose of this book is to set forth in systematic fashion a series of concepts which describe or summarize the important culture traits of a particular culture.

Cultures are distributed spatially over the earth's surface. Usually a culture occupies a specific portion of this surface; its territory can be delineated on a map. (Occasionally, perhaps because of military conquest, two or more cultures will occupy the same territory.) The members of most cultures are to be found living as members of specific local groups (Linton 1936:209–230). A *local group* is a geographically distinguishable aggregate of people. It may be as small as a single family or as large as a city. Thus local groups within a culture can vary in size and complexity. A culture can be so small —in either territory or population size—that it contains only one local group, or it can be so large that it contains hundreds of local groups. Local groups—as well as cultures—can usually be delineated on a map. One of the first anthropological accounts of a culture to utilize the notion of local group is A. R. Radcliffe-Brown's well-known study of *The Andaman Islanders* (1922); these people lived in small hunting and fishing villages on the Andaman Islands in the Bay of Bengal. If a sufficiently detailed map is available (that is, a map which shows man-made structures), local groups can be delineated by drawing circles around clusters of structures. Cultures, in a similar fashion, can be delineated by drawing circles around the local groups of each culture. This technique is graphically illustrated in Figure 1. The term *local group* is not synonymous with the term *community*. For most anthropologists a community is "the maximal group of persons who normally reside together in face-to-face association" (Murdock *et al.* 1961:89). This definition has been understood to mean that when a local group becomes so large that each adult member does not know every other member of the local group, it ceases to be a community. Hence, large towns and cities—although local groups—are not communities in the sense that the term *community* is commonly used by anthropologists.

The local groups in most cultures are organized into territorial units known as *political communities*. The organization derives from the existence of a leader or leaders who perform tasks which are important to the members of the local groups composing the political community. Sometimes the local groups are not organized into larger

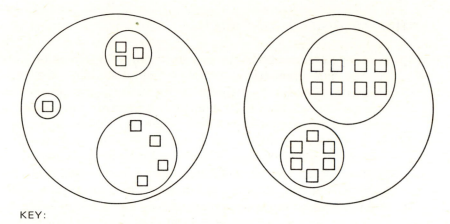

KEY:

Squares represent man-made structures
Small circles represent local groups
Large circles represent cultures

FIGURE 1. Diagram of Basic Concepts—I

units, but are themselves political communities. The functions performed by the leaders of political communities may include ceremonial, economic, and political tasks. Ceremonial tasks may include
the blessing of crops and animals, serving as an intermediary between men and gods, or simply being a symbol of territorial unity.
Economic tasks may include serving as the redistribution agent for
a nonlocal allocative center or the overseer of an economic system
based upon market exchange (see "Economy," in Chapter 3). Political
tasks may include the adjudication of disputes, the enforcement of
decisions, and the initiation and direction of warfare. None of these
tasks is necessarily performed by the leader of a political community. In order to recognize territorial units and their leaders in
accounts written by anthropologists, it is necessary to have a definition of political community. Such a definition has been provided by
Raoul Naroll (1964:268): "A group of people whose membership is
defined in terms of occupancy of a common territory and who have an
official with the special function of announcing group decisions—a
function exercised at least once a year." Although this is Naroll's
definition of a "territorial team," it is preferable for semantic reasons to call territorial units *political communities*—it is difficult to
conceptualize large states as teams—and to call the officials or
leaders of such territorial units political leaders. A further defini-
tional requirement of a political community is that it is a maximal
territorial unit; that is, it is not included within a larger unit.

ANTHROPOLOGICAL RESEARCH

In order to learn about the way of life of a particular group of people, an anthropologist undertakes field research in that culture. Ideally this involves living with the members of the culture for a year or more and learning their language. A year of "fieldwork" is desirable in order that events which occur only once annually can be observed. A minimal facility in the language is necessary of course in order to talk with people. The time-honored method of conducting fieldwork is to take up residence with a local group. This may consist of living with a family, building a house, or pitching a tent. The location should be as advantageous as possible for watching daily activities. From this vantage point the anthropologist absorbs as much information as he can about the way the members of the local group live. He keeps a diary which describes both daily activities and special events. One of his first tasks is to map the location of structures and important landmarks. A census i̅ also taken. The individuals from whom an anthropologist obtains his information are known as *informants*. The two major techniques of gathering information about a people's culture are observation and interviewing. These methods go hand in hand: the anthropologist asks his informants questions about a forthcoming event, he observes the event, and then he asks further questions concerning what he has observed. What he both sees and hears he records. Sometimes he is assisted by a camera and a tape recorder. Other more specialized techniques of data gathering may also be used (Edgerton and Langness 1974: 1–56). After gaining familiarity with the culture through his residence in one local group, the anthropologist may visit or change his residence to other local groups. However, an anthropologist usually spends most of his time studying the culture of a single local group.

Upon returning from "the field," the anthropologist begins the task of analyzing the massive amount of information which he has collected. This information is contained in his diary, in his maps, in his census reports, in his notes, in his photographs, and in his tape recordings. The first step in analysis is to index the diary and to tabulate the census data. The index, the census tables, and the other information collected are organized by topic. The topics may be ones developed for that particular culture, or they may be taken from a standard list. The list commonly used by American anthropologists is titled *Outline of Cultural Materials* (Murdock *et al.* 1961). This list is sometimes used to organize information as it is being collected in the field. The topics discussed in this textbook may also serve as a standard list. The next step consists of reading and rereading the information by topic. At this point the anthropologist begins to "see" the outline for his report coming into focus. The order of the topics may be changed. Eventually the list of topics becomes the outline for his report. The third step is to write the report, utilizing the information which has been organized by topic. The final product is a book which describes the culture of a particular group of people. Since the anthropologist is likely to have spent most of his time living with a single local group, the book is a description not of the lives of all members of the culture, but of the culture of a particular local group. Such a descriptive account is an *ethnography*. The book may also be referred to as an ethnographic monograph, and the information which it contains is known as ethnographic data. And not surprisingly, the anthropologist who conducted the field research and wrote the report is called an *ethnographer*.

My own ethnography, although titled *The Andros Islanders*, deals with a settlement district, known as Long Bay Cays, which extends along the eastern coast of southern Andros (Otterbein 1966:viii). There are seven villages within the district, which had a population of 1247 in 1959. Although I frequently visited all the villages, I lived in one village in 1959 and in another village in 1961. In addition to these two villages, census reports were collected in two other adjacent villages. Together these four villages formed a community of 356 people and 85 households in 1961 (Otterbein 1966:21). Thus my account is not a description of the way of life of all people on Andros Island, and of course it is not a description of any other island in the Bahamas. Although it was strongly suggested to me that I title the book *Family and Kin in Long Bay Cays, Bahamas*, I opted—with hesitation—for the more encompassing title since I felt that the settlement district did represent Andros culture, or at least the southern third of the 100 mile long island.

The content of ethnographies varies. Some provide information on every conceivable subject, including virtually every topic discussed in this book; others emphasize one or several related topics, giving little or no attention to many subjects. I call the former *general* ethnographies, and the latter *focused* ethnographies. An ethnographer wishing to produce a general ethnography will probably consult a standard list to determine if he has given adequate coverage to most topics deemed important to anthropologists; that is, he will include in his report information on topics which other anthropologists have included in their ethnographies. In addition, he will probably include information on topics which are intrinsically interesting to him. The general ethnography has been said to use the "standard style" by Edgerton and Langness (1974:57–67). A focused ethnography is usually said to be "problem-oriented" in the sense that the ethnographer desires to explain the culture trait which he has focused upon. He solves his problem, so to speak, by including in his report topics which he believes, or other anthropologists believe, are causal factors. He also will usually include a description of the subsystem (economic, social, political, or belief system) in which the focus topic is embedded. Most ethnographies written today are focused, but much contextual information is also provided. For example, the Yanomamö ethnography focuses upon marital alliances and warfare, yet data are provided on all thirty-four topics discussed in this book.

Why do anthropologists go to all the trouble of doing fieldwork and writing ethnographies? There are, of course, personal reasons. The fledgling anthropologist may wish to get away from nagging parents, while the mature field researcher may wish to escape from academic pressures. Some anthropologists derive an immense thrill from visiting far-off, exotic places. Others are disenchanted with their own country. There are also various professional reasons for conducting field research. Each new description of a culture adds to the total number of cultures which have been adequately described by anthropologists. Much of what is known about the peoples of the world has been observed by and recorded by anthropologists in ethnographies. (I personally derive great satisfaction from realizing that in the twenty-first century, if someone wishes to know what life was like on Andros Island in the Bahamas 50 to 100 years before, there is only one source to which he can turn—my ethnography.) Each new monograph provides additional information to which fellow anthropologists may turn if they are conducting research that requires extensive ethnographic data from a large number of cultures. Another professional reason for doing fieldwork is to investigate a particular research problem. Such problems can range from the specific to the general. One anthropologist may wish to discover the effects of Westernization upon a particular culture; another may wish to use information about a particular culture to test a complicated theory of culture change.

In the writing of an ethnography, the anthropologist frequently employs concepts that represent the reality which he observed or had described to him by an informant. For example, an anthropologist observes that the members of the local group in which he is residing live in separate houses, each dwelling containing a married man and woman and their children. His census reports confirm this observation. Moreover, he learns that each adult has only one marriage partner and that newly-wed couples establish themselves in a dwelling separate from that of their parents. Because anthropologists refer to such family groups as "independent nuclear family households," this term is used in the ethnography. (The greater part of this book discusses the various concepts that have been utilized by anthropologists.) Each concept is a useful way of designating, in one to several words, a complex phenomenon—a culture trait—which might take several pages to describe. These concepts are often used at the ends of sections or chapters to summarize ethnographic data. In no instance should the concepts be used as a substitute for a detailed description of the culture traits.

Once he has completed the ethnography, the anthropologist may choose to undertake comparative research rather than to initiate another ethnographic study. Comparative research may be undertaken for any one of several purposes. First, the anthropologist may compare his description of the culture he studied with descriptions of other cultures in order to derive new problems for research. For example, if a culture with a nomadic settlement pattern is contrasted with a culture which has year-round settlements, and it is noted that the former is a hunting and gathering people while the latter is an agricultural people, it can be inferred that the mode of subsistence is responsible for the type of settlement pattern. Moreover, the anthropologist may speculate that it is the sufficiency of food obtained or grown which is producing the greater permanence of settlements, since the local groups of the agricultural people do not have to move frequently to obtain enough to eat. Although there are no rules or special techniques for conducting comparative research of this type, usually the anthropologist compares cultures which are dissimilar and attempts to arrive at explanations for the cultural differences. Sometimes it is helpful for two anthropologists to work together in conducting the research. They may thus compare the cultures which each has studied.

Anthropologists may compare two or more cultures to simply discover similarities and differences; they may compare the same culture at two points in time in order to ascertain the amount of culture change which has occurred; they may compare a large number of cultures in order to determine the frequency with which different culture traits occur, either on a worldwide or regional basis; they may compare culture traits themselves in order to establish whether the traits cluster geographically. Underlying each of these endeavors, however, is usually the desire to explain cultural phenomena: Why the similarities and differences between cultures? Why does a culture change over time? Why are some culture traits common and others rare? Why are some culture traits found only in specific geographic regions? The tentative answers to these questions propose a relationship between two phenomena—either two culture traits or a culture trait and some other phenomenon, such as a geographic factor.

The most basic purpose, though, for undertaking comparative research is to test proposed relationships between two phenomena —relationships proposed either from data in ethnographies or from comparative research. Different techniques have been devised for testing these proposed relationships, or hypotheses. One technique, known as the method of *controlled comparison*, consists of comparing two highly similar cultures. (This technique is described in the "Conclusion" of this book.) Another technique, which requires a knowledge of research methodology and statistics, is known as the *cross-cultural survey* method. Usually as many as thirty different cultures, often more, are compared simultaneously. Research reports emanating from this method are known as *cross-cultural studies*. Comparative research, whether it involves the use of the controlled comparison, the cross-cultural survey, or some other technique, is referred to as ethnology. *Ethnology* is the comparative study of cultures. The term is often used to contrast comparative research with ethnographic research.

HOW TO USE THIS BOOK

This book is designed to be read in conjunction with several ethnographies. It presents a technique for simultaneously learning both the basic concepts of cultural anthropology and much of the important ethnographic information for several cultures. The technique is simple: one seeks in the ethnographies for examples of culture traits which correctly illustrate the concepts defined in the book. The concepts indicate what to "look" for in the ethnographies, and in finding appropriate ethnographic examples, one learns the definitions of the concepts. (A more detailed explanation of the rationale behind this technique is provided in the Preface.) The procedures set forth below describe how this technique can be employed.

The first step is to read this book, using the Study Guide Questions at the end of each chapter to check comprehension. Each of the five main chapters is divided into sections; each section deals with a major topic in cultural anthropology. Each section builds upon previous sections; that is, concepts defined in one section are likely to be used in subsequent sections. Each section contains a question;

the "answers" to the questions are concepts which have been defined in the sections. The questions are so phrased that they are inquiries about various aspects of the culture of a people. They are to be used as guides in discovering what culture traits are present and what culture traits are absent in a culture which is being studied. At the end of each section are three ethnographic examples which illustrate one or more of the concepts defined in the section. The examples are taken entirely from three ethnographies: (1) *The Andros Islanders: A Study of Family Organization in the Bahamas* (1966) by Keith F. Otterbein. The Andros Islanders are a fishing and farming people who are the descendants of freed plantation slaves who migrated to southern Andros from other islands in the Bahamas during the latter half of the nineteenth century. I have chosen my own ethnography because the Andros Islanders, who are speakers of English, illustrate many culture traits shared by many readers of this book (a complete annotated, ethnographic bibliography of the Bahama Islands is available [LaFlamme 1976]); (2) *Yanomamö: The Fierce People* (1968) by Napoleon A. Chagnon. The Yanomamö are a warlike tribe of South American Indians who inhabit the tropical forest region of southern Venezuela and northern Brazil. This ethnography was selected because it contains detailed information on nearly every topic discussed in this book, and it is one of the few reports of a culture which describes warfare that was actually occurring while the ethnographer conducted his fieldwork; (3) *The Qemant: A Pagan-Hebraic Peasantry of Ethiopia* (1969) by Frederick C. Gamst. The Qemant are an agricultural people who occupy a small segment of the mountainous Ethiopian Plateau. This monograph, like the other two, well describes most of the topics discussed in this book, and it provides an account of a culture which is politically absorbed into a modern nation. Thus the three peoples contrast greatly with each other. The questions used to elicit the ethnographic examples are listed on a form, labeled "data sheet," which appears at the end of this book. In order to place the ethnographic examples in their full cultural context, it is recommended that the Andros, Yanomamö, and Qemant monographs be read in their entirety.

The next step is to read an ethnography other than the descriptions of the Andros Islanders, the Yanomamö, and the Qemant, and to note the passages which illustrate concepts listed on the data sheet. Tentative decisions as to how to classify various culture traits should be made as the ethnography is read. Notes can be made in the margins of the ethnography and on a blank data sheet. On occasion it will be necessary to reread, and even to read a third time, sections which define the concepts. When the reading of the ethnography is completed, a final decision as to what culture traits are present and what ones are absent must be made on the data sheet. The numbers preceding the appropriate "answers" themselves can be underlined or circled. The basis for each decision should also be stated. It is also advisable to either paraphrase or quote relevant passages from the ethnography; page numbers should, of course, be given. Information to answer all questions with assurance is probably not available in the ethnography. When the analysis of the culture of a local group in terms of its culture traits is completed, one is ready to proceed to the analysis of other cultures. To help such analysis, Case Study Questions for Seven Cases—Navajo, Washo, Tiwi, Cheyenne, Ulithi, Vice Lords, and Swazi—have been included in Appendix 2.

STUDY GUIDE QUESTIONS

Aim of the Chapter

Two basic themes are presented in this chapter. The first theme is to introduce the reader to several of the basic concepts which are fundamental to the understanding of anthropological research. These basic concepts will serve as the foundation for the introduction of additional concepts in the subsequent chapters of the text.

The second theme is to explore the rationale underlying anthropological studies as well as to give the student some appreciation for the problems confronting the anthropologist. In addition, the author presents a brief review of the variety of research techniques which are employed by anthropologists while they conduct their behavioral research.

Basic Concepts

1. What are the two ways in which the term *culture* is used?
2. If you were trying to distinguish one group of people from another, what two criteria would you probably use? Using these two criteria, how might *culture* be defined?
3. Identify the four typical subsystems of a culture. Why are the various subsystems said to overlap and influence each other?
4. What is the narrow definition of a culture trait? the broad definition?
5. Identify five culture traits of our culture. (answer not in text)
6. What is a local group? Can you identify any local groups in your area of residence? (answer not in text)
7. How does a *community* differ from a *local group*?
8. What are *political communities*, and how are local groups related to them?

9. What are the three main functions of leaders of political communities? Can you provide any examples of these functions as carried out by our political leaders? (answer not in text)

Anthropological Research

10. During a year of fieldwork an anthropologist does a number of things. What types of activity does he typically engage in?
11. Define the terms *ethnography* and *ethnographer.*
12. Compare and contrast the information gathered in *general* and *focused ethnographies.*
13. The author asks "Why do anthropologists go to all the trouble of doing fieldwork and writing ethnographies?" What justifications does he suggest that anthropologists frequently give for their work? Do you think that anthropological work has any value to modern society or is it merely representative of an intellectual exercise? (answer not in text)
14. What is an anthropological *concept*, and why is it useful to the ethnographer?
15. For what purposes do anthropologists conduct *comparative research*, and what types of comparisons might they possibly make?

How To Use This Book

16. What suggestions are made for the most productive reading of this text?

Qemant men harvesting barley while a leprous minstrel plays his one-stringed instrument.

2

LAND AND PEOPLE

The People
Language
Physical Environment
History

In order to become oriented toward any culture and its local groups, either as a reader of an ethnography or as an anthropologist about to "step into the field," it is necessary to know the answers to several basic questions: What kind of group of people are they? What language do they speak and do they speak more than one language? Where are the people located geographically and in what type of physical environment are they living? How long have they been living where they are now located? Because this information is so important to understanding the various subsystems of the cultural system, these topics are discussed in the first few pages of most ethnographies.

THE PEOPLE

An ethnographer studies the way of life of a particular group of people and reports the results of his fieldwork in an ethnography. Usually the ethnographer resides with a local group within a culture. Local groups are typically—particularly if they are small—culturally homogeneous in the sense that the members are native speakers of only one language. Linguistic distinctness, it will be recalled, is one of the defining criteria of a culture. In addition to being located within a culture, the local group studied by the ethnographer will be either a political community or a territorial unit within one. Thus, the anthropologist in "the field" must simultaneously concern himself with three entities: the local group, the culture, and the political community. In the introduction to most ethnographies, the anthropologist informs his reader where and when he conducted his fieldwork. He often identifies the actual name of the local group, describes what language or languages are spoken, and designates the name and nature of the political community which controls the region. It is the task of the student who is reading *Comparative Cultural Analysis*, as well as an ethnography, to discover what kind of group of people the anthropologist studied.

Since the development of anthropology in the late nineteenth century, the interests of anthropologists have expanded from the study of small, isolated *primitive cultures* to that of large, modern nations and the peoples within them. The first ethnographers, who were primarily Americans and Britishers, chose native peoples who had been "discovered" by explorers, missionaries, and traders in remote spots of the globe. Sometimes the people chosen for study were small groups of hunters and gatherers, and sometimes they were peoples organized into complex political units known as states. In either case, the first ethnographers chose—if possible—peoples who were politically autonomous; that is, the people had not been conquered and absorbed into a modern nation. Almost invariably the peoples chosen had no written language. For an anthropologist, the term "primitive" means most often that the people being referred to speak an unwritten language. Thus the expression "primitive culture" does not refer to degree of cultural or political complexity, nor does it mean that the people are in any way backward or inferior. In fact, the large complex kingdoms of East Africa, whose peoples spoke unwritten languages, were classified as primitive. For example, George P. Murdock in a volume which describes the culture of eighteen different nonliterate peoples, including the kingdom of the Ganda of East Africa, titled his book *Our Primitive Contemporaries* (1934). More recently E. Adamson Hoebel (1954) titled a book *The Law of Primitive Man*.

This interest of anthropologists in primitive cultures, which were either politically simple or complex, gave rise to the recognition of an important distinction, the distinction being between those cultures possessing governmental institutions and those which did not. In *African Political Systems*, Meyer Fortes and E. E. Evans-Pritchard (1940:5) classify cultures "which have centralized authority, administrative machinery, and judicial institutions—in short, a government—in which cleavages of wealth, privilege, and status correspond to the distribution of power and authority" as "primitive states," and they classify cultures "which lack centralized authority, administrative machinery and constituted judicial institutions—in short which lack government—and in which there are no sharp divisions of rank, status, or wealth" as "stateless societies." Although their typology has been widely criticized, it has remained a starting point for many discussions of types of political systems. The *state* will be defined in this book as a political community headed by a king or dictator. In contrast, the leaders of stateless political communities are chiefs or headmen (see "Political Leaders," in Chapter 5). One characteristic of states is to be expansionistic; they usually have efficient military organizations which engage in the conquest and incorporation of surrounding peoples. F. G. Baily (1969) has used the graphic term "encapsulation" to describe this process. Sometimes the conquering state is a primitive culture; sometimes it is a modern nation. If the conquest took place before the late nineteenth century and the state had a written language, the conquering people should be thought of as a preindustrial state, not a modern nation.

Although the first ethnographers preferred to study politically autonomous cultures, often of necessity the peoples they studied had been encapsulated by states. By the twentieth century only in a few remote places in the world could anthropologists find native peoples who had not been deprived of their political autonomy. This process of conquest and incorporation of peoples without written language created *dependent native peoples*. Ethnographers studying such peoples have sometimes focused upon what their culture was once like before it was conquered by a state. The period between the time that Europeans first discovered and observed a culture and the time that the culture's political communities were absorbed into the conquering nation is known as the *ethnographic present* (Holmes 1971:193). Thus some ethnographic accounts of dependent native peoples deal with the ethnographic present rather than with the culture the way it was when more recently visited by the anthropologist. Ethnographers writing such accounts rely heavily upon the reports of explorers and missionaries as well as the memories of aging informants. In some cases, anthropologists have written ethnographies without conducting fieldwork. This is, of course, necessary if the people lived centuries ago and there is no way of getting information about the culture except through historical documents and archaeological investigations. Such ethnographies are known as *ethnohistorical studies.*

Peasant communities have been studied by ethnographers since the late 1920s. One of the first studies of peasants was conducted by Robert Redfield in the Mexican village of *Tepoztlán* (1930). This village of peasants, who were Nahuatl-speaking Indians, was politically incorporated into the modern nation of Mexico. The peasants engaged in agricultural subsistence pursuits which benefitted them as well as the holders of political power. Eric R. Wolf, who describes peasants as "rural cultivators," asserts that "it is only when a cultivator is integrated into a society with a state— that is, when the cultivator becomes subject to the demands and sanctions of power-holders outside his social stratum—that we can appropriately speak of peasantry" (1966:11). Both modern nations and primitive states may contain peasant communities. Usually, however, peasant communities are incorporated into modern nations; whether the peasants were once members of a primitive culture or simply the poor within a culture which has privileged classes, literacy—in an elementary form—is likely to be present. This will not be the situation, however, if a primitive state, which by definition does not have a written language, has incorporated agricultural peoples into its political community.

During World War II the interest of anthropologists expanded to include modern nations, both those whose peoples were our allies and those who were our enemies. New methods were developed for studying these state level political communities. In the case of enemies or those peoples conquered by our enemies, techniques had to be devised which permitted, as the title of one book stated, *The Study of Culture at a Distance* (Mead and Métraux 1953). Since fieldwork, thus, was not possible in many instances, members of those cultures resident in the United States were interviewed about their way of life as it had been before they immigrated. This opened up to anthropologists what had previously been a research domain of sociologists and political scientists—modern, complex nations. After the war was over anthropologists "refused to go home." They continued to study modern states and the peoples within them. Interest expanded from studying rural cultivators to studying nonrural peoples who were engaged in occupations other than agriculture. Often the peoples studied had recently immigrated to the United States, but the focus had shifted from what their way of life had been like in their countries of origin to what it was now like in the cities where they currently lived. Thus there is today a growing interest among anthropologists in studying what are perhaps most commonly called ethnic groups; these are peoples of culturally diverse backgrounds who usually reside in large urban centers. Since they speak languages which often differ from their urban neighbors, they are culturally distinct peoples. They are not cultures, since the second criterion for defining a culture—geographic separation—is not met.

Several different kinds of groups, all of which are now studied by anthropologists, have been described above. It is the task of the student reading an ethnography to ascertain what kind of group is described in the monograph. Since ethnographers today study a wide variety of different kinds of groups, it is possible that the ethnography describes a group which does not fit one of the above categories. If this occurs, the student should note succinctly what kind of group it is.

1. **What did the ethnographer study?**
    1. a state
    2. a primitive culture
    3. a dependent native people
    4. a peasant community
    5. an ethnic group
    6. other: _____

Using the data sheet which lists the questions (see p. 215), the student should record the kind of group of people the ethnographer studied. It is important to know this, since many of the questions depend upon a clear understanding of the following three entities: the local group, the culture, and the political community. At the top of the data sheet are several blanks which should also be filled in at this time. They include the name of the culture, the name of the ethnographer, the geographic location of the people, when the ethnographer studied them or the date of the ethnographic present, the name of the local group or groups in which the ethnographer resided, the language or languages spoken by the people, and, of course, the title of the ethnography. All this information will probably be included in the introductory chapter or sections of the monograph.

———

The Andros Islanders are difficult to classify in terms of the kinds of groups delineated above. Before attempting a classification, the local group, the culture, and the political community will be identified. Fieldwork was conducted in a single local group (Otterbein 1966:viii):

During the summer of 1959 I lived in Long Bay Cays, a settlement district which extends from the south bank of the Southern Bight south along the eastern coast of Andros for a distance of eight and one-half miles. . . . The district is composed of seven villages—from north to south, Drigg's Hill, Long Bay, Congo Town, Motion Town, Duncombe Coppice, High Rock, and The Bluff. I lived in Motion Town, the administrative and communication center of Long Bay Cays. . . . I returned to Long Bay Cays in the summer of 1961 and stayed in Congo Town.

The inhabitants of the entire island appear to constitute the culture. Both criteria for defining a culture appear to be met: language distinctness and geographic separation. They are geographically separated from other English speakers by water. Andros Island is one of twenty-two inhabited islands in the Bahamas (Otterbein 1966:vii); a map of Andros (see p. xvi) indicates that the nearest neighboring island is approximately thirty miles away. The political community is the Bahamas. Although the Bahamas were a British possession at the time of fieldwork, the colony functioned in many respects as a modern nation. On July 10, 1973, the Bahamas became an independent nation within the British Commonwealth.

Since the focus of the study was not the Bahamas, it should not be concluded that a state was studied. As the English-speaking descendants of freed plantation slaves, they are not a primitive culture nor a dependent native people. Neither are they peasants since they are not primarily cultivators; fishing has always played an important role in their subsistence. And finally, their apparent status as a culture precludes classifying them as an ethnic group. Thus, it is perhaps best to classify "the people" as a fishing and farming community within a modern nation.

The Yanomamö of southern Venezuela and northern Brazil are a primitive culture. They are unquestionably politically autonomous.

The nearly 10,000 Yanomamö live in "some 125 widely scattered villages. . . . Many of the villages have not yet been contacted by outsiders, and nobody knows for sure exactly how many uncontacted villages there are. . . . The Yanomanö are still actively conducting warfare" (Chagnon 1968:1). The ethnographer's several field trips span the years 1964–1968. Chagnon spent most of his time in the village of Upper Bisaasi-teri, a local group numbering 85 people. The Yanomamö are a culture since they are linguistically and geographically distinct (see map, Chagnon 1968:iv). It is also clear that they speak their own language. Chagnon states (1968:1–2):

I spent nineteen months with the Yanomamö, during which time I acquired some proficiency in their language and, up to a point, submerged myself in their culture and way of life.

Furthermore, there are many Yanomamö words included in the ethnography. Each village or local group is a political community (see Question 20 in Chapter 5 for quotation).

The Qemant are both peasants and a dependent native people (Gamst 1969:2–3):

The Qemant are called peasants in this work [ethnography] because they are cultivators who produce a small surplus partially exchanged in market-places and partially paid as taxes to maintain members of a literate secular and clerical administrative hierarchy of the Ethiopian civilization. . . .
    The Qemant peasants have been politically subordinate, for at least the last six hundred years, to the elite of the much larger Amhara and Tegre ethnic groups of Ethiopia, each with its own peasantry.

The ethnographer studied the Qemant, "a previously un-studied division of the Agaw peoples," for twelve months, beginning in September 1964 (Gamst 1969:ix):

My study was conducted principally in a community called Karkar, until recently the chief religious center of the Qemant. . . . I also visited most of the forty or more other Qemant communities at one time or another.

The culture appears to be the Agaw; the Qemant are one of eight Agaw groups. "All Agaw speak either mutually intelligible or nearly mutually intelligible dialects of the Agaw language. . ." (Gamst 1969:6). The criterion of language distinctness, thus, pertains to the Agaw, not the Qemant. The political community is Ethiopia (see Question 20 in Chapter 5 for discussion and quotation).

LANGUAGE

The members of a local group communicate with each other by means of at least one language and through a mutually understood set of rules for the conduct and interpretation of speech. These two criteria define what is known as a speech community (Gumperz 1972:16; Hymes 1972:54). Thus local groups are speech communities. If neighboring local groups share the same language and their members employ it in the same ways, they form a culture. Although anthropologists who specialize in linguistics caution us that we may not find a one to one relationship between a speech community and a wider social unit, such as a culture (Gumperz 1972:16), it is highly likely that upon examination most cultures, particularly primitive cultures, will constitute a speech community. Gumperz (1969:435) has stated that "we continue to think of speech communities as discrete, culturally homogeneous groups whose members speak closely related varieties of a single language. To be sure, no human group of any permanence can exist without regular and frequent communication."

While there are many cultures in which the members speak only one language, there are perhaps even more in which at least two languages are spoken. Cultures in which only one language is spoken are *monolingual*, and cultures in which two or more languages are spoken are *multilingual*. If only two languages are spoken, the culture is generally termed *bilingual* rather than multilingual. To refer to a culture or speech community as multilingual does not mean that *all* members of the culture know two or more languages: "All that is required is that there be at least one language in common . . ." (Gumperz 1972:16). Furthermore, it is possible to have a culture in which several languages are spoken, but no single member knows more than two. Those members who speak two languages are called bilinguals. In a multilingual speech community, bilingual individuals shift from one language to the other depending upon the social context. Since the analysis of multilingual speech communities requires sophisticated methodological techniques beyond the scope of this book, the student is referred to recent works, such as the one edited by Gumperz and Hymes (1972).

Although the study of multilingual speech communities is a recent interest of anthropologists and linguists, anthropologists have long been interested in a different but related phenomenon— the use of a simplified language, which cuts across many different speech communities, to facilitate trade and other forms of intergroup relations. Such "trade languages" are known as *lingua francas* or "pidgins." Trade languages or pidgins are simplified in the sense that they "typically have few inflectional endings or irregularities, and their vocabulary may be limited" (Burling 1973:113). "Pidgins are truly simple. Nobody speaks a pidgin as his first language, and they are used in only a limited range of circumstances" (Burling 1973:120). The use of a trade language by some members of a culture, usually the adult males, does not make the speech community multilingual, since the trade language is spoken between members of different cultures and not normally between members of a single speech community. The best known trade languages are "pidgin English" spoken in New Guinea, "bush Hausa" spoken in West Africa, and Swahili spoken in East Africa.

In some parts of the world, in particular the Caribbean, the peoples speak what are known as "creole" languages. These are not pidgin languages in that their vocabularies are extensive and their grammars and pronunciations "assume the more elaborate and regular patterns that all people seem to invest in their native languages" (Burling 1973:113). A creole is in every sense a complete language, and for the people speaking a particular creole it may be their only language. Creole languages, however, are currently viewed as having originated in pidgin languages. For the Caribbean, the following theory has been set forth: During slave trading days, various pidgins developed. "On plantations, where the slaves had varied native languages, they must have used the pidgin not only to communicate with their masters, but, even more often, to communicate with each other" (Burling 1973:113). After the passage of many generations, the pidgin language developed into a full-fledged language, which nevertheless carried traces of its pidgin origins. In spite of such origins, creole languages are strikingly similar to the languages spoken by the slave owners. The conditions under which pidgins and creole languages arise have been well stated by Gumperz (1972:3):

Conquest, population migration, or other less dramatic forms of social change can lead to the disappearance of old languages and the spread of others. Similarly, new languages, pidgins, and creoles may be created as a result of forced population resettlement and intensive intergroup contact.

Multilingual speech communities arise primarily through conquest and incorporation. When a culturally different people are incorporated into a conquering political community, two languages will be spoken by the peoples residing within the political community. In time many members of the political community, in particular those conquered, will learn a second language. Such a situation gives rise to a bilingual speech community. Another way in which multilingualism can arise, however, is through marriages between the members of different cultures. The capturing of women and children in warfare and raiding can also have the same effect.

States, either primitive or modern, are likely to be multilingual speech communities. On the other hand, a politically autonomous native people is not usually multilingual. If a native people becomes politically dependent, a multilingual speech community arises, usually of the bilingual variety. Peasant communities may be either monolingual or multilingual. If the peasants are the rural poor within a state whose privileged classes speak the same language, the speech community will be monolingual; if the peasants were formerly a dependent native people who have learned the language of their conqueror, the speech community will be multilingual. If the people are an ethnic group, they will initially be monolingual; as the young learn the language of the dominant culture, the ethnic group will become bilingual.

2. **Is more than one language spoken by the members of the culture?**
    1. no
    2. yes, the culture is multilingual
    3. yes, a trade language or pidgin

If the student has already recorded the name of the language or languages spoken by the people on the data sheet, it is an easy task to determine the nature of the speech community. It should be noted, if more than one language is spoken, whether both adult men and women or just the members of one sex know the second language. As mentioned above, only men may know the trade language; while women, if they are from other cultures, will know two languages.

The Andros Islanders speak only one language—English. Although I never explicitly state this in the monograph, there is internal evidence for this conclusion: an engagement letter written in English (Otterbein 1966:40); books used by the people, including *The Statue Law of the Bahama Islands* (quotations are in English); and dialogue between informants which is given in English. No mention is made of any other language being spoken.

The discussion of creole languages in the Caribbean raises

the question of whether the English spoken by the Andros Islanders is a creole. In the nineteenth century conditions existed in the Bahamas for the development of such a language. However, Daniel Crowley's recent collection of Andros folktales makes no reference to Bahamian speech as being a creole; rather, the "Andros dialect" is referred to as being "nearly incomprehensible to speakers of standard English" (1966:6). It took me approximately three weeks on Andros Island before I could listen to and understand a conversation in the dialect. Whether Bahamian speech is or was once a creole language is a topic for future investigation.

The Yanomamö speak only their own language. Chagnon never mentions that any language but Yanomamö is spoken, and their isolation at the time of fieldwork precluded the development of a trade language or pidgin.

The Agaw, including the Qemant, are multilingual (Gamst 1969:6):

Almost all Agaw are bilingual, also speaking Amharic or Tegrenya. Today, however, not all of the Qemant still speak their native Agaw dialect, called Qemantinya. One-third of them speak Qemantinya well; one-third have little knowledge of the dialect and speak Amharic only; and the other third falls in between.

PHYSICAL ENVIRONMENT

Environmental location of a culture is one of the most important factors influencing the culture. The way of life of the members of a culture can be influenced by the opportunities which its environment presents, such as abundant animal life which may lead to a well-developed hunting technology, fertile soils which permit the development of horticulture and agriculture, and grasslands which provide excellent grazing grounds for herds of animals. Or the way of life may be influenced by the limitations which the environment presents, such as scarcity of animal life, cold temperatures which prohibit the growing of crops, and dry lands which provide little or no pasturage. This point of view, which looks upon the physical environment as providing both opportunities and limitations, is known as *environmental possibilism*. Although this approach has only recently come to be known by this phrase, environmental possibilism has been accepted as a valid point of view by most anthropologists since the end of the nineteenth century. Anthropologists who subscribe to this position argue that the environment does not determine a people's way of life by forcing the members of every culture located in a particular type of environment to seek their livelihood in the same manner, but rather they argue that most environments provide several options or alternatives. For example, abundant wildlife, fertile soils, and grasslands may be available in a particular environment. Some cultures within the environment may utilize one or more of the options, and other cultures may utilize other options. Thus within this same environment some cultures may practice hunting and gathering, and other cultures may grow crops and graze animals (Vayda and Rappaport 1968:477–497; Sahlins 1964:132–147).

When anthropologists speak of a culture adapting to its environment, they mean that the culture has utilized one or more of the options available in the environment. Why a particular culture has selected certain options and not others is an important research problem for anyone attempting to understand that culture. Therefore, one of the first tasks confronting a person who is just beginning to read an ethnography is to note what type of physical environment the culture is located in and the options and opportunities available to the members of the culture.

Eight different types of physical environment are distinguishable. The description of the various environments, the limitations present, the opportunities available, and the location of the environments has been derived from Chapple and Coon's book *Principles of Anthropology* (1942:73–95).

Deserts or dry lands are characterized by an annual rainfall of less than ten inches. The resulting dryness produces substantial bare areas between plants. Extreme daily changes in temperatures prevail in most desert regions. The greatest limitation presented to the inhabitants of deserts is the scarcity of water. Root vegetables and animal life, both limited because of the water shortage, provide practically the only means of subsistence. Where oases are found or rivers flow through deserts, the possibility of agriculture exists. The five great desert areas of the world are North Africa and the Middle East, the Kalahari Desert of South Africa, central Australia, the North American Southwest, and the western coastal region of South America.

Tropical forests include both rain forests and semideciduous forests. Rain forests have heavy daily rainfall which results in dense vegetation. Temperatures remain high, approximately 80° Fahrenheit, throughout the year, with little daily variation. Semideciduous forests, although they may be classified as tropical forests, have a dry season in which many trees lose their leaves. Tropical forests provide only a few fruits and seeds, and there is little game to be hunted. Agriculture is difficult because soils are poor and clearings are hard to make and to keep weeded. The dense vegetation makes travel difficult except on rivers where canoe travel may be possible. The three major areas of tropical forest are the Amazon-Orinoco basin of South America, the Congo basin of Africa, and the forested regions of Southeast Asia and Indonesia.

Mediterranean scrub forests are characterized by mild, rainy winters and hot, dry summers. Vegetation consists of scrub forests of broadleaf evergreens and oaks. The forests provide abundant nuts and wild fruits; small game is plentiful. Many different crops and fruits can be grown. The five main areas of Mediterranean scrub forests are the coastal regions of the Mediterranean Sea, the western coast of the United States, part of the coastal region of Chile, the tip of South Africa, and southwestern and southeastern Australia.

Temperate forests of broadleaf and coniferous trees obtain their growth from plentiful rain. These forests are further from the equator than either tropical forests or Mediterranean scrub forests. Great seasonal changes occur when these forest regions are located near the centers of continents. Animal life is moderately abundant, but there is little natural vegetable food. Soils are good and water is ample. Although hunting and agriculture are possible, cold winters make these modes of subsistence difficult. Any crops grown must be introduced from other environments. The three major regions of temperate forests are the eastern United States, most of Europe, and most of China.

Grasslands are characterized by rich subsoil, covered with grasses. One type of grassland, savanna, is dotted with trees, while another type of grassland, prairie and steppe, is usually treeless. There is great seasonal change in vegetation and foliage, and rivers crossing grasslands alternately flood and dry up. Grasslands usually support herds of large animals, such as antelope and buffalo, and they provide excellent pasturage for domestic animals. Savannas, in contrast to prairies and steppes with their thick sod, are easier to farm using simple farming implements. The six major grasslands are the midwestern region of the United States; the Ukraine region of Russia; the South American pampas of Argentina, Uruguay, and southern Brazil; the Brazilian highlands; central Africa north and south of the Congo basin; and northeastern Australia.

Boreal forests, consisting primarily of conifers, are cold, swampy tracts in which the temperature is usually below 50° Fahrenheit throughout the year and rainfall is slight. An abundant animal life flourishes, but agriculture is virtually impossible. Boreal forests extend in a belt around the northern hemisphere between 50° and 70° of latitude, including northern Canada, Scandinavia, and Siberia.

Polar lands include tundra, polar deserts (bare ground between patches of tundra), and permanent ice caps. Little snowfall and no forests, except for scrub vegetation and dwarf trees, characterize these lands. Animal life abounds, particularly fish and sea mammals. Hunting is the only type of subsistence possible. Polar lands fringe the border of the Arctic Ocean in North America, Europe, Asia, and the islands of the Polar Sea. The entire uninhabited continent of Antarctica is an ice cap.

Mountains, if they are located near the equator, may have all seven types of physical environments described above. What makes them interesting to anthropologists is that mountains in low latitudes have slopes and plateaus of moderate temperature and rainfall which are ideal for the development of intensive agriculture. In both the Old and the New World the domestication of many plants and animals occurred in mountain regions. The three great chains of mountains are the range which runs westward from Tibet to the Pyrenees, the chain which runs along the west coast of both North and South America, and the partially submerged chain which extends southeastward through the Malay Peninsula and out into the Pacific Ocean as far as New Zealand.

3. **In what type of physical environment is the culture located?**
    1. desert
    2. tropical forest
    3. Mediterranean scrub forest
    4. temperate forest
    5. grassland
    6. boreal forest
    7. polar land
    8. mountains

Most ethnographies either directly or indirectly describe the physical environment in which the culture is located. Since mountains may have other types of physical environment associated with them, it is possible to have more than one "answer" to this question— mountains and one or more other types of physical environment. In order to confirm one's judgment, the culture can be located on a climatic or environmental map in a standard world atlas.

The physical environment of the Andros Islanders closely approximates the above description of a tropical forest of the semi-deciduous type (Otterbein 1966:1):

The Bahamas have a subtropical oceanic climate. The annual mean daily temperature is 77° F. . . . Andros, the largest island in the Bahamas, is approximately 100 miles long and 40 miles wide. A rocky ridge, composed of oölitic limestone, extends along the east coast, except at the extreme southern end of the island. This ridge supports a hardwood growth called the "coppet," and a pine forest, known locally as the "pine-yard," lies west of this growth. A mangrove swamp, called the "swash," makes up the west coast of the island; in contrast, the eastern shore is bordered by sandy beaches and coconut trees. Between the "pine-yard" and the "swash" are level prairie-like stretches resembling savannas. . . .

The Yanomamö live in a tropical forest region interspersed with mountains (Chagnon 1968:18):

The general area around Kaobawä's [the headman] village is a low, flat plain interrupted occasionally by gently rolling hills and, more rarely, by a few low mountain ridges. The land is entirely covered with jungle, even the tops of the mountain ridges.

The jungle is relatively dense and characterized by numerous species of palm and hardwood trees. The forest canopy keeps the sunlight from penetrating to the ground, but scrub brush and vines manage to grow in relatively great abundance in most places, making it difficult to walk along the trails. Thorny brush is especially heavy along the banks of streams, where adequate sunlight and a constant supply of water provide ideal circumstances for its growth.

The Qemant live on the Ethiopian Plateau, a physical environment which can be classified as mountains (Gamst 1969:18):

Qemantland, a somewhat rugged part of the northwestern region of the plateau lying 18 miles to the north of Lake Tana, varies in altitude from 4000 to over 10,000 feet. Irregular in shape, it measures approximately 30 miles by 50 miles.

Photographs depict the mountainous terrain (Gamst 1969:21,27,80). Several types of physical environments are associated with the plateau—desert, grassland, and temperate forest (Gamst 1969: 20):

The ecological zones of the Qemant area are also found throughout much of the Ethiopian Plateau. These zones are best explained by the Ethiopians' own system of categorization as follows:

1. *Qolla*. Ranging from sea level to 7000 feet. Warm to hot climate: often disease ridden. Some parts are humid during the big rains. Characteristic crops are white *tef* (an important cereal with grains the size of fine sand and indigenous to northern and central Ethiopia), sorghums, cotton, and finger millet.
   a. *Baraha*. Lowest and hottest of the *qolla*. Said to have spontaneous grass and forest fires, and thought to be excessively unhealthy.
   b. *Medera bada* (land with nothing). Driest of the *qolla*. Refers to true desert, whereas *baraha* is semidesert.
2. *Wayna dega*. Ranging from 6000 to 9000 feet. Temperate climate. Characteristic crops are red *tef*, wheat, barley, and peas.
3. *Dega*. Ranging from 8000 to 15,000 feet. Cool to cold zone. Barley is the principal *dega* crop, but lentils, edible flax, and broad beans will also grow, although frost kills them in certain years. *Chowqe*, ranging from 12,000 to 15,000 feet, is the coldest and highest projections of the *dega*. Descriptive of the uninhabited higher mountain slopes, such as Ras Dajan and Guna. No farming and little grazing is done here.

HISTORY

Since most peoples once lived somewhere else, the history of a people must consider such basic questions as: where did the people come from and how long have they been living where they are now? In the introduction to his ethnography, an anthropologist usually attempts to provide answers to such questions. The answers are an account of the historical movements or migrations of the people. Reports of early travelers, linguistic evidence, archaeological remains, and the oral traditions of the people are all used, if available, to reconstruct their migration history. Migration, as it will be discussed in this section, will deal only with large-scale movements of peoples, and not with the migration of individuals or families within or outside of their culture, nor will it deal with the systematic movement of nomadic peoples who shift from one section of their territory to another throughout the year (see Settlement Pattern in Chapter 3). (For a recent brief review of migration as a topic of anthropological investigation, see Kasdan [1970]).

The mass migration of a people can take several forms. First, the people can expand territorially while retaining control of the region they initially occupied. The people thus are more widely dispersed and occupy more of the earth's surface. Usually this is accompanied by an increase in their numbers. The expansion of the English-speaking peoples from Elizabethan times onward is an example of this form of mass migration (Churchill 1956–1958). Second, a people can move en masse from one region to another. The exodus of the Hebrews from Ancient Egypt and their migration to the Promised Land illustrates this form of migration. (Of course, a people can stay, though it is unlikely, in one location for millennia with their territorial boundaries remaining approximately the same. It is also possible for their boundaries to shrink [Otterbein 1970a: 93].) The migrating people may enter land which is uninhabited by other peoples. Thousands of years ago this was common. However, in the last one hundred years—that is, during the period in which anthropological field research has been conducted—there has been almost no unoccupied land for people to enter. In the previous several hundred years there were a few uninhabited regions into which primitive cultures migrated. Perhaps the best known of these cultures are those Polynesians, known as the Maori, who settled New Zealand, which was uninhabited by other peoples when they arrived in their sea-going canoes (Vayda 1961, 1970).

The causes of migration are varied. Changing climatic factors, such as a prolonged shortage of water, may lead to the desiccation of a region and make it less habitable. Overpopulation resulting from an increase in population density (i.e., the number of people per sq mi or km) and/or a decrease in the productivity of the land can be another cause of territorial expansion. The development of a new subsistence technology which allows the exploitation of a previously unexploitable physical environment can be yet another cause of territorial expansion. Probably the most common reason for the mass migration of a people, at least in the last few centuries, is war. The territorial displacement of peoples due to war is a recurring event which explains why many peoples live where they do. If a people lose a war, several things can happen to them: they can be annihilated, they can be incorporated into a conquering political community, or they can flee. If the losers flee, they will probably seek uninhabited land, but will be unlikely to find it; or, if they find land which is inhabited, they may be assimilated into the culture of the occupants. What is likely though to happen is that they in turn, through war, displace other peoples from their land (Otterbein 1970a:92–103).

When the members of a culture migrate to a new physical environment, they bring with them a cultural system which is adapted to their original environment. The longer a culture has been located in one particular environment, the more likely that the opportunities and limitations of that environment have shaped its cultural system and the culture traits which compose the system; and by the same token, the more likely that the people have modified the environment. With the passage of time a "fit" develops between a culture and its environment. For example, the seafaring Polynesians became primarily an agricultural people after they settled New Zealand. In turn, they deforested New Zealand to obtain land for fields (Vayda 1961). This adaptation over time to a particular environment is called specific evolution (Sahlins 1960; Otterbein 1972). When a people migrate profound changes are likely to occur to their cultural system. It may take decades, perhaps even centuries, for a new adaptation to fully develop.

However, a careful researcher can often discover culture traits within a cultural system which have survived intact from a time when the culture occupied another environment. Oliver (1962), in a study of the buffalo hunting Indians of the Great Plains of North America, found that the various Indian peoples who had migrated onto the Great Plains several centuries ago retained within their cultural systems culture traits which were indicative of their way of life before they entered the plains. In summary, the longer a culture has remained within a region, the more likely that it will be adapted to its environment. When such a culture migrates to another region, assuming that the physical environment is different, changes in its cultural system are likely to occur as it adapts to the new region. Therefore, a culture which has recently migrated is likely to have had profound changes occur in its cultural system, and it will not be as well adapted to its environment as other cultures already occupying that region.

The migration itself may have a profound effect upon the culture even before it has an opportunity to become established in a new region. When an entire people migrate, they do not migrate as individuals but as social and political units. If they migrate into a region which is inhabited by other peoples, it is highly likely that war will occur. Indeed, it is quite likely that the culture was forced to migrate in the first place to avoid annihilation or encapsulation by a victorious enemy. Migration and warfare go hand in hand; and in the process the sizes of populations are altered, population densities increase or decline, the new physical environment itself may become altered, and, as has apparently happened many times in the past, entire peoples have disappeared from the earth. The Great Plains well illustrate the interrelationship of migration and warfare (Secoy 1953); the Indians did not cease to wage war until conquered by the United States Army (Fried 1952).

The warfare which occurs between the original inhabitants of a region and the migrating culture which is attempting to establish itself in the region creates a situation in which it is advantageous for each culture to cease internal fighting, whether it be feuding or internal war (see "Feuding" and "Warfare" in Chapter 5). If the internal fighting stops, each culture can concentrate upon fighting the other. William Divale (1974a, 1974b) has argued that for such a switch to take place, changes in the social systems of the cultures must occur. Specifically, he argues that marital residence changes from patrilocal residence (i.e., men bring their wives to live with them) to matrilocal residence (i.e., men to go live with their wives' families). This change in residence leads to a cessation of feuding and internal war (the reasons are described in the sections on Feuding and Warfare in Chapter 5). Over time the cultures become adjusted to each other; as the warfare between them declines, patrilocal residence reemerges. In support of his theory, he demonstrates in two separate cross-cultural studies that cultures which have recently migrated are likely to be matrilocal, while cultures which have long remained in one region are likely to be patrilocal. The following question is adapted from Divale's research (1974a).

4. **When did the members of the culture enter
    the region where they are now living?**
    1. original inhabitants
    2. ancient migrants (over 500 years ago)
    3. recent migrants (within past 500 years)

If all available evidence, according to the ethnographer, indicates that the culture has always been located in the same region or has been there for over two thousand years, the people should be classified as original inhabitants. If the information available indicates the culture has been there for less than that period of time, but more than 500 years, the people should be classified as ancient migrants. And if they have migrated within the past 500 years, they should be classified as recent migrants. If the ethnographer gives an approximate date for the migration, the date that the fieldwork was conducted or the date of the ethnographic present—not the current date—should be used to obtain the length of time the culture has been in its present location. If information on migration is not to be found in the ethnography, this should be noted on the data sheet.

The Andros Islanders are recent migrants to the island (Otterbein 1966:6, 9):

First Settlements on Northern Andros. The earliest settlements on Andros were established in the latter half of the eighteenth century by a few white families and their Negroes, followed by a number of Loyalists and their slaves. . . .

First Settlements on Southern Andros. Many grandparents and great-grandparents of the present inhabitants of southern Andros came from the Exumas and Long Island, 100 miles to the southeast of Andros, during the latter half of the ninteenth century in search of free land. . . . The desire for virgin soil led the migrants to choose southern Andros, which seems to have been uninhabited, for their new home. . . .

The Yanomamö villages which Chagnon studied are recent migrants to southern Venezuela, having crossed the Orinoco River around the turn of the century (1968:41–43). It appears that the region was unoccupied prior to 1900. Greater information on the movements of the Yanomamö are described in Chagnon's doctoral dissertation (1966:27–31).

The Qemant are the original inhabitants of their territory (Gamst 1969:5):

The Agaw . . . are the original inhabitants of most of the region, with a population of about 25,000, and the group to which the Qemant belong.

STUDY GUIDE QUESTIONS

Aim of Chapter 2

This chapter deals with the initial information which is generally collected during an ethnographic study. Basic to an understanding of a people is a knowledge of the history and development of their culture. The history of a people frequently includes the study of their language, physical environment, migrations, and contacts with other cultures. In conducting historical research anthropologists must not only be aware of changes which have occurred to a culture due to either internal of external causes, but they must also view the physical environment as a setting which provides opportunities or limitations for a culture as well.

Finally, as the primitive world has shrunk with the expanding frontiers of the twentieth century, it is pointed out that anthropologists have been increasingly forced to turn their attention from primitive cultures to modern ethnic cultures as units to study.

The People

1. What does the anthropologist mean when he uses the terms *primitive* and *primitive culture*?
2. Define the concepts of *state* and *dependent native peoples* and explain in what way the two are related.
3. What sources of information are frequently relied upon by anthropologists who study the *ethnographic present* or conduct *ethnohistorical studies*?
4. What are the several characteristics which may be used to identify a *peasant community*?
5. Discuss the development of anthropology since World War II in terms of the peoples studied by the anthropologist. Contrast this recent emphasis with that of the nineteenth and early twentieth century anthropologists.

Language

6. Define what is meant by the concept *speech community*.
7. Cultures may be described as *monolingual, multilingual,* or *bilingual.* Give an example to illustrate your knowledge of each term.
8. Contrast the complexity and development of pidgin and creole languages.
9. What conditions might give rise to pidgen and creole languages? Contrast and compare these factors with those which are associated with the development of multilingual speech communities.

Physical Environment

10. Does the environment force a way of life on a society?
11. Cultures adapt to their environments. Illustrate this statement with examples from your background of knowledge. (answer not in text)
12. Which physical environments would probably support the greatest populations? the least?

History

13. On a map of the world locate the various physical environments.
14. Identify the sources of information which might be used by the anthropologist in order to trace the historical movements of a people.
15. Contrast the two primary forms of mass migration.
16. What do anthropologists see as the main causes behind the large-scale migrations of populations?
17. What problems frequently are encountered by a people who migrate into new physical environments, and what consequences might this have for their culture?
18. Why are migration and warfare said to go hand in hand?

A Yanomamö *shabono* and its surrounding plantain garden.

3

TECHNOLOGY AND ECONOMY

Subsistence Technology
Population Density
Division of Labor
House Form
Settlement Pattern
Settlement Size
Economy
Stratification

Being human sets certain requirements which must be met if the members of a local group are to survive and reproduce. The physical environment must be capable of providing nourishment and, in other ways, supporting human life. Whether people can live in a particular region will depend upon the subsistence technology and the division of labor which they employ to exploit their environment. Exploiting the physical environment results in certain spatial consequences which are reflected in population density, house form, settlement pattern, and settlement size. The products which are produced are allocated differentially according to economic principles; if inequality results social stratification occurs.

SUBSISTENCE TECHNOLOGY

The various options within a physical environment lie dormant until they are exploited technologically. Therefore, those options which will be utilized are determined by the subsistence technologies available to the people. Subsistence technologies are the activities which people perform to exploit their environment in order to gain a livelihood. In anthropological terms, the subsistence technologies utilized by a culture are the means by which that culture adapts to its physical environment. There are five basic subsistence technologies: hunting and gathering, animal husbandry, horticulture, agriculture, and industrialism. Some cultures rely almost exclusively upon one of these basic technologies, while others rely upon a combination of two or more. Cultures which utilize two of the basic subsistence technologies are probably taking greater advantage of the options provided by the physical environment than are cultures which utilize only one subsistence technology (Bohannan 1963:212–216; Chapple and Coon 1942:142–197).

Hunting and gathering (including fishing) consists of techniques of obtaining natural foodstuffs—animal and vegetable—from the environment, using implements fashioned from materials obtained directly from the same source. Hunting, which is usually a male task, requires skill in the use of implements such as clubs, throwing sticks, bolas, spears, harpoons, spear throwers, bows and arrows, blowguns, slings, firearms, nets, snares, deadfalls, pitfalls, stakes, box traps, and spring traps. Hunters may work alone or in groups, depending upon whether the cooperation of several hunters is advantageous. Gathering, on the other hand, is usually performed by women and children. Often it requires less skill and fewer implements than hunting. Gatherers use knives, digging sticks, bags, baskets, wooden bowls, or other simple containers. Frequently they work together for companionship and for joint child tending. Fishing, a form of hunting, may be carried out by men, women, and children. Skill is required in the use of hooks and line, fish spears, bows and arrows, canoes, boats, dams, weirs, seine nets, casting nets, basketry traps, and fish poisons. Fishing may be done individually or in groups.

Animal husbandry is the practice of breeding and raising domesticated animals. Such animals require constant attention. Animals may be used for food, as a means of transportation, in hunting or herding other animals, and for their skins, hair, or feathers. The food use of animals includes not only meat, but also milk, eggs, and blood; the transportation use includes riding, packing, hauling, and plowing. Except for small animals which live near or within the family homestead, men and older boys usually tend animals.

Horticulture is the technology of farming or raising crops with the use of hand tools such as a digging stick or hoe. Fields or gardens are usually prepared by clearing the land of grass, bush, and trees. Often the vegetation removed from the land is heaped and burned, and the ash used to fertilize the soil. This is referred to in ethnographies as *slash-and-burn agriculture*. The soil is prepared by being hoed or by being broken up with a digging stick. The types of crops planted, using this technique, include grains (such as Indian corn or maize, wheat, millet, and sorghum) and roots (such as manioc, cassava, yams, and potatoes). As the crops grow they are weeded, and when the plants are mature they are harvested. After two or three years the fertility of the fields has usually declined; they are allowed to return to fallow, either bush or jungle. New fields must then be cleared. Anthropologists call this practice *shifting cultivation.* Men usually do the tasks of felling trees, cutting bush, and breaking up the soil, while women do the tasks of planting, weeding, and harvesting.

Agriculture is the technology of farming with a plow and draft animal. Before the discovery of the New World by Europeans, this technique was confined to the Old World where the plow was invented. The use of the plow distinguishes agriculture from horticulture. Usually agriculture is a more intensive form of cultivation than horticulture. Fields are permanent and are kept fertilized with animal and human refuse. Grains, rather than root crops, are more likely to be planted. Men do the plowing and usually assist their wives in planting, weeding, and harvesting. Agriculture is a more efficient method of cultivation than horticulture because more crops can be raised per unit of land.

Industrialism is the technology of producing foodstuffs and goods in large quantity at a manufacturing site. Factory industrialism dates from the beginning of the industrial revolution, which is well defined by Webster's unabridged dictionary (1973:935) as "the change in social and economic organization resulting from the replacement of hand tools by machine and power tools and the development of large-scale industrial production: applied to this development in England from about 1760 and to similar later changes in other countries." Industrialism, unlike the other four types of subsistence technologies, involves a shifting of the means of livelihood away from the home and the local group. Thus cultures characterized by industrialism will usually contain local groups whose adult membership is divided between working the land and working in factories; that is, some individuals stay home and farm, others seek their livelihood in industrial centers—often hundreds of miles away.

5. **What subsistence technology is dominant (or codominant)?**
   1. hunting and gathering
   2. animal husbandry
   3. horticulture
   4. agriculture
   5. industrialism

If the members of a culture gain their subsistence largely through one of the above technologies, that subsistence technology should be noted as being dominant. One may find that two technologies are approximately equal in importance in terms of the direct or indirect contribution which they make to the food supply. The technologies are said to be codominant. Four such systems of codominance which the student should be on the lookout for include: (1) hunting and gathering/horticulture, (2) animal husbandry/horticulture, (3) animal husbandry/agriculture, and (4) agriculture/industrialism.

———————

The Andros Islanders have a codominant subsistence technology based on fishing, a form of hunting and gathering, and horticulture. Many of the men, for part of their lives, leave Andros to seek employment. Some may find work in factories. (Otterbein 1966:23–28):

Local agriculture and offshore fishing furnish the subsistence of the inhabitants of Long Bay Cays. Local produce, however, does not provide a cash crop. Ever since southern Andros was first settled, temporary absenteeism has been necessary for most men to supplement the subsistence economy. Today, just as in the past, men must leave their homes and engage in work which provides the money for purchasing clothing, groceries, and building materials. Before 1940 the money was earned by sponging; today it is earned largely through crawfishing and working as agricultural laborers in the United States. . . .

Agriculture. The fields, which are used in shifting cultivation, are often located several miles back in the "bush" on the oölitic limestone ridge which runs the length of the island. . . .

Shifting cultivation, as practiced in southern Andros, is based on a slash-and-burn clearing technique. Following the selection of the uncleared area to be used for the new field, the brush is chopped down with a "cutlass" (machete), heaped into piles, and burned. The brush which does not burn is repiled and burned again. The soil is then prepared for planting by being turned over with a short-handled hoe or with a cutlass. . . . Tubers are planted by hand. A "plantin' stick" (a long pointed pole) is used in planting seeds. The farmer pokes around in the ashy earth until he finds a soft spot in which he can make a hole. After two or three grains have been dropped into the hole, it is closed with the heel of the bare foot. Once the plants start to grow, they are weeded carefully with a cutlass. . . .

After the crops are harvested, the field is weeded in preparation for a second planting. A field will be used two or three times, after which it will be allowed to remain fallow for approximately six years. However, weeding may be so difficult after a harvest that it is easier to start a new field. . . .

Fishing. Fishing provides not only another basic source of food for the Andros Islanders but also a cash income. Several kinds of fishing are carried on. Since the late 1930s sponge fishing has been of no importance in the economy. However, another type of fishing, nearly as lucrative, has taken its place—crawfishing. . . .

Some fishermen engage in "scale-fishing" (fishing for any fish with a scaly exterior) after the crawfish season closes. These men spend approximately two weeks fishing and a third week delivering the fish to market in Nassau. A "smock-boat"—a vessel with an enclosed well for keeping the fish alive—carries the crew to the fishing area. . . .

Fishing close to shore with hand lines provides most of the fish which are consumed locally and which form an important part of the diet. A man will go out in the morning in his dingy and return in the mid-afternoon in order to sell the fish he has caught. . . .

Horticulture is the dominant subsistence technology for the Yanomamö (Chagnon 1968:33–36):

Although the Yanomamö spend almost as much time hunting as they do gardening, the bulk of their diet comes from foods that are cultivated. Perhaps 85 percent or more of the diet consists of domesticated rather than wild foods—plantains are by far the most important food in the diet. . . .

The first operation in making a new garden is to cut the smaller trees and brush; the bigger trees, *kayaba hi*, are left standing until the underbrush is removed. Then the big trees are felled with axes and left lying on the ground to dry out in the sun. . . .

After the brush has dried out and the larger trees felled, the portable timber and brush is gathered up into piles and burned, each man having several fires going in his own patch, to which he hauls the brush as he gathers it up. Usually, the fires are built under or next to one of the larger logs. In this way the logs dry out even more completely and can be easily chopped up by the women for firewood. The ashes are not scattered to improve soil fertility. . . .

Each man's garden contains three or four varieties of both plantains and bananas. The larger portion of the cultivated land will contain plantains, as they produce a higher yield than bananas. The garden will also have a sizeable patch of sweet manioc, a root crop that is boiled or refined into a rough flour by grinding it on a rock and then converting the flour into thick, round cakes of baked cassava bread. . . .

Next in importance are three other root crops: taro, sweet potatoes, and mapuey. All of these resemble potatoes; they are usually boiled, but occasionally they are roasted directly over the coals. . . .

The dominant subsistence technology for the Qemant is agriculture (Gamst 1969:2):

The fertile soils of Qemantland support an economy based upon agricultural technology, including the plow, draft animals, and other livestock which are secondary to the crops in the subsistence pattern. Cereals, legumes, oil seeds, and root crops are the staples of the economy, some being first domesticated as early as five thousand years ago by the ancestors of the Qemant.

POPULATION DENSITY

Population density is dependent upon the basic problem of human behavior—the obtaining of food, and thus it has been viewed as "the most critical single ecological datum" (Bartholomew and Birdsell 1953:488). Furthermore, "population density normally is a complexly maintained equilibrium, dependent upon environmental as well as behavioral (and in the case of man, cultural) forces" (Bartholomew and Birdsell 1953:492). The most important cultural force affecting population density is subsistence technology—previously defined as an activity which people perform to adapt to and exploit their physical environment in order to gain a livelihood. Thus population density must be considered in conjunction with available resources, which in turn are dependent upon the physical environment and the subsistence technology employed.

The population density of a culture is strongly influenced by the adaptation which the culture has made to its environment. Since the cultures within a particular environment utilize the different options provided by the environment in different ways, the population density of the cultures will vary depending upon their mode of adaptation. Thus it is not possible to predict accurately the population density of a culture simply from a knowledge of the type of physical environment in which the culture is located, although Mediterranean scrub forests, temperate forests, grasslands, and some mountains are more suited to human habitation than are deserts, tropical forests, boreal forests, and polar lands. Since the various types of subsistence technologies provide for different modes of adaptation, it is to be expected that the population density of a particular culture will depend to a large extent upon the type of subsistence technology practiced. Of the five basic types of subsistence technology, agriculture and/or industrialism can support the most dense population and hunting and gathering the least dense population. Animal husbandry and horticulture, in terms of the density of population which they can support, occupy an intermediate position between agriculture and/or industrialism and hunting and gathering. Hence, population density varies with the manner in which a culture adapts to its environment, as mediated by the type of subsistence technology practiced. For example, the population density of various local groups of Andaman Islanders (see "Basic Concepts" on p. 6) has been shown to be related to territorial size —which provides hunting grounds—and length of coastline—which provides access to marine life; the greater the coastline, holding territorial size constant, the greater the population density (Erickson and Beckerman 1975).

The magnitude of the population density and the extent of available resources have an influence upon the members of a culture as well as upon their political communities. Territorial expansion may result from an increase in population density and/or a decrease in the productivity of the land (see "History," Chapter 2). Other relationships between the density of a population and the availability of resources have also been proposed by anthropologists. In lower primates, such as Rhesus monkeys, a high population density and scarcity of resources has been shown to lead to interpersonal aggression (Southwick 1972). In man, it appears to lead to both intra-group conflict (e.g., brawls) and inter-group conflict (e.g., feuds and war) (Vayda 1968). It has also been argued that states will form if there is a high population density and resources are plentiful (Stevenson 1968; Carneiro 1970). Statehood appears to be a necessary consequence of organizing a densely populated people with ample resources.

6. **What is the population density of the culture?**

If the population density figure for the culture is not given in the ethongraphy, it can be computed by dividing the number of square miles or kilometers occupied by members of the culture into the population size of the culture. The formula is as follows:

$$\text{Population Density} = \frac{\text{Population Size}}{\text{Square Miles (or Kilometers)}}$$

The resulting figure will give the population density in terms of the number of persons per square mile. Usually the population size of the culture is presented in the introductory section of the ethnography. Since some ethnographies give the population size at different time periods, the student should note which time period his data pertain to. If the population size is not given, the calculation cannot be performed.

The population density of Andros Island is, according to the 1953 Bahamas census, "4.46 persons per square mile on Andros" (Otterbein 1966:24).

For the Yanomamö the ethnographer estimates that "in total numbers their population probably approaches 10,000 people, but this is merely a guess" (Chagnon 1968:1). He also provides a frontispiece map, p. iv, which shows the location of the Yanomamö. The scale for the map is given in kilometers (1 kilometer = .62 miles); if desired, the scale can be converted to miles. Estimating from the map, Yanomamö territory is approximately 200 miles by 200 miles, or roughly 40,000 square miles. Using the formula one can compute the population density at .25 persons per square mile.

Gamst estimates the population of the Qemant between 20,000 and 25,000 (1969:1). In another place (see Question 1 in Chapter 2) he describes their territory as measuring 30 miles by 50 miles—in other words, 1500 square miles. Utilization of the formula yields a population density of approximately 15 persons per square mile.

DIVISION OF LABOR

The division of labor in a culture is based upon the allocation of tasks. In all known cultures different tasks are allocated to different individuals on the basis of sex, age, and sometimes specialized training. The division of labor by sex is universal; the greater strength of males makes it easier for them to carry out strenuous technological activities. Thus men hunt, raise animals, cut bush, and plow, while women gather, plant, weed, and harvest. Women are also responsible for the rearing of children, since they are the ones who bear children and nurse them. The division of labor by age is also universal; the human infant matures slowly over a long period (approximately fifteen to twenty years) in which it is dependent upon its parents. Therefore, the activities of a child differ from those of an adult. As a person grows old and his faculties deteriorate, he can no longer perform the tasks which adults in his culture normally perform. Hence, all cultures recognize at least four stages in a person's life: infancy, childhood, adulthood, and old age. There is no culture known to anthropologists which does not have a division of labor which is based upon at least the two criteria of age and sex.

These two criteria, when considered together, generate eight age-sex categories, seven of which are used by all known cultures (Linton 1942:593):

In spite of the wide range of variation in the delimitation of age and sex categories, there is a minimum of seven groupings which appear to be basic to all systems of age-sex classification. These are: Infant, boy, girl, adult man, adult woman, old man, old woman. Even in these primary differentiations cultural as well as physiological factors are recognizable. Cultural factors are least important in connection with the infant category, which is established primarily by the infant's helplessness and complete dependence upon adults. Sex differences are of little importance at this stage, a fact reflected in most age-sex terminologies.

In some cultures, in addition to the criteria of age and sex, there is found a division of labor by a third criterion: specialized training in different techniques. In these cultures individuals, usually men, specialize in performing different tasks. They may perform the tasks as a part of a joint productive effort, or an individual alone may perform a task which results in a single product, such as a pot, a rug, a canoe, or a basket. These products or the performance of the techniques used to produce the products are either sold or traded to other members of the culture for goods and services. If these specialists devote only a part of their time, either daily or seasonally, to their tasks, they can be classified as *part-time specialists.* If they devote all of their time to their tasks, they can be classified as *full-time specialists.* A culture, of course, can have both part-time and full-time specialists (Chapple and Coon 1942:250–256).

Anthropologists and sociologists both have been interested in the division of labor because of its relationship to the growth and development of cultures. It is in the simplest of cultures that one finds a division of labor based upon age and sex only. In the most complex cultures, such as the industrial nations which now dominate the earth, the division of labor is based upon full-time specialists. In other words, as cultures grow in size and complexity their division of labor changes from being based on age and sex to being based on full-time specialists. This increase in the degree of specialization is seen as being both a result of and a cause of the development of particular cultures.

7. What is the division of labor?
    1. age and sex only
    2. part-time specialists
    3. full-time specialists

If there are no specialists, either part-time or full-time, in the culture, then the division of labor will be based upon age and sex only. On the other hand, if there are specialists in the culture, then the division of labor cannot be based upon age and sex only. Since both part-time and full-time specialists can be present in the same culture, it is best to list every specialist and then to make a decision as to whether he is part-time or full-time. If both types of specialists are present, both categories should be recorded. Simple counting will provide the ratio between the number of part-time and full-time specialists.

The Andros Islanders have both full-time and part-time specialists. For the community of four villages covered by the census, a table listing the "occupations of adults" is given (Otterbein 1966: 29–30):

Only the schoolteachers, the telegraph operator, and the constable-postmaster are employed full-time. One man has a part-time job looking after the warehouse at the end of the dock. . . . All the bartenders, as well as the constable-postmaster, the preacher, and the mason, work fields.

> Detailed information on the "division of labor by age and sex" is also given in tabular form (Otterbein 1966:96–97). It covers occupations not represented in the community but available to residents of southern Andros. They include nurse, carpenter, and ship builder; only the nurse is full-time.

> The Yanomamö have part-time specialists who prepare items for intervillage trade (see Question 9 below). Two of the major items produced for trade are hammocks manufactured from cotton and clay pots (Chagnon 1968:100–101).

> The Qemant have both part-time and full-time specialists. Part-time specialists include "local feudal officials" and carpenters, while full-time specialists include the *wambar,* "a full-time politico-religious specialist," and itinerant traders (Gamst 1969:79,81,83).

HOUSE FORM

> The house is a vital link between man and the physical environment —vital in the sense that some form of dwelling or shelter is a necessity for survival in most geographical regions. As an important aspect of man's culture, it has permitted him to adapt to such harsh environments as polar ice lands or windswept deserts. Given a suitable house, man can inhabit nearly any region on the earth's surface. Houses or dwellings are man-made structures which protect people from the elements. Usually associated with a house is a fire-place or hearth. Thus, those who occupy a dwelling are provided with shelter, warmth, and arrangements for cleanliness—basic needs of the individual (Malinowski 1960:103–104). The house in many cultures also protects its inhabitants by providing barriers between them and potential animal and human enemies: domestic animals are often kept within dwellings in order to deny predatory animals a meal, and personal enemies from within the same local group are kept from stealing or injuring the inhabitants, particularly while they are sleeping. Also, in some cultures the houses are built to withstand the attacks of enemies from other political communities.
>> Basically, a house consists of walls and a roof, the materials for which are usually taken from the physical environment. Although

building materials such as clay, wood, and thatch are part of the environment, they are not determinants of house form. The point of view known as *environmental possibilism* pertains to the construction of houses just as it does to the types of subsistence technology utilized to exploit the physical environment. This point of view has been well stated by Rapoport (1969:47):

House form is not simply the result of physical forces or any single causal factor, but is the consequence of a whole range of sociocultural factors seen in their broadest terms. Form is in turn modified by climatic conditions (physical environment which makes some things impossible and encourages others) and by methods of construction, materials available, and the technology (the tools for achieving the desired environment).

Two common-sense observations can be made concerning the relationship between the walls and roofs of houses. First, it has been noted in a cross-cultural study that circular shaped houses have conical roofs and rectangular-shaped houses have flat, gabled, or hipped roofs (Whiting and Ayers 1968:120–121). Second, another similar study notes that if the walls are made of relatively permanent materials such as stone or adobe clay, the roof may be either of a permanent material (such as tile) or an impermanent material (such as thatch); but, if the walls are made of an impermanent material, the roof will be nearly always of impermanent material (Griffiths n.d.). Except for tents, whose upright poles may be found at each new camp site, impermanent walls, obviously, are not erected to support permanent roofs.

Houses or dwellings of some sort are a cross-cultural universal (Murdock 1944:124); that is, they are found in some form in all known cultures. Even peoples organized into small groups of hunters and gatherers build shelters or huts. Perhaps the simplest of such physical structures are the crescent-shaped windbreaks of the no longer surviving native inhabitants of the island of Tasmania (Murdock 1934:5–6). Many important activities take place within the house: the preparation of food, the eating of meals, sleeping, the sexual act, bodily hygiene, childbirth, rearing of children, making of craft products, raising of animals, tending the ill and infirm, and preparation of the dead for burial. These are activities which are normally associated with the hearth.

Houses or dwellings are occupied by households. A *household* may be defined as one or more persons who live together in the same dwelling and cooperate in a variety of domestic affairs (Solien 1960). In most cultures the typical household contains a married man and woman and their children. A marital or sexual relationship between two members is not a prerequisite for the existence of a household; households do not necessarily contain related individuals. In fact, the members may be all of the same sex. Furthermore, in some cultures a few residential units may contain lone individuals. An anthropologist analyzing the census of a local group should record such single person residential units as households. Since the house is a cross-cultural universal, so is the household. In all known cultures the members of local groups are organized into households or domestic groups. It is the domestic group that participates in the activities which take place within the house. Members of a household who cooperate in domestic affairs are said to share a common hearth. A domestic group is organized for carrying out certain activities which require a leader or head; and thus, the ethnographer in the field should, while taking a census, identify the head of each household.

The house, a physical structure with walls and a roof, is in most cultures occupied by a single household or domestic group. Such single household dwellings, thus, are the most common type of house form. In cultures with *single household dwellings*, the house and the household are coterminous. However, in some cultures the household—that is, the group living and cooperating together— may actually occupy several buildings, which are usually adjacent. Typically, the buildings are small and clustered together at one site, often surrounded by a fence or wall. Such buildings usually contain one room; the room being used either for cooking, eating, sleeping, or storage. Anthropologists refer to such clusterings of buildings as *compounds.* In other cultures the households of a local group reside within sections or units of large man-made structures. Each household occupies its own set of rooms or apartment. Sometimes the entire population of the local group lives within a single dwelling. These *multihousehold dwellings* assume various forms. Some commonly occurring types include: (1) the long house, in which households are arranged side by side in a chain, typically separated by partitions (in some cultures the chain may form a circle enclosing a plaza, patio, or dance ground); (2) the apartment house, in which households are located at different levels within the structure.

Single household dwellings and compounds within the same local group can vary greatly in size. If a household is large in terms of number of members, it is likely to occupy a large dwelling with many rooms or a compound consisting of a cluster of many small buildings. Unless the culture provides precise rules as to where such dwellings and compounds are to be located, the household heads in these cultures have a choice of where to locate their dwellings. If differences of wealth, privilege, and status are recognized by the culture, the sizes of houses as well as their location can be used by household heads to demonstrate their social position. Thus the size of a house is influenced by both the size of the household and the social position of the household head. These relationships have been demonstrated in a recent ethnographic study of changing house forms in a community on Andros Island in the Bahamas (Otterbein 1975:87–89, 97–101). On the other hand, multihousehold dwellings are likely to contain household units which are approximately equal in size. Furthermore, it is unlikely that the household heads will have much choice in where their units are located. Consequently, household heads in cultures with multi-household dwellings have difficulty in demonstrating their social position through the size and location of their houses. Although apparently never tested in a cross-cultural study, it appears that there might be a correlation between cultures which have multihousehold dwellings and cultures in which differences of wealth, privilege, and status are not highly important. If differences do not exist or are slight, it is easy, from an architectural point of view, to erect long houses or apartment buildings using identical or similar residential units. Kings and commoners do not live side by side in row housing. Furthermore, if the entire population of a local group lives within one dwelling, the local group itself—which is probably a community in the sense of being a face-to-face group—becomes sharply defined, both in a spatial and a social sense. The structure in which the community lives symbolizes the local group.

8. **What house form is present?**
    1. compounds
    2. single household dwellings
    3. multihousehold dwellings

In most cultures there are clearly defined households: each domestic group occupies a house, and every one knows to which household he belongs. Since household members cooperate in some, if not all, domestic activities, membership can be determined by ascertaining who shares a common hearth. In cultures with compounds and multi-household dwellings it may be more difficult to delineate households. The criteria of sharing a common hearth, however, should be employed to the fullest extent possible.

The Andros Islanders live in single household dwellings (Otterbein 1966:33, 85, 89–90):

The House. A man who grows up in Long Bay Cays learns that he must build a house for his wife; this requirement becomes a primary value to every adult male in the community. . . .

Houses are nearly identical except for size. They are box-shaped with white limestone walls and shingle roofs, which give them a structure that can well withstand the impact of late summer hurricanes. Porches, usually of wood, extend across the fronts of some houses. Windows, which seldom have glass panes, are often screened to keep out "varmint" (insects); they are always framed by wooden shutters, usually green, which are closed at night.

Two basic types of households are characteristic of the domestic system of Long Bay Cays: those containing a cohabiting man and woman and those containing only an adult woman. The former type are classified as male-headed and the latter type as female-headed.

Each Yanomamö local group consists of one multihousehold dwelling (Chagnon 1968:25–26):

The Yanomamö permanent house—*shabono*—is probably the most sophisticated manufacture produced by these people. . . . Each individual builds his own section of the *shabono*. . . . The village looks like a series of individual houses arranged in a more or less neat circle, a gap of about 3 feet separating the individual houses from each other. These gaps are roofed over by the men whose houses are adjacent to them, and the village then looks like a continuous roof surrounding an open plaza. . . .

An aerial photograph of a multihousehold dwelling from Chagnon's book *Yanomamö: The Fierce People* (1968) is shown on p. 38.

The dwellings of the Qemant are compounds which are often clustered into what the ethnographer calls homesteads. A typical homestead consists of "three closely spaced houses and several smaller structures" (Gamst 1969:24). Each house is occupied by a family, one house by the father and each of the other houses by a married son; each house has one or two hearths for cooking. Although I would not classify the homestead itself as a compound because each family has its own hearth, I would classify the houses themselves as compounds (Gamst 1969:25–26):

Erada's homestead, like others, has one or more cylindrical huts with undaubed wattle walls and thatch roofs for goats and donkeys, and particularly for young animals of all species raised. . . . Each dwelling has an adjoining granary, which may be a cylindrical structure placed on stilts, with wattle-and-daub walls and a thatch roof, or a cylindrical subterranean pit located outside the house. One-man sleeping huts for mature, unmarried sons are common. They are small, rectangular, and constructed from the same materials as the houses. Malke sleeps in one of these just outside his father's house and next to those once used by his two brothers. . . .

SETTLEMENT PATTERN

The physical distribution of the members of a culture within its territorial boundaries constitutes its settlement pattern. All peoples reside in local groups of various sizes, from small families to large cities. At any particular point in time each local group has a particular geographical location. Some local groups remain permanently at one location, while others move seasonally. Settlement patterns can be classified according to the size and spatial distribution of the local groups within the culture.

If the members of the culture are grouped into bands of approximately twenty to sixty individuals which shift from one section of their territory to another throughout the year, the culture can be categorized as having a *nomadic* settlement pattern. Whether individual bands own sections of the territory or not is an empirical problem which must be investigated for each culture. For many nomadic peoples the bands move within a prescribed annual cycle; that is, every year at the same time they return to the same section of their culture's territory. Other nomadic peoples have large bands which break up into smaller bands for several months out of the year. The members of some cultures spend part of the year, often winter, in permanent settlements and the remainder of the year migrating as bands. Such a settlement pattern is known as *seminomadic*.

Many cultures have settlement patterns in which the local groups remain at relatively permanent locations. Natural catastrophe, warfare, or depleted soils may on occasion force local groups to move, but once moved, the settlements again become relatively permanent and take on the characteristics typical of the former settlements—provided the physical environment is similar to that previously occupied. Neighborhoods of *dispersed homesteads* characterize some cultures whose technology is horticulture. Fields lie between the homesteads, which may be from several hundred feet to several hundred yards from each other. Thus neighborhoods are spread over several square miles. In contrast to neighborhoods of scattered homesteads are settlements of homesteads or houses which are close to each other. The local groups are *hamlets* or *compact villages*, which often have a social, economic, and ceremonial center—a market or a village square may serve these functions. The reason for distinguishing between hamlets and villages is that in some cultures there are compact villages with outlying satellite hamlets. Thus the settlement pattern is based upon both hamlets and compact villages. In terms of population size, any settlement under 5000 persons can be considered a hamlet or compact village. Settlements of over 5000 persons can be considered *towns* or *cities.* Although the figure of 5000 persons is arbitrary, it is an attempt to quantitatively distinguish between settlements which have a primarily local character and those that are urban and serve the needs of all the members of the culture (and in some cases also individuals from other cultures). Towns and cities have a cosmopolitan character. Artisans, traders, and merchants gather in number. Since most urban dwellers do not know each other, administrative offices are needed to regulate the relationships between individuals. A distinction is made between towns and cities because in some cultures there are cities with outlying satellite towns. Thus the settlement pattern is based upon both towns and cities.

The settlement pattern of a culture is influenced by a number of factors, several of which have already been discussed. The physical environment, the subsistence technology, the population density, the division of labor, and house form all play a role in determining the size and spatial distribution of local groups. Hunting and gathering and animal husbandry both predispose a culture to being nomadic or seminomadic. Horticulture and agriculture, on the other hand, favor the more permanent settlement patterns of dispersed homesteads, hamlets, and villages. If there is a high population density and the division of labor is based on specialists, towns and cities are likely. Warfare may also affect the settlement pattern by causing the members of the culture to live in fortified villages, towns, and cities, rather than dispersed homesteads.

9. **What is the settlement pattern?**
    1. nomadic
    2. seminomadic
    3. dispersed homesteads
    4. hamlets and/or compact villages
    5. towns and/or cities

Most ethnographies indirectly describe the settlement pattern. It should be noted whether combinations of hamlets and villages or towns and cities occur, and it is possible to have a culture in which all of these are present. Furthermore, there are other possible combinations, such as neighborhoods of dispersed homesteads, hamlets, and villages.

The Andros Islanders live in dispersed homesteads (Otterbein 1966:14–17):

The seven villages which compose Long Bay Cays are connected by a path, 50 to 200 yards back from the shore line. Between the path and the shore are the coconut groves. . . .
    The houses in each village are scattered along the main path, so that settlement patterns are lineal. Many houses are built on the side of the path away from the shore, the trees and bush providing some protection from the impact of hurricanes. . . .

Sketch maps of the four villages covered by the census disclose that three villages have widely dispersed houses (Otterbein 1966:15, 19, 20) and one has a more compact settlement pattern utilizing paths that connect the main path to a back path (1966:16). However, because of the "lineal" nature of the settlement pattern and the occasional presence of fields between the houses, I would classify the "villages" of the Andros Islanders as neighborhoods of dispersed homesteads. In a recent highly focused monograph I have described how the settlement pattern on southern Andros has slowly changed since the nineteenth century, but with its character remaining essentially the same (1975).

The Yanomamö live in compact villages (Chagnon 1968:88–89):

Kaobawä's village is oval-shaped. His house is located among those of his agnatic kinsmen; they occupy a continuous arc along one side of the village. Each of the men built his own section of the village, but in such a way that the roofs coincided and could be attached by simply extending the thatching. When completed, the village looked like a continuous, oval-shaped lean-to because of the way in which the roofs of the discrete houses were attached. Each house, however, is owned by the family that built it.

Moreover, the village is fortified (Chagnon 1968:29):

The permanent village is complete when the palisade of logs is erected around its circumference. This is placed some 3 or 4 feet behind the roof, allowing space for a path around the village inside the palisade. The palisade itself is about 10 feet high and usually made of a mixture of palm and hardwood logs.

The settlement pattern of the Qemant is based upon dispersed homesteads (Gamst 1969:1, 22):

Qemantland does not have compact villages. Instead, one to four wattle-and-daub walled houses topped by peaked thatch roofs constitute semi-isolated homesteads that are scattered across pastures and cultivated fields throughout the length and breadth of the land. Anywhere from one to four hundred of these homesteads are united socially to form a widely dispersed community.

As previously mentioned all Qemant live in dispersed settlements, and the Qemant of Karkar and Shelga are no exception. Homesteads consisting of single houses or clusters of two to four houses are located anywhere from 300 to 3000 feet from other homesteads. Clusters of ten to twenty houses are rare among the Qemant, and villages . . . do not exist.

SETTLEMENT SIZE

A complete picture of the settlement pattern is not available until the population of the largest settlement is known. This figure provides more information about a culture than does that of the average settlement size. Naroll (1956:693) has argued:

To know the size of the largest settlement is usually to know the size of the largest and most diverse collection of specialists, and very often the size of the center of political and economic organization also. Here is usually the largest center of information. In a crude sense—although we cannot press the analogy too far—the largest settlement is the brain of the ethnic unit.

Size in population gives a measure of the degree of urbanization or cosmopolitanism of the largest settlement. In other words, the greater the population, the greater the degree of urbanization. If the population of the largest settlement is, say, over 50,000 persons, we have evidence of a large urban concentration of people.

Having available information on the size of the largest settlement makes it possible to differentiate between villages (under 5000 persons) and towns (over 5000 persons). It also provides an indication of the maximum possible size of a nomadic band; the size of the permanent settlements when the settlement pattern is seminomadic; and the size of the largest neighborhoods of dispersed homesteads when the settlement pattern is dispersed homesteads.

**10.   What is the population of
the largest settlement?**

It is not always easy to obtain this information directly from the ethnography. If census data for several local groups are given, then the population of the largest of these local groups should be listed. Often, however, the ethnographer simply states vaguely that settlements range in size, say, from 50 to 100 persons. When this is done, the maximal figure—in this case 100—should be noted. Sometimes it is simply necessary to guess, or approximation techniques can be used: (1) multiplying the number of homesteads in a large local group by the average number of persons in a household; (2) dividing the number of settlements into the total population.

The size of each village in Long Bay Cays is listed in a table. The largest village, The Bluff, had a population of 337 in January, 1959 (Otterbein 1966:21).

The ethnography dealing with the Yanomamö provides both a table showing the size of selected villages and a statement of the range in settlement size. The size of the largest village in the table is 232 (Chagnon 1968:74). The maximal figure for the range is 250 (Chagnon 1968:1):

Some 125 widely scattered villages have populations ranging from 40 to 250 inhabitants, with 75 to 80 people the most usual number.

Since the figure of 250 is close to the figure of 232 and is Chagnon's approximation for the maximum village size, 250 should be listed as the population of the largest settlement.

An important Qemant community is Karkar, "until recently the chief religious center of the Qemant" (Gamst 1969:ix). Although not explicitly stated to be the largest settlement, its importance and size leaves little doubt that it is the largest Qemant community (Gamst 1969: 22–23):

A detailed study was made of the community of Karkar, which is divided into three subcommunities by a range of hills and an escarpment. One of these three segments, called Karkar Anchaw Mikael, was the actual site of the fieldwork. . . . The population of this segment in 1965 was 650, while the population of "greater" Karkar was 2640.

Thus the population of the largest settlement is 2640.

ECONOMY

Economics deals with the allocation of goods and services, whereas technology deals with the production of goods and foodstuffs. In studying an economy one is interested in the manner in which goods and services are transferred from one party or group to another. The exchange and movement of goods and services can either be within the local group, between different local groups within the culture, or between different cultures. Anthropologists are indebted to Karl Polanyi, an economic historian, for identifying three different modes of allocation or principles of exchange, or as Polanyi called them, "forms of integration": reciprocity, redistribution, and market exchange (Polanyi 1957). Every economy is characterized by at least one of these principles. Many economies are based on two or all three, though usually one principle will be dominant.

Reciprocity is the exchange of goods and services between units of the same kind, such as individuals, households, kinship groups, or local groups. Such exchanges usually occur between units which are already linked by social and ceremonial obligations; thus, reciprocity follows rather than creates such relationships. Reciprocity often takes the form of gift exchange since the distribution of goods of material value is not usually the purpose of reciprocity. The main reason for exchanges of this type is the maintenance of the obligations which exist between the units. Two types of reciprocity can be distinguished (Sahlins 1965).

Balanced reciprocity is direct exchange in which goods and services of commensurate worth are traded within a finite period. That is, one unit in the exchange gives the other unit a gift; the gift must be "repaid" by a gift of comparable value, probably within a period of one year. There cannot be a one-way flow of goods—if the gift returned is of significantly less value or if it is not returned within the appropriate period of time, the social relationship upon which the exchange is based is disrupted. Thus balanced reciprocity is a way of maintaining relationships between units. (When reciprocity between local groups occurs, it is likely to be balanced reciprocity, and the members of the local groups carrying out the exchanges are likely to be nonkinsmen.)

Generalized reciprocity, on the other hand, is exchange in which goods and services flow predominantly one-way, with appreciation and respect flowing from the recipient. That is, one unit gives a gift; the gift need not be repaid within a finite period, and if it is repaid, the gift returned need not be of commensurate worth. Appreciation and respect, and sometimes deference, however, must be shown to the donor. Generalized reciprocity frequently occurs between close kinsmen who are members of the same local group. The sharing of large game animals which is common in hunting and gathering cultures and the distribution of meat from large domestic animals which sometimes occurs in cultures that practice animal husbandry, horticulture, or agriculture is a form of generalized reciprocity. The hunter or owner of the slaughtered animal receives prestige in exchange for his ability or generosity.

Redistribution is the systematic movement of goods and services toward an administrative center and their reallocation by the authorities. Redistribution may be voluntary on the part of the members of the culture or it may be involuntary, in that the administrative center uses agents to force the members to contribute goods and services to the authorities. The goods may be used to support the needy, to reward followers, to support armies, or simply to ensure the comfort of the authorities. The redistributive center can vary from the head of a band to the ruler of a large kingdom.

Market exchange is the exchange of goods and services according to the law of supply and demand. In market exchange, goods and services have a value or price which is established by supply and demand. General purpose money makes this possible, while authorities are necessary to enforce financial commitments. General purpose money, by definition, provides a medium of exchange, a standard of value, and a means of discharging obligations. Limited purpose money, on the other hand, serves only one or two of these functions. Both general purpose money and enforceable contract law need to be present for market exchange to operate efficiently. Marketplaces may or may not be present. The mere fact that markets occur is not evidence that market exchange is present. And by the same token, market exchange can occur without market sites being a part of the culture.

The economic integration of cultures has received theoretical discussion by Elman Service (1962). In his book *Primitive Social Organization: An Evolutionary Perspective*, he has employed three different types of integration—social, political, and economic—within cultures as the defining characteristics of four different evolutionary stages. The types of integration are seen as the major factor forcing cultures to higher levels of evolutionary development. Bands, the lowest level, occur when no form of social, political, or economic integration exists between local groups. Tribes, the next level, are defined by the existence of pantribal sodalities which are kinship groups including in their memberships individuals from different local groups. Reciprocity between local groups may occur at this level. Chiefdoms exist, by definition, when there is redistribution through a nonlocal allocative center. A chief presides over the administrative center. Political force need not be present for redistribution to occur. States arise when there develops a government with the legitimate use of force. Market exchange is often characteristic of states. Although Service uses social and political criteria, as well as an economic criterion, for establishing his different forms of integration, he has made a strong argument for the importance of studying the economic integration of a culture, particularly integration based upon redistribution through a nonlocal allocative agency.

One or more of the three principles of exchange may be found. That principle which transfers the greatest number of goods and services from one party or group to another can be considered dominant. Usually redistribution will be more dominant than reciprocity, while market exchange will be more dominant than redistribution. Nevertheless, the dominant principle of exchange must be ascertained through empirical investigation.

11. **Which principle of exchange is dominant?**
    1. balanced reciprocity
    2. generalized reciprocity
    3. redistribution
    4. market exchange

If households or homesteads exchange goods and services, including gifts, and redistribution and market exchange do not or only rarely occur, then reciprocity is the dominant principle of exchange. If there is a two-way flow of goods and services, the reciprocity is balanced; if the flow is one-way, the reciprocity is generalized. If there is an agency, such as a political leader or a religious official, who receives services and goods which are reallocated, and this is the dominant principle of exchange, then it should be noted that redistribution occurs. In some instances it may be difficult to distinguish between redistribution and generalized reciprocity, since with both these principles of exchange there is a one-way flow of goods and services. They can, however, be differentiated: almost invariably the recipient in redistribution is a leader with high standing, whereas the recipient in generalized reciprocity is likely to be a person of low standing, perhaps a child (Sahlins 1965:163–164). If general purpose money is present and the law of supply and demand operates, then market exchange is dominant.

The economy of the Andros Islanders is based almost solely upon market exchange. There are repeated references throughout the monograph to earning and spending money both within the Bahamas and the United States as well as in Long Bay Cays (Otterbein 1966:10–12, 23–24, 27–32, 33–34, 39, 44–45, 50–51, 93–94, 99–101). Redistribution occurs in the form of government old age pensions of £ 2 ($5.60 U.S.) a month to people over sixty-five years old (1966:100–101). No information is provided as to how the Bahamas government obtains revenue. (It is obtained primarily by imposing high duties on imports. There is no reference to taxing the Andros Islanders because they are not directly taxed, neither their property nor their incomes.)

Generalized reciprocity occurs on a limited basis. Relatives supply labor to a young man building a house, and at the time of his marriage they may provide tables, chairs, and trunks (Otterbein 1966:33–34). Providing rent-free homes to the elderly is another example of generalized reciprocity (Otterbein 1966:91):

Most widows continue to live in their home even though their children have grown up and moved away. They do not move in with their children or with other relatives even if their own home has fallen into ruin. At any given time there are always several vacant houses in the community. These vacancies result, in part, from families moving to Nassau on a relatively permanent basis. Since most owners believe that a house lasts longer if it is inhabited, they are willing to allow someone else to live in and take care of the house. An older woman who has had to abandon her home is permitted to live in one of these houses rent-free.

A brother is expected to financially assist his sister if the need arises (Otterbein 1966:122):

When he is older he is expected to contribute financially to the rearing of his sister if necessary, and once she is married he sees that her husband properly provides for her. If her husband cannot do this the brother ought to assist in her support. . . . In actual practice, however, brothers contribute little to their sisters' welfare because the money they earn must be used to provide for their wives and children. Still, if a sister is in desperate need, she may legitimately call upon her brother for assistance and will probably receive help.

On the other hand, balanced reciprocity characterizes the godparent-godchild relationship (Otterbein 1966:132–133):

The godparent-godchild relationship is considered by the inhabitants of Long Bay Cays to be of importance to the child because it provides him with "relatives" who will at times assist in his upbringing. . . . Since godparents give presents such as clothes and food to their godchildren, parents choose people they think will help the child. . . . They should and usually do give presents to their godchildren, and they have the right to discipline them. The godmother, who is more important than the godfather, is supposed to give the child a Bible and a hymnbook, and to teach the child the Lord's Prayer and the Ten Commandments. In turn, the godchild must carry wood and water for the godmother, and also at times help her clean and wash. The godchild is expected to perform errands for the godfather. The godparent-godchild relationship also implies that when the child becomes an adult this pattern of reciprocity should continue. Thus godparents and godchildren frequently exchange goods and services.

Both generalized and balanced reciprocity within the local group occur among the Yanomamö. Generalized reciprocity occurs in the following situations (Chagnon 1968:33,91):

On other [hunting] trips, we often managed to collect enough game in one day to feed the entire village. It is a happy occasion when one of the hunters bags a tapir, for everyone gets a large share of it.

On the other hand, balanced reciprocity also occurs (Chagnon 1968:7):

Nor could I enter into their system of reciprocities with respect to food: every time one of them gave me something "freely," he would dog me for months to pay him back, not with food, but with steel tools. Thus, if I accepted a plantain from someone in a different village while I was on a visit, he would most likely visit me in the future and demand a machete as payment for the time that he "fed" me. I usually reacted to these kinds of demands by giving a banana, the customary reciprocity in their culture—food for food—but this would be a disappointment for the individual who had visions of that single plantain growing into a machete over time.

> Moreover, a man who has married into the village hunts for his wife and her parents, and in turn he is provided with plantains by his in-laws (Chagnon 1968:91,93).
> Although it is difficult to reach a decision as to which principle of exchange is dominant, the entire tenor of Yanomamö culture leads one to infer that nothing is ever given without an expectation of a return. Therefore, it can be concluded that balanced reciprocity is the dominant principle of exchange in the local group.
> Balanced reciprocity occurs between Yanomamö local groups (Chagnon 1968:100):

Three distinct features of Yanomamo trading practices are important in the context of alliance formation. First, each item must be repaid with a different kind of item. . . . Secondly, the payment is delayed. . . . The consequence of these two trading features is that one trade always calls forth another and gives the members of different villages both the excuse and the opportunity to visit each other. . . . The third significant trade feature is the peculiar specialization in the production of trade items. Each village has one or more special products that it provides to its allies. These include such items as dogs, hallucinogenic drugs (both cultivated and collected), arrow points, arrow shafts, bows, cotton yarn, cotton and vine hammocks, baskets of several varieties, clay pots, and in the case of the several contacted villages, steel tools and aluminum pots.

> Intervillage feasting, in addition to trading, is also an example of balanced reciprocity (Chagnon 1968:97):

The chief purpose of entertaining allies is to reaffirm and cultivate intervillage solidarity in the intimate, sociable context of food presentations, thereby putting the ally under obligation to reciprocate the feast in his own village at a later date, bringing about another feast and even more solidarity.

Market exchange is dominant in Qemantland, both within the local group and between local groups. Gamst states (1969:81–83):

The Qemant have at least four modes of distributing their production. Allocation of goods and services may be by formal market exchange inside of a marketplace, by informal market exchange outside of a marketplace, by collection and redistribution in connection with ritual, and by reciprocity. . . .

Means of transportation and communication in the Qemant region are poorly developed, and the Qemant peasant has access only to his own regional marketing system, which is little affected by conditions outside Qemant society. Marketing, formal and informal, is the exchange of goods and services at prices arrived at by supply and demand.

Money is almost always used in formal marketing and is sometimes employed in informal marketing. Today the official Ethiopian copper and paper currency is used as the principal medium of exchange. . . .

Formal marketing is held at fixed times in marketplaces, usually little more than vacant clearings when the market is not being held. . . .

For the Qemant peasant, trading at a marketplace is a means of exchanging a commodity of which he has a slight surplus for another commodity which he lacks. . . .

In the marketplace, one might additionally . . . hear the latest of the customary pronouncements from the local feudal officials. These officials have long guaranteed the peaceful existence of the marketplace so that their region will prosper, and produce taxes, through trade and commercial traffic to centers of trade. . . .

Informal marketing consists of exchange between two persons in which middlemen are not involved, and money is seldom used. This trade may be transacted anywhere in a community at almost any time. In most transactions, a certain amount of one commodity is deemed equal in value to a certain amount of another commodity and the two are exchanged. Before livestock is exchanged, however, the price of the beasts is agreed upon in Maria Theresa dollars. If one of the parties in the transaction receives an animal worth less than the one he has given, he receives additional produce priced at the number of Maria Theresas needed to balance the exchange.

It appears from the above description that "formal marketing" occurs between local groups and that "informal marketing" prevails within local groups.

Both types of reciprocity also occur within local groups. Balanced reciprocity is described in the first paragraph below, and generalized reciprocity is described in the second paragraph (Gamst 1969:84):

Qemant distribute a significant part of their goods and services through modes of reciprocity. It may be a bond of reciprocity between breast father and breast child, between a man and his fictive mize brothers, among all members of a community mahebar association, or simply between two neighbors, interacting in a very limited context, who help one another with house repairs.

The items involved in reciprocal exchange are not easily equated. For example, a priest may use his influence on behalf of and give special blessings to a peasant who regularly feeds and occasionally labors for the priest. Two families might engage in a continuous round of giving gifts, including meals, to one another. A rich man may build up his social credit in the community by feeding and entertaining people and by giving rather generous compensation to those who occasionally till his fields for him.

> In addition to market exchange, which is integrative for the entire culture of the Qemant, redistribution through a nonlocal allocative center also occurs (Gamst 1969:83):

The third mode of distribution [the first two described were formal and informal marketing] ties in with Qemant religious practices and kinship, and consists of collection and redistribution, in connection with ceremonies, of beverages and raw and processed foods. Peasants contribute animals and food used by the wambar and the priests for sacrifices and feasts. Contributions are made according to a person's means, the wealthy donating more than the poor. However, at ceremonies every participant consumes to his capacity or until the supply is exhausted. At certain times in the year, everyone in a community is thus guaranteed a feast that includes meat, which is not ordinarily part of a poor person's diet.

> Gamst continues by describing a phenomenon which he considers to be redistribution, but what is more properly classified as generalized reciprocity within the local group, since a local allocative agency is absent and since the recipients are apparently not due what they receive and the givers are apparently not obliged to give (1969:83 –84):

Collection and redistribution of food for use in rituals is sometimes based on kinship and membership in associations. For rites of passage, food is collected from people who are related to the persons undergoing the rites, and distributed among the members of the community.

> Taxation by the Ethiopian government is also another form of redis-

tribution, which tends however to integrate the Qemant into a modern nation rather than to integrate Qemant culture (Gamst 1969: 20,71).

STRATIFICATION

Stratification refers to an arrangement of noticeable layers or strata, one on top of the other in a hierarchical manner. In the natural sciences it can usually be inferred that the upper layers have formed more recently than the lower layers. However, in the social sciences stratification does not refer to noticeable physical layering, but to the noticeable differences in attributes of different groups of people. It is the differences within each attribute which create the hierarchical order. Inequality is the term used to describe these differences between the layers or strata in social stratification. Inequality is seen by both anthropologists and sociologists in terms of three attributes: wealth and property, privilege and power, and status and prestige. Therefore, the upper or higher strata are characterized by more wealth, privilege, and status than are the lower strata.

States are political communities in which sharp cleavages in wealth, privilege, and status are found (see "The People," in Chapter 2). While there is not complete agreement among social scientists, the trend recently is to consider stratification based upon inequality as a feature exclusive to the state, whether the state be a primitive culture, a preindustrial country, or a modern nation. Nonstate cultures are viewed as not being stratified, but as being ranked. This position has been strongly enunciated by Fried (1967) who argues that "rank societies" have a fixed number of positions of valued status. On the other hand, a "stratified society is one in which members of the same sex and equivalent age status do not have equal access to the basic resources that sustain life" (Fried 1967: 186). Fried believes that it is almost impossible to find stratified societies lacking state institutions (1967:185, 224).

Three types of stratification will be identified: castes, classes, and slavery. There are other forms of stratification, but because they are rare and restricted to particular geographic regions they will not be described. Systems of stratification are built from the kinds of peoples which are found within state level political communities. Thus, dependent native peoples, peasant communities, and ethnic groups are the elements by which systems of stratification are constructed. These groups of people are politically incorporated into the state.

Castes and classes are frequently described and defined by contrasting them. That approach will be followed here. Castes are considered to be "closed" and classes "open." For sociologists this means that in caste systems social mobility is rare to nonexistent—an individual is born into and generally dies a member of the same caste; in class systems there is both upward and downward mobility for individuals—by gaining or losing property, power, and prestige one can raise or lower his status (i.e., move into another stratum). Furthermore, in terms of distinctiveness castes are sharply defined, but classes are not (Tumin 1973:43–139). For anthropologists closed or open is interpreted in terms of kinship and marriage. In a caste system an individual must marry someone of his own stratum or caste. Thus castes are frequently referred to as "closed endogamous classes" (Harris 1975:421), endogamous meaning marrying within a particular social group. In a class system an individual can marry someone of either a higher or lower stratum. But the fundamental difference between caste and class goes beyond these differences. They are two ways of ordering occupational or ecomonic roles. *Castes* represent an "ascriptive occupational role system found in preindustrial state systems" (Gould 1971:8); caste members are restricted in their occupational choices and frequently have the same occupation. *Classes,* on the other hand, are found in modern nations with industrialism, market exchange economy, and achieved placement in occupational roles; they typically are composed of individuals with similar broad categories of occupations, such as the laboring class.

Historically, according to Gould (1971), castes arose gradually in the ancient Middle East out of "ethnic diversity" and "technological variety," while classes developed in Western countries after the emergence of the industrial revolution. Thus, castes are characteristic of what were once conquering primitive states; those conquered became dependent native peoples. Classes are characteristic of modern industrial nations. Since individuals are grouped into classes by occupational roles or specialties, they draw their membership from dependent native peoples, peasant communities, or ethnic groups.

A third type of stratification is slavery. Unlike caste and class systems which are based upon occupational roles, slavery is a form of servility; it is a relationship in which one "individual has legal rights in another, if these rights are held to the exclusion of other persons and are not derived from either contractural or kinship obligations" (Bohannan 1963:179). Such a definition excludes apprentices and indentured servants. In slavery the essential element of the arrangement is the right of the master or owner to command his slave to labor or render other services for him (Moore 1964:642). A slave, unlike a member of a caste or class, is kinless; he is attached to his master's kinship group through his master. The two most common ways of becoming a slave are to be sold by one's kinship group or to be captured in war. In some regions warfare is conducted for the purpose of obtaining slaves, which are then sold to the members of other cultures. Slaves thus form a single stratum typically found at the lowest level of the hierarchical order. Slavery may be found in cultures which have either caste or class systems or neither.

12. **What types of stratification are present?**
    1. absent
    2. castes
    3. classes
    4. slavery

The first step is to determine if the political community is a state. If it is not, stratification as defined above is absent. If the political community is a state, then the student should examine closely the economic system for evidence of stratification. If the state is a primitive culture or a preindustrial country, it is likely that castes and slavery will be present. If the state is a modern nation with industrialism, it is highly likely that classes will be present. If a type of stratification is found which does not correspond to one of the three types of stratification identified in this section, it should be noted in some detail on the data sheet.

Economic differences between households, based largely upon occupational differences between household heads, exist in Long Bay Cays. These differences indicate the existence of classes (Otterbein 1966:111):

The procedure followed in demonstrating economic differences between household types consists of constructing an economic index that will permit the ranking of individual households and household types. The method used is derived from the technique developed by W. Lloyd Warner, Marchia Meeker, and Kenneth Eells (1960) for constructing an index (known as the Index of Status Characteristics) to measure an individual's social class. For Long Bay Cays, house type, property, and occupation were found to be suitable indicators for distinguishing economic differences between household types.

> All the male-headed household types, except for one case of a father-child household, rank higher than any of the female-headed types (Otterbein 1966:114). The ethnography describes how a man over time raises his "level of economic well-being."

> Since Yanomamö political communities are not states, stratification is absent.

> The Qemant stratification system is described by Gamst as feudal (1969:3):

The use of the term "feudal" in this book closely parallels the use of the word by historians, who employ it to mean relationships of lord and vassal such as once existed in Europe. Indeed the feudal system of Christian Ethiopia, which persists largely unmodified to this day, is similar to the feudal system once prevalent in Christian Europe.

> Since the Qemant do not appear to have castes, classes, or slavery, their feudal system should be briefly described (Gamst 1969:20–21):

The Qemant peasant communities were integrated into first the Abyssinian and later the Ethiopian nation by administrative and economic bonds, and thus their ties with the nation are ancient. An Amhara-Tegre feudal elite today controls and taxes the Qemant, as it does all of the ethnic groups of the nation. This feudal structure is gradually being transformed into a modern bureaucracy on the industrial-urban model, but at present the Qemant, who are in a lower stratum of the feudal structure, are still in direct contact with feudal administrators.

STUDY GUIDE QUESTIONS

Aim of Chapter 3

> This chapter discusses the relationship between a population and its technology and economy. Anthropologists in conducting their studies search for the ways in which the subsistence technology affects a population, and they typically find expressions of this influence in such areas as population density and settlement patterns.

> In addition, the anthropologist also attempts to develop an understanding of a culture in terms of its principles of stratification and eco-

nomic exchange systems as well as its fundamental economic breakdown via the division of labor.

Subsistence Technology
1. What are subsistence technologies? Illustrate your understanding of this term with examples from your background of knowledge.
2. Identify the five basic subsistence technologies. Who does the primary work in each?

Population Density
3. How is population density tied to subsistence technology? Which technologies would support the greatest population? the least?
4. If a culture has 3000 members and a territory of 12,000 square miles, what is the population density?

Division of Labor
5. On what basis is the division of labor made? Illustrate with examples how the division of labor has changed in the United States during the past few decades. (answer not in text)
6. At what subsistence levels would you expect to find part-time and full-time specialists? What seems to be the key factor which is necessary before specialists emerge?

House Form
7. Identify the various functions which are associated with the house or dwelling.
8. Distinguish between the terms house and household.
9. What should the anthropologist be aware of when he studies the size and locations of houses?

Settlement Pattern
10. What variables influence settlement patterns?
11. What type of settlement would you expect for a hunting and gathering culture? An agricultural based culture?

Settlement Size
12. What is the value in knowing the size of the largest settlement in a culture?

Economy
13. Differentiate between *balanced* and *generalized reciprocity*.
14. How does redistribution differ from market exchange?
15. Elman Service is cited as suggesting three different types of integra-

tion: social, political, and economic. Give examples of each type of integration for (a) your school as a cultural unit, and (b) your community. (answer not in text)

Stratification

16. Define how the anthropologist uses the term *stratification* and identify the attributes and political community which most often lead to this social ordering.
17. Compare and contrast *caste* and *class* in terms of social mobility, distinctiveness, marriage opportunities, and occupational or economic roles.
18. Contrast the development of castes and classes.
19. In what ways does slavery differ from membership in a caste system?

The procession leaves the church after a wedding on Andros Island.

4

FAMILY AND KINSHIP

Residence
Marriage
Household Type
Descent Groups
Kindreds
Cousin Marriage
Kinship Terminology

One of the most difficult problems facing an enthnographer is to be able to distinguish between ideal and real behavior. Since much of the data collected in the field comes from the verbal accounts of individuals, it is necessary that the ethnographer ascertain whether the information is a statement of what ought to be or a recounting of what does occur. Informants will often describe the ideal behavior of the members of their culture in a manner which allows the interviewer to construe the response as a statement of the actual behavior. This is not usually a deliberate attempt to lie and deceive, but rather it arises from the embarrassment that the informant would feel if he told of practices which he was not proud. The skilled ethnographer avoids confusing the ideal and the real by checking his data with other informants, by collecting cases in detail, by observing as much behavior as possible, and by collecting census and genealogical data. If this is done, the monograph prepared by the ethnographer will distinguish between those statements describing what ought to be and those describing what is.

In no realm of anthropology is it more important to distinguish between ideal and real behavior than in the study of the family and kinship. An informant may tell the ethnographer where a person should live, what kind of household he should live in, how many wives he should have, whether he should marry a first cousin, what descent groups he should belong to, and how he should address certain relatives. Yet in every instance, only a small minority of the members of the culture may be actually doing what they and others think they ought to be doing. In the sections in this chapter the student should record the real behavior or frequency of occurrence of the practices. If there is an explicit rule, norm, or ideal which does or does not correspond with the actual practice, it should also be recorded.

RESIDENCE

Marital residence has been an important topic of anthropological research since the latter part of the nineteenth century. Edward B. Tylor (1888), in what is probably the most outstanding article ever to be written by an anthropologist, distinguished three types of marital residence and showed their relationship to several different kinship customs. The three types of residence were also related to stages of cultural evolution. According to Tylor (1888:247), at the lowest stage of cultural development the husband took up "his abode with the wife's family permanently," at a higher stage he did so "temporarily and eventually to remove with her to his own family or home (the reverse of this does not occur)," and at the highest stage "the husband takes his wife to his home." Today these modes of residence are known respectively as matrilocal, matri-patrilocal, and patrilocal residence. For Tylor matri-patrilocal residence was referred to as transitional or removal; the other two types were left unnamed. The recent "classic" statement on residence comes from George P. Murdock in his book *Social Structure* (1949). He defines *matrilocal* residence as occurring if the groom leaves "his parental home and live[s] with his bride, either in the house of her parents or in a dwelling nearby" (1949:16). *Patrilocal* residence occurs if "the

bride regularly removes to or near the parental home of the groom"
(1949:16). Murdock proposes the term *matri-patrilocal* residence
for the combination in which matrilocal residence occurs "for an
initial period, usually for a year or until the birth of the first child,
to be followed by permanent patrilocal residence" (1949:17). He
considers this form of residence "only a special variant of patrilocal
residence" (1949:17).

In addition to defining the above three modes of residence,
Murdock describes several other forms of marital residence. In
avunculocal residence the couple "reside with or near a maternal
uncle of the groom rather than with the parents of either spouse
or in a separate home of their own" (1949:17). The most difficult
form of residence to understand is *bilocal* or *ambilocal* residence,
since the practice refers not to a single couple but to all the married
couples in the culture or the local group. "Some societies permit
a married couple to live with or near the parents of either spouse,
in which case such factors as the relative wealth or status of the
two families or the personal preferences of the parties to the union
are likely to determine whether they will choose to reside matrilocally or patrilocally" (1949:16). Thus individual couples practice
either patrilocal or matrilocal residence—they themselves do not
practice ambilocal residence. This form of residence pertains to the
frequency of both patrilocal and matrilocal residence in the culture
or local group. Murdock (1967:156) has helped to clarify the situation by stating that ambilocal residence is "residence established
optionally with or near the parents of either the husband or the
wife . . . where neither alternative exceeds the other in actual frequency by a ratio of greater than two to one." For our purposes, the
phrase "with or near" in the above definitions is interpreted to mean
within the household of the parents.

The types of residence described above involve a move by
one of the marital partners from his or her parental home to the
parental home of the other partner (or to the home of the groom's
maternal uncle). Thus new households are not formed. What occurs
is a change in the composition of the membership of the parental
households. (The nature of the changes which occur will be discussed in the section titled "Household Type.") On the other hand,
there are four types of residence which do lead to the formation of
new households. Best known of these types is neolocal residence.
Murdock has defined *neolocal* residence as "normal residence apart
from the relatives of both spouses or at a place not determined by
the kin ties of either" (1967:156). Two other types of residence,
which produce new households, are virilocal and uxorilocal resi-

dence. *Virilocal* residence means that the "married couple customarily becomes part of the male's natal residence group"; *uxorilocal* residence means that the "couple customarily becomes part of the female's natal group" (Service 1962:30). The use of the term natal is ambiguous since it can refer either to the household or the local group into which one is born. Here, "natal" will be interpreted to mean within the local group, but not within the household. The need to distinguish between household and local group in the use of terms for types of residence has been recognized by Carrasco (1963).

All three of the above definitions can be rendered more precise by considering the various logical alternatives open to a married man and woman who are establishing their own household. They may establish their household in a local group other than the local group or groups where their parental homes are located (neolocal residence). They may establish their household in a local group in which the man's parental home is located, but not the woman's parental home (virilocal residence). They may establish their household in a local group in which the woman's parental home is located, but not the man's parental home (uxorilocal residence). A fourth logical alternative exists—they may establish their household in the same local group in which the parental homes of both the man and the woman are located. For this type of residence I propose the term *commonlocal.* Although marriage within the local group has been referred to as "local endogamy," the expression does not distinguish between residence involving the establishment of a new household and residence in which one partner moves into the parental home of the other partner.

An ethnographer in the field is faced with the task of ascertaining what form of residence is being practiced by each married couple in the local group or groups he is studying. (Criteria for identifying marital unions will be discussed in the next section.) When this is completed he must tabulate the frequency with which each type of residence occurs. The frequencies are used for classifying a culture as to the type of residence which prevails. Table 1 shows the classification of cultures, based upon the frequency ranges (in percentages) of practices followed by individual couples. (The frequency ranges are derived from Murdock's definition of ambilocal residence.) In order to determine the residence practice of a culture, it is necessary to locate in the ethnography the most detailed enumeration of the types of residence practiced by individual couples. Sometimes this information is found in a table, sometimes in a statement to the effect that a certain percentage or fre-

TABLE 1   Classification of Cultures by Individual Couples

Type of Residence	Type of Residence Practiced by Couples	Percentage Practicing
Ambilocal	Patrilocal and	33–66
	Matrilocal	33–66
Patrilocal*	Patrilocal* and	67–100
	All other types of residence combined	0–33

* Any of the remaining six types of residence—matrilocal, avunculocal, neolocal, virilocal, uxorilocal, and commonlocal—may be substituted in the formula for patrilocal.

quency of the people reside according to one of the types of residence. In older ethnographies, when it was not the practice for ethnographers to take a detailed census, one may find only a statement that residence is either patrilocal, matrilocal, or neolocal (ambilocal, avunculocal, virilocal, uxorilocal, and commonlocal are newer terms). The residence data, converted to percentages if necessary, are compared with the right-hand side of the chart. For example, if 60 percent of the couples reside patrilocally and 40 percent matrilocally, the culture is classified as ambilocal. However, if 80 percent of the couples reside patrilocally and only 20 percent reside matrilocally, then the culture is classified as patrilocal. If the residence data consists of frequencies of types of residence which do not fit the right-hand side of the chart, these frequencies should be recorded and no attempt should be made to classify the culture according to one of the eight residence practices.

Matri-patrilocal residence presents a problem in classification, since a local group practicing this form of residence would show at a particular point in time some couples residing matrilocally and the remainder residing patrilocally. It would be a mistake to classify the culture as ambilocal, since the couples residing matrilocally will soon be residing patrilocally. If the ethnographer states that couples residing matrilocally will soon be residing patrilocally, then residence can be classified as matri-patrilocal.

13. **What type of marital residence is practiced?**
    1. ambilocal
    2. patrilocal

3. matrilocal
4. avunculocal
5. neolocal
6. virilocal
7. uxorilocal
8. commonlocal
9. matri-patrilocal
10. other _____

The above discussion of residence has focused upon only the real behavior of individual couples, although much of the literature in anthropology which deals with marital residence, including Murdock's treatment, concerns itself primarily with the ideal—that is, with the explicit cultural rules which state what people ought to do. Thus many discussions of residence are discussions of marital residence rules. It is important to know what the rules are (if indeed there are such rules) and whether the actual residence of individual couples conforms or does not conform to the rules. In understanding any culture it is crucial to know why conformity does or does not occur. Thus not only should one record the type of residence practiced, but he should also note what the residence rules are if they are explicitly stated in the ethnography. Such rules will read the same as the definitions of the eight types of residence, with the addition of a phrase such as "the couple should," "custom requires," or "the husband is expected to."

Ideally residence in Long Bay Cays is virilocal. The single household dwellings are, according to explicit cultural rules, erected within the village where the young man grew up and where his parents are living (Otterbein 1966:85):

House Building. The house lot is usually provided by a young man's father from land that he owns in the village. Although the father does not have to contribute financially to the building of his son's house, the community expects him to provide the lot. Sometimes this land is located beside the father's house, but usually it is elsewhere in the village. If the father has no land, some other relative may provide the lot, or if the youth is already courting a girl, her parents may furnish the land.

The actual types of residence practiced by individual couples are enumerated in Table 2 (Otterbein 1966:36):

TABLE 2   Residence Pattern

Form of Residence		Percent
Village endogamy (both husband and wife grew up and are living in same village)		25
Community endogamy (both grew up in one of the four villages in the community)		
Virilocal (live in his village)	14	
Uxorilocal (live in her village)	4	
		18
Community exogamy (either husband or wife came from outside the community)		
Virilocal (wife from outside)	27	
Uxorilocal (husband from outside)	28	
		55
Neolocal (both from outside)		2
Total		100

If the "male's natal residence group" or village of birth is considered to be the local group, rather than the community (i.e., the four villages covered by the census) or Long Bay Cays itself, it can be concluded from the table that 41 percent of the couples reside virilocally, 32 percent uxorilocally, 25 percent commonlocally, and 2 percent neolocally. The frequencies of types of residence do not fit the right-hand side of Table 1, and hence the data should be reported with no attempt to classify the Andros Islanders according to one of the eight residence practices.

A Yanomamö male upon marriage usually establishes his own household within the village in which he grew up (see Question 9, above). His wife is likely to be a cross-cousin (see Question 18 in Chapter 4) from the same village. If she is not a member of his village or he marries a nonrelative in another village, he will probably have to perform bride service, perhaps for as long as three years. During this period the husband lives in his wife's village and hunts for his wife and her parents (Chagnon 1968:79, 93). Hence, for some men residence is initially matrilocal. Some wives are obtained by abduction (Chagnon 1968:73, 98). Thus the vast majority (exact figures are not given) of Yanomamö men reside in their own village. Their wives are from the same or a different village. Many anthropologists would classify the Yanomamö as patrilocal; however, Chagnon refrains from using residence concepts such as patrilocal. Strict adherence to the above definitions requires that the Yanomamö be classified as having both commonlocal and virilocal residence, since a man establishes his own household upon marriage and remains in the local group in which his parental home is located. Since one cannot be certain that over 67 percent of the men are residing commonlocally, the Yanomamö cannot be classified as either commonlocal or virilocal. Hence both types of residence should be recorded.

Marital residence for the Qemant is initially patrilocal, then becomes virilocal or commonlocal (Gamst 1969:109–110):

If a girl is past puberty at the time of her marriage, she usually resides with the groom at his father's house. . . .
After several years of marriage, a couple builds its own house and sets up a household next to that of the groom's parents.

However, if the bride has not reached puberty, she continues to live with her parents while the groom continues to live with his parents (Gamst 1969:109–110).
Gamst describes Qemant marital residence with the following technical terms (1969:69):

Residence after marriage but before the newlywed couple builds a house is duolocal at first, the groom living with his parents and the bride with her parents. Residence then gradually becomes patrilocal or, at times, matrilocal, the married couple living with the groom's parents or with the bride's parents. . . . Residence after construction of a house is usually patrilocal; a son builds a house near that of his father after approximately three to five years of marriage.

Elsewhere Gamst states that (1969:26):

Patrilocality (residence of a married couple with or near the groom's parents) is the nominal rule, although it is followed only about seventy percent of the time. In practice, a man may build his house anywhere, given sufficient incentive (options on the land of his wife's family or a relative's family, or strife within his own family).

Gamst, it should be noted, is using the term patrilocal in its earlier more general sense. Thus his use of the term includes patrilocal, virilocal, and commonlocal. Since information concerning which communities men take their wives from is lacking, it is not possible to determine whether virilocal or commonlocal residence is the prevailing mode of marital residence. Probably—and this is only a guess—most men obtain wives from their own local group; however, some men may be forced to seek wives from other local groups because of restrictions imposed by kinship and religion. Since none of the types of marital residence described above appear to exceed 67 percent, all four types should be recorded—patrilocal, matrilocal, virilocal, and commonlocal. "Duolocal" residence, mentioned by Gamst, should not be regarded as a type of marital residence, since the bride and groom are not living together. In fact, common residence is one criterion for distinguishing marital unions (see "Marriage" below).

MARRIAGE

Marriage is a sexual relationship between a man and woman who share a common residence or household. The relationship is to be distinguished both from casual mating and from relatively permanent sexual relationships which do not involve living together. On the other hand, living together does not constitute marriage unless the man and the woman are sexual partners. For marriage to exist, then, two criteria must be satisfied: presence of a sexual relationship and common residence. Marriage thus is cohabitation—living together as husband and wife. The marital relationship is sometimes referred to as the conjugal tie (Fox 1967:39–40) or the conjugal dyad (Adams 1960:39). Marriage is also referred to as an affinal relationship. When a man and woman enter into marriage, a social unit or entity— a marital group—is formed. The above definition of marriage can be referred to as a common sense definition; it corresponds to what most of us think of as marriage. Some anthropologists, however, do not regard this definition of marriage as satisfactory since there are some cultures—very few—which do not have marriage or marital groups in terms of the above definitions. These anthropologists prefer a definition which is applicable to all cultures (Malinowski 1930: 140; Gough 1959:32; Goodenough 1970:12–13). Although the common sense definition may not be universally applicable, such a definition, based upon two criteria, permits the delineation of different types of marriage, or rather marital groups.

The types of marriage found among the different peoples of the world are known by nearly everyone—monogamy, polygyny, and polyandry. *Monogamy* is the marriage of one man to one woman;

polygyny is the marriage of one man to two or more women at one time; *polyandry* is the marriage of one woman to two or more men at one time. (The term polygamy refers to either polygyny or polyandry and means "multiple mates.") What is not usually realized, however, is that these types of marriage do not pertain to individual marital unions but to the composition of marital groups. That is, the type of marriage does not affect the nature of the marital relationship, as defined above. Rather, the terms refer to the social groups which are formed when individual men and women enter into one or more marital unions. This point can probably be more easily grasped if the composition of each of the three types of marital groups is diagramed. The following symbols, employed by virtually all anthropologists, are utilized in the diagrams: △ (triangle) = male; ◯ (circle) = female; = (equal sign) = marital union; ⧄ or ∅ (slash) = deceased male or female; ⌐──¬ = the sibling relationship.

Type of Marriage	Diagram Showing Composition of Marital Group	Definition
Monogamy	△ = ◯	male married to female
Polygyny	◯ = △ = ◯	male married to two females
Polyandry	△ = ◯ = △	female married to two males

Logically a fourth type of marital group can occur. This would consist of two or more men being married to two or more women at one time. Such a group can be diagramed as follows:

$$\begin{array}{ccc} △ & = & ◯ \\ ‖ & & ‖ \\ ◯ & = & △ \end{array}$$

Following the practice of nineteenth-century anthropologists, this type of marital group can be called *group marriage*. However, ethnographic research has demonstrated that group marriage has never occurred as the prevailing type of marital group in any culture. A fifth type of marital group can be derived from the diagram for group marriage if a marital union does not exist between one of the men and one of the women:

$$\begin{array}{c} \triangle = \bigcirc \\ \parallel \\ \bigcirc = \triangle \end{array}$$

Such a group can be labeled polyandry-polygyny. I know of only one culture in which such marital groups were frequently found—the Marquesan Islanders of the South Pacific (Otterbein 1963).

Some cultures are 100 percent monogamous; that is, only monogamous marital groups are found present in the culture. Such a situation usually occurs because of a rule which prohibits an individual from having more than one spouse at one time. However, a majority of the world's cultures permit men to be married to more than one woman at one time. Thus many cultures contain polygynous marital groups. Sometimes a culture permits a man to take for a second wife only his current wife's sister, a practice which results in what is known as *sororal polygyny:*

$$\bigcirc = \triangle = \bigcirc$$

Since it is rare to find a culture in which every married man has more than one wife (a man usually marries one wife, then later another), most cultures containing polygynous marital groups also contain monogamous marital groups. On the other hand, it is rare to find a culture which permits a man to have more than one wife, and yet which contains only monogamous marital groups. Polyandrous marital groups are rarely found. Few cultures permit a woman to be married to two or more men at one time. When it is permitted, the two men are often brothers. Such a practice is known as *fraternal polyandry:*

$$\triangle = \bigcirc = \triangle$$

When polyandrous marital groups are discovered, the culture is also likely to contain both monogamous and polygynous marital groups. One study of 554 cultures found that 24 percent of the world's cultures were monogamous, 75 percent were polygynous, and 1 percent were polyandrous (Murdock 1957:686).

Two exceedingly widespread marital practices are the levirate and the sororate. If a man marries the widow of his deceased brother, the practice is known as the *levirate*; if a man marries the sister of his deceased wife, it is known as the *sororate*. The levirate, which can also be viewed as the marriage of a woman to her deceased husband's brother, can be diagramed as follows:

$$\triangle = \bigcirc = \triangle$$

The sororate, which can also be viewed as the marriage of a woman to the husband of her deceased sister, can be diagramed as follows:

$$\bigcirc = \triangle = \varnothing$$

These practices serve to maintain kinship ties between intermarrying kinship groups—the new spouse is, of course, a member of the deceased spouse's kinship group. Furthermore, continuity in the rearing of children is maintained: the new husband is providing for his brother's children and the new wife is caring for her sister's children. These two important functions probably account for the widespread occurrence of both the levirate and sororate.

Just as an ethnographer needs to ascertain the type of residence being practiced by each married couple in the local group, he also needs to describe the composition of the marital groups to which the married couples belong. Each married individual will belong to one, and only one, marital group at one time. Monogamous groups, of course, will consist of only two individuals, while polygynous and polyandrous groups will vary in size from three to perhaps hundreds of individuals (if one man has hundreds of wives). Each marital group can be classified according to one of the three types of marriage. Then the frequency of each type of marital group can be tabulated. Although most ethnographers do not present the data in their monographs in terms of the number of marital groups conforming to each type of marriage, they often do provide information on the number of wives each man has. Since each married man belongs to a different marital group, except where polyandry occurs, the number of men with only one wife provides us with the number of monogamous marital unions and the number of men with more than one wife provides us with the number of polygynous marital unions. The figures can be used to compute percentages. If all (100 percent) of the marital groups in the culture are monogamous, the culture is classified as practicing *monogamy*. If the percentage of polygynous marital groups in a culture ranges between 1 and 19 percent, the culture is classified as practicing *limited polygyny*; if the percentage of polygynous marital groups ranges from 20 to 100 percent, the culture is classified as practicing *general polygyny* (Murdock 1957:670–671). Twenty percent is an arbitrary dividing line which roughly separates cultures practicing polygyny into two equal groups. If there are polyandrous marital groups in the culture, the culture is classified as practicing *polyandry.*

14.   What type of marriage is practiced?
    1. monogamy
    2. limited polygyny
    3. general polygyny
    4. polyandry

The type of marriage practiced is determined by the percentage of the different types of marital groups in the culture. The actual percentages should be recorded. If the culture does not have marriage and marital groups are absent—and it is rare to find such cultures—the absence of marriage should be noted.

      Monogamy is practiced by the Andros Islanders. Although the term monogamy is never mentioned, the lengthy discussion of courtship, marriage, and the mating system leave no doubt that they are monogamous (Otterbein 1966:33–56, 67–84). Tables showing ages at marriage, number of separations, age and conjugal condition of the population, number of marriages, and the distribution of the population by household type confirm this conclusion (Otterbein 1966:45, 72–73, 80, 104). The mating system is summarized as follows (Otterbein 1966:83–84):

The mating system of the inhabitants of Long Bay Cays is based on two of the three possible choices in mating . . . : marriage and extra-residential unions. Consensual unions, although common in many areas in the Caribbean and the New World, are unimportant; only separated individuals who cannot remarry cohabit consensually. Since a young man and woman are not permitted to enter into a consensual union, the only mating alternatives open to them are marriage and extra-residential unions. Although the community does not sanction the latter type of union for a young couple, such unions do in fact exist. An engaged couple can be said to be mating extra-residentially when a stable sexual union involving separate residences becomes established following the sending of the engagement letter. Even if his fiancée becomes pregnant, rather than cohabiting consensually the man will wait until his house is finished before marrying, although it may mean that their first child is born out of wedlock.

Once married, the husband will have love affairs and may also succeed in establishing an extra-residential union with a single, separated, or widowed woman. His wife, on the other hand, is not permitted to have a sweetheart. If a man learns his wife is having an affair, a separation results. Separated persons, since they are neither divorced nor widowed, may only mate extra-residentially or cohabit consensually. Widowed persons have all three mating choices open to them. However, if a widowed person should wish to mate with a separated person, only two are permissible. Since separated and widowed persons . . . usually prefer not to enter a conjugal union, the frequency of remarriages and consensual unions is low.

General polygyny is practiced by the Yanomamö. Although exact figures are not given, it appears that well over 20 percent of the marital groups are polygynous (Chagnon 1968:73, 75). A case is described in which the village headman shares his house with his youngest brother, and he also "shares" his younger wife with his brother (Chagnon 1968:14, 89). This appears to be a case of fraternal polyandry. However, the arrangement is probably temporary, and hence the marital group does not warrant being classified as polyandrous.

The Qemant practice monogamy (Gamst 1969:67):

Marriage among the Qemant is monogamous. Concubinage exists, but there is now no polygyny, although Qemant legends, Ethiopic manuscripts, and early European accounts mention this practice.

HOUSEHOLD TYPE

A household, as defined earlier, is one or more persons who live together in the same dwelling and cooperate in a variety of domestic affairs. Usually the group occupies a physical structure with walls and a roof which can be described as a house or homestead. In some instances, however, the household may occupy a unit in a larger structure, or the household may occupy several houses, usually adjacent (see "House Form," in Chapter 3). The people occupying the house must cooperate in some domestic and subsistence tasks for a household to exist. That is, the members of a household cook, eat, sleep, and work together—they can be said to share a common hearth. The basis of this cooperation is usually a division of labor characterized by age and sex. Most households are composed of married men and women and their offspring. Thus, in addition to domestic economic cooperation, the household usually performs three other functions: sexual gratification, reproduction and child care, and socialization of children (Murdock 1949:7–11).

The household or domestic group provides the link between mother-child units and the local group, as well as to the larger culture to which the local groups belong. The mother-child relationship is sometimes referred to as the maternal dyad (Adams 1960:39). The "domestic domain is the system of social relations through which the reproductive nucleus is integrated with the environment and with the structure of the total society" (Fortes 1958:9). From the point of view of the socialization of the child, Parsons and Bales (1955) have emphasized the "expressive" quality of the mother role and the "instrumental" quality of the father role. Expressive roles are emotion/feeling oriented—mother handles internal disruptions and soothes over conflicts. Instrumental roles are task/job oriented —father is primarily interested in getting things done. Expressive roles are more important within the household, while instrumental roles are prominent in relating the domestic group to extra-familial systems. The link between households and the local group can be viewed in terms of interaction; that is, each makes contributions to the other. The household or domestic group serves to integrate its members into the local group and culture, and this function is aided by the instrumental role played by the father (Bell and Vogel 1960:8).

Although it is possible to have households or domestic groups which consist of nonrelated individuals, the types of households described below are composed of individuals related by kinship and marriage. Diagrams will be used to show the social composition of each household type. The symbols introduced in the previous section will be used, plus one additional symbol:

| (a vertical line) = the relationship of descent

The diagrams used to illustrate household composition are enclosed in rectangles which symbolize the physical structure in which households live.

The type of household characteristic of a culture depends primarily upon the type of marital groups present and the mode of residence practiced. Independent nuclear family households are formed when monogamous marital groups and neolocal, virilocal, uxorilocal, or commonlocal residence occur together. By definition monogamy means that there will be only one husband and one wife living in the household, and neolocal, virilocal, uxorilocal, or commonlocal residence means that the couple and any children resulting from the union will reside in a house independent of the parental home of either spouse. A household with the following composition results:

The diagram shows a husband, a wife, and two children, a brother and a sister. The square enclosing the diagram symbolizes the house in which the parents and children reside. Thus an *independent nuclear family household* is a domestic group consisting of a married couple and their child or children who occupy a dwelling which is not part of any other household. A household with only a married couple is usually considered by anthropologists to be an independent nuclear family household since it is likely that the couple will have a child in the near future.

Independent polygamous family households occur when either polygynous or polyandrous marital groups and neolocal, virilocal, uxorilocal, or commonlocal residence prevail within a culture. If the marital group is polygynous, there will be one husband, two or more wives, and their children living in the household. A household with the following structure results:

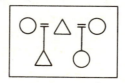

If the marital group is polyandrous, there will be one wife, her children, and two or more husbands living in the household. Such a household can be diagramed as follows:

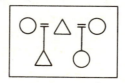

(Although it is usually not possible to determine the biological father of each child when polyandry occurs, one husband is shown as the father of the children in the diagram.) Thus an *independent polyga-mous family household* is a domestic group consisting of either a polygynous or a polyandrous marital group and its children who occupy a dwelling which is not part of any other household. Both independent nuclear family households and independent polygamous family households contain two generations of related individuals.

Extended family households come into existence when marital residence is other than neolocal, virilocal, uxorilocal, or common-local. Either patrilocal, matrilocal, or avunculocal residence can produce extended family households. These three types of residence include in their definitions the statement that the couple live "with or near" either the groom's parents, the bride's parents, or the maternal uncle of the groom. The phrase with or near is interpreted to mean that the couple takes up residence within the household—not necessarily the same dwelling, since a household may occupy several houses—of the designated relative. The practice of either patrilocal, matrilocal, or avunculocal residence draws together into one household three or more generations of related individuals. Extended family households can be classified by the type of residence practiced: patrilocal extended family households, matrilocal extended family households, and avunculocal extended family households. An extended family household of the patrilocal variety can be diagramed as follows:

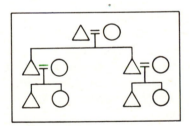

Thus in an extended patrilocal household sons will bring their wives into the household, whereas daughters will leave the household to reside with their husbands. If the type of residence practiced is matrilocal, the household will have the following structure:

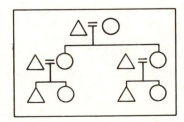

The composition of an extended matrilocal household is opposite the patrilocal form; that is, the daughters will bring their husbands into the household and the sons will leave the household at the time of marriage. In both cases unmarried children of either sex should be considered as members of the household until they marry—at which time they either remain or leave as culturally required.

A culture characterized by ambilocal residence will have extended family households of both the patrilocal and matrilocal variety. There may also occur in such cultures extended family households in which both sons and daughters have brought their spouses to reside in their paternal household. These ambilocal extended family households arise when a son resides patrilocally and a daughter resides matrilocally. (Diagrams of ambilocal and avunculocal extended family households are not presented.) Although it would be possible to distinguish between extended nuclear family households and extended polygamous family households on the basis of the type of marital groups included in the households (as was done for independent households above), anthropologists have not made this distinction. Thus an *extended family household* is a domestic group consisting of three (or possibly more) generations of related individuals, including one or more marital groups in each of two adjacent generations. It does not matter whether the marital groups composing the household are monogamous, polygynous, or polyandrous.

A subtype of the extended family household has been distinguished by anthropologists. The stem family household comes into existence when only one child of a marital group remains in the household and brings his or her spouse to reside there. Either patrilocal or matrilocal residence can produce stem family households. If patrilocal residence is practiced, such households have the following composition:

If matrilocal residence is practiced, the household can be diagramed as follows:

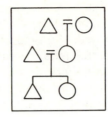

Thus the *stem family household* is a small extended family household consisting of three generations of related individuals, including one marital group in each of two adjacent generations. Such households are usually found in cultures which have a rule of inheritance in which only one child, either a son or daughter, receives his parents' home and possessions. Those children who must leave often seek their fortunes elsewhere, sometimes even in other cultures or political communities.

Two other types of households are occasionally described by anthropologists. One is the *fraternal joint family household* composed of two or more brothers, their wives, and their children (Murdock 1949:33); the other is the *mother-child* or *female headed household* composed of a woman, who is either unmarried, widowed, separated, or divorced, and her children, and sometimes her grandchildren (Otterbein 1965b). The former type is comparatively rare, and the latter type is probably never found as the dominant household type in any culture.

Many ethnographers who collect information on residence and marital groups also collect information on household composition. In some cases the composition of every household in the local group is presented in the ethnography. Other times the ethnographer derives household types for the culture and presents the frequency of each type in a table. Sometimes he simply describes the major household type and any variations from the type. Although households vary greatly in size and in composition, for most cultures one type of household is dominant. That is, most of the households in the culture will conform to one of the major types of households described above..

15. **What types of households
    are present?**
    1. independent nuclear family
    2. independent polygamous family
    3. extended family
    4. stem family

The most frequently occurring type of household should be noted. If there is a less common type occurring with some regularity, it should also be recorded. The type of household that people prefer to live in may not be the most frequently occurring type. Thus the evaluations which members of the culture hold concerning household composition should be noted, if this information is available in the ethnography. The variations on each major household type do not need to be listed, since data on residence and marital groups, recorded for the two previous sections, provide this information.

Since the Andros Islanders are monogamous, with residence being virilocal, uxorilocal, and commonlocal, the households are of the independent nuclear family type. Other types of households, however, are found in the community. They include households headed by single persons, either males or females; children or grandchildren may be present in the households. In addition, there are "grandparent" households. As the following quotation indicates, I chose not to classify them as extended family households (Otterbein 1966:103–105):

The use of the term three-generation or grandparent household rather than extended family is deliberate. In the usual sense an extended family is one in which the eldest son (or possibly the youngest) takes over upon the death of the father. Since sons bring their wives to live in the household, such a family has continuity through generations. However, the grandparent household of the Andros Islanders is not of this type. Sons and daughters leave upon marriage. Sons build their own homes, for even if they inherit their father's house, they do not move into it or repair it. The grandchildren in the household are likely to be daughters' children rather than sons' children. They are considered temporary residents: either their mother may take them away at any time, or they leave when they are able to care for themselves. Since it is unlikely that they will inherit anything, houses and land being of little value, they have no reason for remaining beyond the period of their childhood. Therefore a household has continuity for only the life span of the senior generation. For these reasons the grandparent household of the Andros Islanders bears little resemblance to the extended families found in many areas in the world.

The frequency of household types is presented in tabular form (Otterbein 1966:104): 38 percent of the households are nuclear families, 18 percent grandparent households, 29 percent female-headed (11 percent grandmothers, 5 percent mothers, and 13 percent alone), and

15 percent male-headed (2 percent grandfather, 1 percent father, and 12 percent alone).

Since commonlocal and virilocal residence are practiced by the Yanomamö and many of the marital groups are polygynous, independent polygamous family households occur with great frequency. On the other hand, men with only one wife reside in independent nuclear family households. Thus both types of households are present. Exact figures on household composition are not given. However, since it is unlikely that polygynous marital groups exceed 50 percent of the marital groups, probably independent nuclear family households are the most frequently occurring type.

The virilocal and commonlocal residence of the Qemant, in conjunction with monogamous marital groups, produces independent nuclear family households. Extended family households are also present because both patrilocal and matrilocal residence are practiced. Although exact figures on household composition are not given, independent nuclear family households probably occur with greater frequency. Since Qemant reside patrilocally or matrilocally for only the first few years of their married life, a married man and woman spend the greater part of their lives apart from their parents, with only their children present in the household. Not until one of their children brings a spouse into the household does their nuclear family household become converted into an extended family household.

DESCENT GROUPS

Many cultures have descent groups; membership in these groups is determined by a rule of descent. A descent group is "any publicly recognized social entity such that being a lineal descendant of a particular real or fictive ancestor is a criterion of membership" (Goodenough 1970:51). Descent, on the other hand, refers "solely to a cultural principle whereby an individual is socially allocated to a specific group of consanguineal kinsmen" (Murdock 1949:43). Such kinsmen are descended from a common ancestor. Allocation to a descent group, known technically as filiation, is through either one's father or one's mother. Descent groups and rules of descent go hand in hand; that is, it is impossible to have one without the other. Four basic types of descent groups and rules of descent can be distinguished:

Descent Group	Rule of Descent
Patrilineage	Patrilineal descent
Matrilineage	Matrilineal descent
Ambilineage	Ambilineal descent
Unrestricted descent group	Multilineal descent

All four types of descent groups are similar in their fundamental structure: they are multigenerational; they are headed or founded by an ancestor (sometimes they are referred to as ancestor-oriented groups); and they include in their membership only descendants of the ancestor. These four types of groups differ in their structure or composition because of different rules of descent. With the exception of multilineal descent, rules of descent are a means of limiting membership in descent groups. They prescribe who can and who cannot belong. The members of a patrilineage, a matrilineage, an ambilineage, or an unrestricted descent group are usually referred to by a certain name, and in most cultures they regularly assist each other in economic, political, and religious matters (Befu and Plotnicov 1962).

Membership in a patrilineage is based upon a rule of *patrilineal descent*. This cultural principle automatically filiates a child at birth through his father to a descent group that consists of all kinsmen who are related to him through his male ancestor. An individual will belong to only one patrilineage, and the members of a lineage may reside in different local groups. A patrilineage has the following structure:

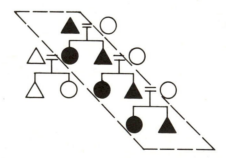

Members of the patrilineage are shown in black, and they are enclosed within a dotted parallelogram in order to indicate that patrilineages are usually nonlocalized groups. In the diagram individuals are shown marrying spouses who are not members of their patrilineage. Thus a *patrilineage* is a descent group whose membership is based upon a rule of patrilineal descent. Because patrilineages are similar in structure to patrilocal extended family households, many anthropologists believe that patrilineages may have developed out of patrilocal extended family households which have grown larger and larger through the birth of individuals who belong to new generations (Titiev 1943).

Membership in a matrilineage is based upon a rule of *matrilineal descent*. This cultural principle automatically filiates a child at birth through his mother to a descent group that consists of all kinsmen who are related to him through his female ancestors. A matrilineage has the following structure:

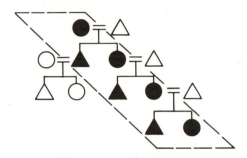

Thus a *matrilineage* is a descent group whose membership is based upon a rule of matrilineal descent. Many anthropologists believe that matrilineages have grown out of matrilocal extended family households, just as patrilineages have grown out of patrilocal extended family households.

Membership in an ambilineage, sometimes referred to as a ramage, is based upon a rule of *ambilineal descent*. This cultural principle filiates an individual through either his father or mother to a descent group that consists of only some of his kinsmen. Filiation does not necessarily occur at birth, but is more likely to occur in adulthood. Residence, which plays no role in determining membership in patrilineages and matrilineages, is usually the deciding factor in determining the parent through whom filiation will be traced. This is because ambilineages are almost always land-owning groups, and an individual must live with other members of the ambilineage and till the soil in order to exercise his right to belong to the ambilineage. In some cultures his membership may be determined by the residence of his parents. If they reside with his paternal grandparents, he will filiate through his father and belong to his father's ambilineage; if they reside with his maternal grandparents, he will filiate through his mother and belong to his mother's ambilineage. This occurs only if he resides with his parents as a child and as an adult. If after marriage he resides with his spouse's parents, he does not

exercise his right to belong to an ambilineage. His children will filiate through their mother. Such ambilineages are said to be of the
· exclusive or irreversible type. There are also ambilineages of a
nonexclusive or reversible type. In the nonexclusive type an individual can always reverse his choice; that is, after having lived with one
ambilineage for several years he can change his membership to the
other ambilineage by making a change of residence. Thus, an individual always retains his rights to belong to two different ambilineages regardless of his residence (Otterbein 1964:32).

Since ambilineages—in contrast to either patrilineages or
matrilineages—have variable structure, two examples are given, one
headed by a male, the other by a female.

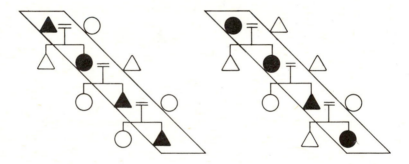

Members of the ambilineages are shown in black, and each ambilineage is enclosed within a solid parallelogram to emphasize that
ambilineages are usually localized groups. Thus an *ambilineage* or
ramage is a descent group whose membership is based upon a rule
of ambilineal descent. Since ambilineal descent groups derive their
structure from the residential choices of individuals, ambilocal residence is usually found associated with ambilineages and ambilineal
descent. (It will be remembered that a culture which has couples
residing both patrilocally and matrilocally is classified as practicing
ambilocal residence.) Presumably ambilineages grow out of ambilocal extended family households.

The unrestricted descent group is based upon a rule of *multilineal descent.* From the point of view of the founder of an unrestricted descent group, multilineal descent refers to all of his
descendants, not his ancestors or collateral relatives. This cultural
principle automatically filiates a child at birth through his father and
his mother (and through his four grandparents, and through his eight
great grandparents, and so on) to every descent group founded by

one of his ancestors. An unrestricted descent group has the following structure:

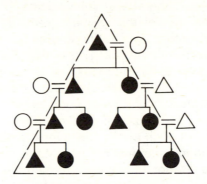

Members of the unrestricted descent group are shown in black, and they are enclosed within a dotted triangle in order to indicate that such descent groups are nonlocalized. An individual can belong to many of these nonlocalized descent groups, and the type of residence which he practices has no effect on his memberships. Thus an *unrestricted descent group* is a descent group whose membership is based upon a rule of multilineal descent (Otterbein 1964).

Students often raise the question: Do we have descent groups in the United States? The traditional answer has been to say, "No, we have kindreds; but, because the father's last name is passed to his children we have something like patrilineages." Generations of students have realized that this is not really an answer. Before attempting to answer the question, it is, I believe, useful to examine the "family tree" of a famous American—John Adams. The following skeleton genealogy omits many female descendants and all affinals.

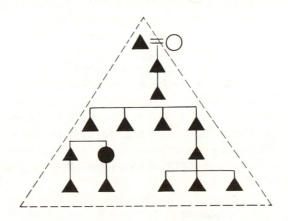

Two features are to be noted. First, the descent group is nonlocalized. Few of the descendants of the founder have lived in Quincy, Massachusetts, the site of John Adams' birthplace and home. Second, one member of the descent group is linked to the geneology through his mother. Unlike the other members of the descent group, his surname is not Adams. (He is the senior author of one of the publications cited in this book.) It is characteristic of Americans who are tracing their ancestry back to Revolutionary War figures to use genealogical links through both males and females. If this family tree is taken as typical of an American descent group, it can be compared with each of the four types of descent groups described above. Although the Adams' genealogy closely resembles a patrilineage, the filiation of one male through his mother rules out classifying it as such. It cannot be a matrilineage because the ancestor is a male (although one could argue that Abigail Smith Adams is the founder of the group) and most of the genealogical links are paternal dyads (father-son). It does not qualify as an ambilineage since it is nonlocalized. The Adams' genealogy does, however, match the structure of the unrestricted descent group. Filiation occurs through both males and females, and the descent group is nonlocalized. Thus it can be concluded that the Adams "family" and many similar descent groups found in America are unrestricted descent groups with multilineal descent.

In cultures with unrestricted descent groups an individual usually has the opportunity—just as he has in a culture with ambilineages of the reversible type—to select the descent group(s) to which he wishes to belong. He will normally select the descent group(s) conferring the greatest amount of privilege and status. Since many Americans regard it as prestigious to be descended from an ancestor who settled the United States before 1800, particularly a Revolutionary War hero, many Americans carefully trace their genealogies, often with the help of national historical societies. In many towns and cities in the United States the stratification system is based in part on who is, and who is not, a descendant of one of the first settlers in the area. Some American Indian peoples also employ similar methods of reckoning descent for the purpose of establishing tribal membership. Hayes (1975:76) has referred to such a descent rule as *ethnolineal:* "Ego will trace descent through the combination of male and female ancestors which provides ego with the most socially valuable descent and present alliances, ignoring the alternative descent paths."

In addition to the four basic types of descent groups, three other types of descent groups—based upon lineages—have been distinguished. The term *lineage* refers to both patrilineages and matrilineages. In many cultures lineages are found joined together into larger descent groups. A *clan* exists when the members of two or more lineages consider their lineages to be units or segments of a larger descent group. Clans are nonlocalized, they are named, and they are based upon the same rule of descent as the lineages which compose them. If clans are united into an even larger descent group which is nonlocalized, which is named, and which is based upon the same rule of descent as the clans composing it, a *phratry* occurs. If there are more than three levels of kinship units in a descent group, ethnographers usually develop their own notational system for describing each level. If the culture has only two clans or two phratries, so that every individual is a member of one or the other, the culture is said to have moieties. Each clan or phratry is referred to as a *moiety*. Since lineages compose clans and clans compose phratries, it is not possible to have phratries without clans and lineages, nor is it possible to have clans without lineages.

16. **What types of descent groups are present?**
    1. descent groups absent
    2. patrilineages
    3. matrilineages
    4. ambilineages
    5. unrestricted descent groups
    6. clans
    7. phratries
    8. moieties

Not all cultures have descent groups, and those that do usually have only one of the above four basic types. There are some cultures, however, which have both patrilineages and matrilineages. These cultures are said by anthropologists to practice *double descent*. Rarely will lineages be found in cultures with ambilineages. Unrestricted descent groups may be found in cultures with ambilineages, but probably never in cultures with lineages. Clans, phratries, and moieties may be based upon either patrilineal or matrilineal descent. It has not been necessary to list patriclans, matriclans, patriphratries, patrimoieties, and matrimoieties above, since information on the type of descent rule followed by one of these groups is contained in the prefix of the type of lineages composing the larger descent group. The above question simply asks what types of descent groups are present—it does not ask how many descent groups of each type are present (except indirectly by asking about moieties), nor does it ask how many members each descent group has. If this latter information is given in the ethnography, it is worth noting.

_____

Unrestricted descent groups characterized by multilineal descent are found on Andros Island (Otterbein 1966:129):

Societies with kindreds may also be characterized by unrestricted descent groups or descending kindreds (Otterbein 1964b:32). Such groups are composed of all the descendants of one person. If the land and property of a person are left to all his descendants, generation after generation, there exists a landholding, unrestricted descent group. In contrast to personal kindreds, these groups have an authority system, since after the original owner dies someone is needed to administer and allocate land to his descendants. Thus relationships based on rights and duties come into existence. Since there is usually more than one household on the land, these relationships will extend beyond the individual household. In this way, the members of several households belong to one corporate group.

Groups with this structure are found in the Bahamas. Although a group of this kind is unnamed in Long Bay Cays, the land which it holds in common is called "generation property" and is under the direction of an "executor." "Generation property" comes into existence when a man leaves a will naming all his male and female descendants, generation after generation, as his heirs and his eldest son as the "executor." The will usually states that the land is never to be sold and that the executor can appoint his successor. The executor is considered to be a powerful person who can provide plots of land to any of his father's relatives in any manner which he chooses. Since the population is sparse and there is no shortage of land in Long Bay Cays, a person has no difficulty in being able to exercise his right. In fact, siblings' descendants of the original owner and affinal relatives, who have no actual rights, may be allowed to live on the land rent-free (Otterbein 1964b:32–33).

Nevertheless, it is noted that unrestricted descent groups are uncommon in the community; this has occurred in Long Bay Cays because many individuals did not establish generation property and thus many residents of the community do not belong to any unrestricted descent groups (Otterbein 1966:129–130).

Patrilineages are the only type of descent group which the Yanomamö have. Two important features of their lineage system are as follows (Chagnon 1968:61):

First, people reckon descent through males and are grouped into exogamous, patrilineal lineages. These are called *mashi* by the Yanomamö, although none of them bear distinctive names. Second, members of these lineages tend to intermarry with members of a second lineage over a number of generations, being bound to them by obligations to reciprocate women in marriage. This results in a dual organization of kinsmen within the village, whose residents fall into one or the other of the two lineages.

> The term *dual organization* is often used to describe moieties. If approximately half the Yanomamö lineages were joined together into a larger descent group and the remaining lineages were joined together into another descent group, then moieties would be present. But such second-order descent groups are not present, and therefore, the Yanamamö should not be classified as having moieties. Since there are no second-order descent groups, clans are absent.
>
> The "local descent group" described by Chagnon is a smaller kinship group than the patrilineage. It cannot be classified as a lineage, or an unrestricted descent group, since coresidence, in addition to patrilineal descent, is a criterion for membership (Chagnon 1968:68–69):

Local descent groups have three characteristics. First, membership in them depends on patrilineal descent. . . . Second, the members of the group live in the same village. If, for example, a young man leaves his village to seek a wife elsewhere, he is no longer a member of the local descent group that includes his brothers and father. He can rejoin them later and again become an active member, but while he lives in a different village he does not participate in the political affairs of that group. Third, the group is *corporate* with respect to the functions of arranging the marriages of the female members.

> The Qemant have patrilineages, clans, and moieties (Gamst 1969:3):

The males of each homestead are closely related through paternal lines to one another and to males in some of the nearby homesteads in their community. The paternal lines lead back to the oldest living male among them or to an ancestor of these men from one or two generations earlier. These paternal lines can be traced back through time, along with many other such lines of descent from part of the remainder of the community and from parts of other Qemant communities, until they ultimately merge into the person of a culture hero who is the common ancestor of this vast number of men and the founder of the clan to which they belong. Therefore, a clan is a kinship group whose members trace descent unilineally, through the line of one parent—in this case, the male line—to an ancestor who is usually mythical.

The many Qemant clans, each composed of several lineages, or segments of the clan, are united on a greater structural level to form two moieties, a fundamental dual social division into which an ethnic group may be organized. All Qemant belong to either one or the other of the two moieties, and they must marry, according to Qemant marriage laws, outside of their own moiety and into the other one; these moieties are therefore exogamous.

Gamst uses the concept of ambilineal in his discussion of land tenure and the inheritance of property (1969:70):

Rights to the use of land are based upon kinship traced ambilineally, as in the following sentences which explain ambilineality. In justifying or establishing claims to use land, any of the sixteen great-great-grand-parents may be used, and rights to land are usually traced to still more distant ancestors. Claims are made through a single line of descent traced generation after generation back and forth in any way from male to female ancestors, hence ambilineally, to the ancestor who first cultivated the land.

Although he speaks of a person's "ambilineal descent group," the Qemant appear not to have ambilineages, since distinct ancestor-oriented groups based upon a rule of ambilineal descent are not discussed. What Gamst describes as an ambilineal descent group should probably be classified as a kindred (see Question 17, below).

KINDREDS

In contrast to descent groups, which are ancestor-oriented, are kindreds, which are ego-oriented social categories of individuals. A kindred is a social category rather than a social group because its membership is composed of individuals who define their respective membership in the category in terms of their relationship to a particular individual, technically known as *Ego*. In a group, on the other hand, each individual has a relationship with every other member of the group. In a kindred the only relationships are those between Ego and every other member of the category. A kindred may consist of any of an individual's relatives, including descendants, ancestors, and collaterals such as siblings and cousins; however, it need not contain them all. Some anthropologists consider in-laws, since they are affinal kin, to be members of kindreds; but, since most do not, kindreds will be considered here to include only consanguineal kin. As described in the previous section, a descent group consists of only the descendants of a particular individual, who headed or founded the group. Until approximately fifteen years ago, kindreds were considered to be descent groups, which were characterized by a rule of bilateral descent. But since their structure differs markedly from the structure of descent groups, anthropologists today consider kindreds to be a distinct kinship phenomenon which should not be classified with descent groups. Since kindreds are not descent groups, they cannot be characterized by descent; hence, the notion of bilateral descent is disappearing from usage (Buchler and Selby 1968:88–89; Mitchell 1963).

Kindreds vary in type. On one hand, kindreds may be so simple that they are only *named* categories of kin. That is, a kindred may consist of all recognized relatives of an individual, and Ego has one generic name or label for these relatives. The individual, of course, knows or can find out from senior relatives who should belong to his kindred and their relationship to him. Most English-speakers refer to the members of their kindred as "family." The members of such a kindred constitute a social category which an individual can usually scan in order to find support or assistance for any activity or difficulty in which he has become involved. On the other hand, kindreds may take on the characteristics of groups. Kindreds of this type, which can be referred to as quasigroups (Pospisil 1963:32–37, 101), consist of those relatives of an individual who have identical rights and obligations with regard to the individual. The rights and obligations can include hospitality, responsibility for the individual's actions (such as debts and homicides), and required attendance at important ceremonial events (such as the individual's birth, initiation, wedding, and funeral). The rights and obligations are mutual since an individual belongs to the kindreds of each relative who belongs to his kindred. Kindreds, as quasigroups, are probably named, but need not be. It is possible to have more than one kind of kindred of this type (Appell 1967).

Both types of kindreds are ego-oriented categories of relatives. It is usually stated in anthropological literature that only brothers and sisters with the same mother and father (that is, full siblings) have the same kindred. This is true for kindreds of the former type. It is not necessarily true for kindreds which are quasigroups, since the descendants of two siblings are related differently to each of the siblings. For example, a grandson is two genealogical links away from Ego, while a brother's grandson is three links away.

If only relatives two links away or less are responsible for an individual's actions such as debts and homicides, the grandson and not the brother's grandson is responsible; hence, the grandson, but not the brother's grandson, is a member of Ego's kindred. The following diagram shows a kindred that extends for two genealogical links from Ego:

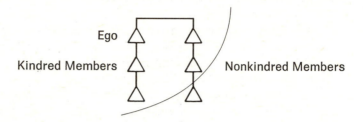

Thus there may be one kindred of the quasigroup type for each member of the culture. Kindreds overlap in their memberships. That is, each individual will belong to many different kindreds. Kindreds have traditionally been thought of as being characteristic of cultures without patrilineal or matrilineal descent groups. Although kindreds probably are more commonly found in such cultures, they nevertheless are found occasionally in cultures with descent groups.

17.   Are kindreds present?
   1. absent
   2. present

Determining whether kindreds are present in the culture will be a difficult task, since many ethnographers studying cultures without descent groups state that kindreds are present and that descent is bilateral. The statements of these ethnographers must be ignored. A decision as to whether kindreds are present must be made, first, on the basis of whether there is a term for all of an individual's relatives and, second, on the basis of a careful study of the rights and obligations between relatives. Careful analysis may reveal more than one kind of kindred of the quasigroup type. One must also look for kindreds in cultures with descent groups.

The Andros Islanders have kindreds which regulate marriage and serve as a basis for forming friendships (Otterbein 1966:34–35, 127, 128):

A man is not permitted to court, or mate with, any female member of his kindred, which extends bilaterally as far as genealogical connections can be remembered by his oldest relatives. Therefore, his kindred includes all known consanguineal relatives, who are referred to by the community as being "family to him." Thus cousin marriage of any degree is prohibited. Since a kindred may have several hundred members, possibly some relatives will be unknown to the man. If he selects for a prospective wife a girl distantly related to him, his mother informs him of the relationship. Since he has not begun courting the girl, it is unlikely that there has been time for an attachment to form, so that the young man will not be disappointed and attempt to disregard the wishes of his parents.

The relationships between cousins show great variability. If they live near each other they may become very good friends; in fact, if they are of the same age they may become closer than brothers. On the other hand, they may never meet, and furthermore, if they are distantly related they may not know of the consanguineal tie between themselves. . . .

Kinship systems based on bilateral kindreds, of which the one just described is a case in point, permit consanguineal relatives to form the kinds of relationships that they want with each other, provided they are not members of the same household. In other words, the kinship bond may or may not be used as a basis for friendship. If two persons want to be friends, the consanguineal tie gives them a starting point on which to build a relationship. But if they do not wish this, there are no sanctions or mechanisms to bring them together and force the relationship upon them. This seems to result from the fact that kindreds are ego-oriented networks of kin or "categories of cognates" (Freeman 1961:202–203), rather than corporate groups. Since corporate units involve individuals performing activities together, leadership and authority emerge. Thus the relationships between members become structured to the extent that rights and duties supported by sanctions control the behavior of the individuals. The kindred has no such structure, and therefore relatives can choose the way they want to act toward each other without having to fear that sanctions will force them to alter their behavior.

Kindreds appear to be absent in Yanomamö culture; no evidence for their existence can be found in the Yanomamö ethnography.

Kindreds of the quasigroup type are present in Qemant culture. Although Gamst refers to a person's kinsmen as "ambilineal kin," the social relationships described in the following paragraph are entirely ego-oriented (1969:70):

A person allows his ambilineal ties to wax and wane in strength according to his needs for labor and for support in claiming rights to use land. A Qemant may rely on local ambilineal kin to give assistance in projects requiring labor and when he is involved in a dispute. Ambilineal kin who live far away attend weddings, funerals, and other rites of passage, but may not be depended upon for labor. It is the duty of the ambilineal kin group to avenge a member's murder or to raise blood money that must be paid by a member of the group. A Qemant may be injured or murdered in revenge for an act committed by a member of his ambilineal descent group. ·

It can be concluded that the category of kin described above is a kindred.

COUSIN MARRIAGE

In some cultures first cousins marry. Two types of cousin marriage have been distinguished by anthropologists. Parallel cousin marriage is the marriage of the children of two brothers or two sisters. An individual's father's brother's child or his mother's sister's child is his *parallel cousin.* Cross-cousin marriage is the marriage of the children of a brother and a sister. Two forms of cross-cousin marriage occur: matrilateral and patrilateral. An individual's mother's brother's child is his *matrilateral cross-cousin,* and his father's sister's child is his *patrilateral cross-cousin.*

Cross-cousin marriage may occur because there are explicit rules which state that men must or should marry a particular type of cross-cousin; on the other hand, cross-cousin marriage may occur incidentally as a result of a rule of exogamy. Many descent groups practice *exogamy;* that is, the members of a descent group follow a rule which states that a person may not marry a member of either his lineage, clan, phratry, or moiety. The practice of exogamy produces exogamous descent groups. Exogamy may lead to cross-cousin marriage since an individual's cross-cousin is not a member of his descent group and is also a nephew or niece of one of his parents. Thus a cross-cousin is probably a likely individual for him to marry.

Matrilateral cross-cousin marriage is the marriage of a man to his mother's brother's daughter. The structure of such a marital union is shown in the following diagram:

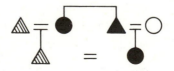

Three patrilineages are shown in different shades. In the diagram, matrilateral cross-cousin marriage is associated with lineage exogamy. Although exogamy may produce matrilateral cross-cousin marriage whether the descent groups are patrilineages or matrilineages, patrilineages are shown in the diagram, since matrilateral cross-cousin marriage is more frequently found associated with patrilineages than with matrilineages. The possible reasons for this association have created a lively debate for the last twenty-five years (Lévi-Strauss 1969 [orig. 1949], Homans and Schneider 1955, Needham 1960, Spiro 1968).

Patrilateral cross-cousin marriage is the marriage of a man to his father's sister's daughter. This form of marriage can be diagramed as follows:

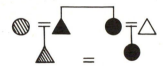

Three matrilineages are shown in different shades. Patrilateral cross-cousin marriage may occur whether matrilineages or patrilineages are present. Matrilineages are shown in this diagram since patrilateral cross-cousin marriage is more frequently found associated with matrilineages than with patrilineages. Since matrilineal descent groups occur with less frequency than patrilineal descent groups, it is to be expected that patrilateral cross-cousin marriage is a more rare form of cross-cousin marriage than the matrilateral variety. A cross-cultural study of thirty-three cultures which practice either one or the other form of cross-cousin marriage has shown that nine of the cultures had matrilineal descent groups while only seven cultures practice patrilateral cross-cousin marriage (Homans and Schneider 1955:34).

The question should be asked at this point: Why does any culture practice cross-cousin marriage? The classic answer is that cross-cousin marriage, which is associated with the practice of exogamy, is the means by which descent groups unite themselves with other descent groups (Tylor 1888:267):

Among tribes of low culture there is but one means known of keeping up permanent alliance, and that means is intermarriage. Exogamy, enabling a growing tribe to keep itself compact by constant unions between its spreading clans, enables it to overmatch any number of small intermarrying groups, isolated and helpless. Again and again in the world's history, savage tribes must have had plainly before their minds the simple practical alternative between marrying-out and being killed out.

Tylor's theory has recently been subjected to testing in a cross-cultural study, and no support was found for the theory (Kang 1976*b*). Indeed, it was found that exogamy was associated with fighting and feuding between local groups. Based on these results, I suspect that although the members of a culture may believe that intermarriage makes them militarily less vulnerable, they in fact become—without knowing it—more vulnerable. Why then does any culture practice cross-cousin marriage? My guess—and it is only a guess—is that men tend to marry women whom they know. In cross-cousin marriage the woman is a parent's sibling's child; a man has probably known his cross-cousin for years. If many men in a particular culture marry cross-cousins, an explicit rule may develop. Most of the theoretical literature on cross-cousin marriage has dealt with rules; however, it has been observed that most cultures practicing either matrilateral or patrilateral cross-cousin marriage "are cases in which the practice of this custom represents a personal preference of the actors rather than compliance with a rule" (Spiro 1968: 113).

Parallel cousin marriage, in comparison with cross-cousin marriage, is rare, and only the patrilateral form occurs with any frequency. Patrilateral parallel cousin marriage, usually referred to simply as *parallel cousin marriage*, is the marriage of a man to his father's brother's daughter. As is shown in the following diagram, such a marriage must—for reasons of logic—occur between members of the same descent group, provided that descent is patrilineal.

One patrilineage is shown in black. If the members of a descent group follow a rule which states that a person must marry a member of either his own lineage, clan, or phratry, a rule of *endogamy* exists. The practice of endogamy produces endogamous descent groups. Endogamous groups of course are not united by marriage with other descent groups. If it is true, as argued by Tylor, that endogamous descent groups are not likely to survive in fighting between descent groups, then groups practicing endogamy will be rare. Since parallel cousin marriage produces endogamous unions if the descent groups are patrilineal, it is to be expected that parallel cousin marriage is rarely found among the world's cultures. The only region where parallel cousin marriage occurs with any frequency is the Semitic Near East. Ethnographies which describe the cultures of the region indicate that endogamy is practiced by brothers as a technique for retaining all their inheritance within the patrilineage.

18. What types of first cousin marriage are practiced?

1. first cousin marriage absent
2. matrilateral cross-cousin marriage
3. patrilateral cross-cousin marriage
4. parallel cousin marriage

Many cultures do not practice any form of first cousin marriage. Some cultures practice only one of the types; others, a combination of both matrilateral and patrilateral cross-cousin marriage (known as bilateral cross-cousin marriage). Conceivably parallel cousin marriage can be found in association with one or both forms of cross-cousin marriage. Some Iranian villages, which are characterized by patrilineages and patriclans, practice both parallel and bilateral cross-cousin marriage (Noland 1976). Although the frequency with which each one of the types of first cousin marriage occurs within a given culture is important for that culture, most ethnographies do not provide the information. Frequencies, however, should be noted if they are given. In addition to frequencies, it should be noted whether an explicit marriage rule exists.

_____

For the Andros Islanders first cousin marriage is absent. In fact "cousin marriage of any degree is prohibited," and the rule is followed and enforced (Otterbein 1966:35):

Marriage between kin is condemned because "it is wrong." Apparently there is no thought that such a union might result in the birth of defective children, nor is there a fear of punishment by eternal damnation. There are only three known cousin marriages in Long Bay Cays. One couple did not learn they were distantly related until after their wedding. Since they did not intentionally violate community standards, they were not condemned. Another couple, who are first cousins, married despite strong opposition from the woman's mother; since the daughter was more than twenty-one, her mother could not legally prevent their marriage. The man was a widower in his forties. They avoid the pressure of community sanctions by living in Nassau. Even several years after the wedding, the woman's mother was embarrassed and ashamed when she told me about her daughter's marriage. I was unable to get data on the third couple, who were also first cousins.

Both matrilateral and patrilateral cross-cousin marriages are practiced by the Yanomamö, and there is an explicit rule which states that a man should marry a cross-cousin (Chagnon 1968:61):

Men are obliged to marry a woman of a single, specific category, *suaböya.* This category defines a variety of women, two subcategories of which can be translated into the English biological equivalents MoBrDa and FaSiDa. Yanomamö men prefer to marry women of these subcategories because they are relieved of much of the discomfort of avoiding their mother-in-law.

The ethnographer presents a table which shows that out of sixty-nine marriages, forty-four men married a cross-cousin (Chagnon 1968:73).

Neither cross-cousin nor parallel cousin marriage is practiced by the Qemant (Gamst 1969:67–68).

The incest taboo, or marriage prohibitions, among the Qemant applies to all persons in one's moiety and once included all consanguinal (blood) relatives of the other moiety less than eight degrees removed from the person. During the past forty years. Qemant have gradually reduced the prohibition to relatives only four degrees removed from one, but they still speak of the old rule as proper.

Hence, first cousin marriage is absent.

KINSHIP TERMINOLOGY

Kinship terminological systems are classified by the terms which are employed in referring to first cousins. Although the study of kinship terminology may appear to be an obscure and esoteric subject, many of the major figures in anthropology—including Lewis H. Morgan (1871), W. H. R. Rivers (1924), A. R. Radcliffe-Brown (1952), and George P. Murdock (1949)—have considered the analysis of terminological systems crucial to an understanding of kinship and the family. Kinship terminology is viewed by most anthropologists as being a fundamental aspect of many cultures which they study. The

labels for the six types of kinship systems described below are de-
rived from the names of particular cultures or regions. Hawaiian and
Eskimo stem from the Hawaiian Islanders and the Eskimo of the
Arctic coast of North America. Sudanese derives from Sudan, a
region south of the Sahara Desert in Africa. Iroquois, Crow, and
Omaha are the names of North American Indian tribes.

The most simple terminological system is the *Hawaiian* type.
All male cousins are referred to by the same term which an individual uses to refer to his brother, and all female cousins are referred
to by the same term which he uses to refer to his sister. If the terms
for cousins differ, but are clearly derived from those for siblings, the
system is still classified as Hawaiian. In the following diagram abbreviations for brother (Br) and sister (Si) are used to show that all
first cousins are referred to as brother and sister.

(The use of English kinship terms is done in order to facilitate
understanding of the diagrams. The student should not assume that
the emotional connotations attached to the English terms pertain in
other cultures. In the first diagram it would be more accurate to state
that a single term—it is irrelevant what it is—is used for all male
children provided they are the offspring of siblings. In the other
diagrams the definitions would be even more pedantic [Bohannan
1963:67–71]).

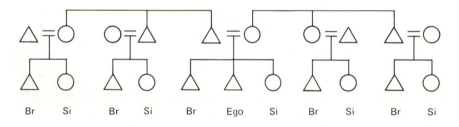

The next simplest system, familiar to most Americans, is the
Eskimo type. Cousins are referred to by a distinctive term which is
different from the term used to refer to brother and sister. In the
following diagram an abbreviation for cousin (Co) is used to show
that all cousins are referred to by the same term.

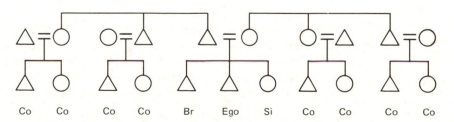

Another simple system is the *Sudanese* type. Each category of cousin is referred to by a distinct term. If the distinct terms are composed of terms used to refer to other relatives, the terminological system is said to be *descriptive*. Descriptive terminology is employed in the following diagram. Abbreviations for father (Fa), son (So), mother (Mo), and daughter (Da), in addition to brother (Br) and sister (Si), are used to show that each type of cousin is referred to by a distinct term.

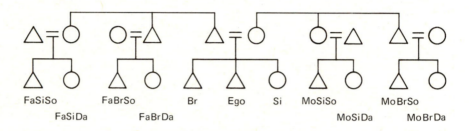

FaSiSo   FaBrSo   Br   Ego   Si   MoSiSo   MoBrSo
FaSiDa   FaBrDa   MoSiDa   MoBrDa

The three remaining systems are more complex than those just described. Simplest of these is the *Iroquois* type. Parallel cousins are referred to by the same terms used to refer to brother and sister, while cross-cousins are referred to by a different term.

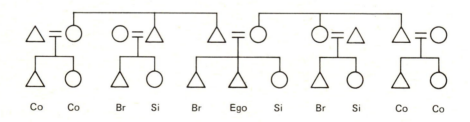

Co   Co   Br   Si   Br   Ego   Si   Br   Si   Co   Co

In the *Crow* type system, parallel cousins are referred to by the same terms used to refer to brother and sister, while both patrilateral and matrilateral cross-cousins have distinctive terms. Father's sister's son is referred to by the term used to refer to father, and father's sister's daughter by the term used to refer to father's sister; on the other hand, mother's brother's son is referred to as son or brother's son, and mother's brother's daughter as daughter or brother's daughter. Crow kinship systems are usually associated with matrilineal descent groups.

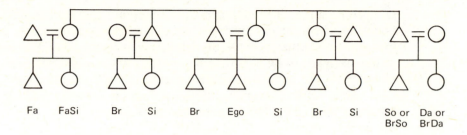

Fa   FaSi   Br   Si   Br   Ego   Si   Br   Si   So or   Da or
                                                         BrSo   BrDa

In the *Omaha* type system, parallel cousins are referred to by the same terms used to refer to brother and sister, while both patrilateral and matrilateral cross-cousins have distinctive terms. Father's sister's son is referred to by the term used to refer to son or sister's son, and father's sister's daughter by the term used to refer to daughter or sister's daughter; on the other hand, mother's brother's son is referred to as mother's brother and mother's brother's daughter as mother. Omaha kinship systems are usually associated with patrilineal descent groups.

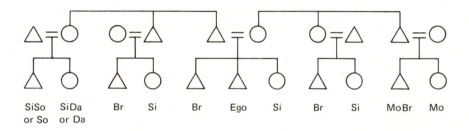

SiSo   SiDa   Br   Si   Br   Ego   Si   Br   Si   MoBr   Mo
or So   or Da

**19. What type of kinship terminology
for first cousins is employed?**
    1. Hawaiian
    2. Eskimo
    3. Sudanese
    4. Iroquois
    5. Crow
    6. Omaha

Most ethnographies include kinship terms, either in a table or on a diagram. If the diagram is similar to the type used in this section, a direct comparison with the above types can be made. If the diagram is not similar or a table of terms is given, the terms can be written below an unlabeled diagram of the above type and then the comparison can be made. If the kinship terminological system being studied does not fit one of the six types, the student needs to make a judgment as to whether it could be derived from or is a variation of one of the six types. If he cannot make a judgment, the system cannot be classified and it should be recorded in full detail. (For practice in the analysis of kinship systems the exercises in Schusky's *Manual for Kinship Analysis* [1972] are recommended.)

The kinship terminological system of the Andros Islanders is Eskimo. Ego refers to his brother and sister as "brother" and "sister." In addressing them different terms are used (Otterbein 1966: 120–21):

A boy calls all his older brothers "Bulla" or "Bulla (name)" and all his younger brothers by their name or a "pet name" (nickname). Parents sometimes call their eldest son "Bulla." The term seems to imply respect for age but little more. . . .

The eldest daughter . . . is called "Tita" by the members of the household. The term is one of respect which carries the connotation of "the boss." Even people outside the household are apt to recognize her position by calling her "Tita." The next eldest daughter is called "Sister." The youngest daughters are called by their names or "pet names.". . .

Ego refers to his cousins as "cousins" or by the exact genealogical relationship, and he addresses them as "cousin" (Otterbein 1966: 126–127):

Two siblings' children are "first cousins." A first cousin and a child of a first cousin are "second cousins." The children of first cousins are "third cousins." A third cousin and the child of a third cousin are "fourth cousins." In other words, cousins are not described as being once or twice removed. This terminology, however, is not used to describe relationships, since exact genealogical connections are used to trace degrees of kinship. For example, a person would not say, "He is my second cousin," but rather, "He is my mother's sister's daughter's son." The number of degrees of consanguinity determines the feeling of closeness or distance between two relatives, i.e., the fewer the degrees, the closer the consanguineal bond is felt to be. . . .

In addressing each other the young cousin calls the older person "Cousin" or "Cousin (name)"; in turn the older cousin calls the younger person by his name or a "pet name." The spouse of a cousin is also addressed in the same manner. The term "Cousin" denotes respect for age.

Iroquois kinship terminology for first cousins is employed by the Yanomamö (Chagnon 1968:56):

Their kinship system is called the "bifurcate merging" type with "Iroquois" cousin terms (see Glossary). Within each generation, all the males of one lineage call each other "brother," and all the women call each other "sister." Males of lineage X call males of lineage Y "brother-in-law" and are eligible to marry their sisters. In fact, the males of lineage X call the females of lineage Y "wife" *whether or not they marry them.* This is likewise true for the males of lineage Y with respect to the females of lineage X. [Italics in the original.]

The Chagnon glossary contains a definition of "Iroquois kinship terms" which is essentially the same as the definition given in this section.

Gamst provides a complete list of kinship terms for the Qemant (1969:73). The appropriate terms can be written below an unlabeled diagram.

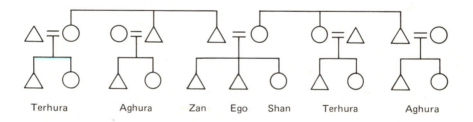

Terhura   Aghura   Zan   Ego   Shan   Terhura   Aghura

Comparison of this diagram with each of the six diagrams fails to reveal a complete correspondence. It is most similar, however, to the diagram illustrating Eskimo terminology, since brother and sister are differentiated from both types of cousins. In fact, Gamst classifies the system as Eskimo (1969:72):

According to the widely used Spier-Murdock classification, based principally upon terms for cousins, kin terms of the Qemant are of the Eskimo type. The Yankees also have the Eskimo system in which terms for siblings are distinct from terms for cousins.

Although the kinship terminology can be described as Eskimo, it should be noted that parents' brothers' children (Aghura) are differentiated from parents' sisters' children (Terhura).

STUDY GUIDE QUESTIONS

Aim of Chapter 4

The aim of this chapter is to introduce the student to a series of terms which are used by anthropologists when they analyze family and kinship structures. Such an analysis generally takes in at least seven areas—residence, marriage, household type, descent groups, kindreds, cousin marriage, and kinship terminology.

It is essential that the anthropologist, as well as the student, have a firm grasp on the methods and categories of family and kinship organization for these elements lie at the heart of the social order of the culture.

Residence

1. Contrast *matrilocal* and *patrilocal* residence.
2. What is *ambilocal* or *bilocal* residence? When is it said to exist? On what basis is residence chosen?
3. Contrast *virilocal* and *uxorilocal* residence.
4. Compare and contrast *neolocal* with *commonlocal* residence.
5. Why do you think that anthropologists are concerned with determining the ideal and real residence patterns of a culture?

Marriage

6. When is marriage said to exist?
7. Contrast *monogamy, polygyny*, and *polyandry*.
8. Identify the key symbols which are employed by anthropologists to diagram family structures.
9. Define the terms *sororal polygyny* and *fraternal polyandry*. In what ways are these two forms of marriage similar?
10. Contrast the *levirate* and *sororate* marriage customs. Why are they probably so widespread?

Household Type

11. What is a *household* and what are its functions?
12. How would you illustrate your household if asked to diagram it? (answer not in text)
13. Contrast an *independent nuclear family household* with an *independent polygamous family household*.
14. Contrast an extended *patrilocal household* with an *extended matrilocal* household.

15. What is a *stem family household*? Under what conditions do they generally occur?

Descent Groups

16. How is a *descent group* defined? What functions are provided by descent groups? (answer not in text)
17. Contrast *patrilineal* and *matrilineal* descent.
18. What is an *ambilineage* and how does it operate?
19. Discuss what is meant by *multilineal* descent.
20. How do *clans* differ from *phratries.*
21. Can you identify any ambilineages or unrestricted descent groups in your genealogy? (answer not in text)

Kindreds

22. How is the term kindred defined by the anthropologist? What functions are provided by kindreds?
23. How do kindreds differ from descent groups?
24. Compare the kindred as a category of kin to the kindred as a quasi-group.

Cousin Marriage

25. Contrast *parallel cousin* and *cross-cousin* marriages.
26. What is the difference between *exogamy* and *endogamy*? which form is associated with cross-cousin marriage? with parallel cousin marriage?

Kinship Terminology

27. Identify the basis for kinship terminological systems.
28. Diagram the terminological system used by members of your kindred or descent group. What type of kinship terminology is employed?

Yanomamö allies demonstrating their solidarity and friendship by joining together and getting ready for a raid on another village.

5

LAW AND WARFARE

Political System
Political Leaders
Legal System
Military Organizations
Feuding
Warfare
Causes of War

Anthropologists study the political systems of cultures. In such studies the term "politics" is used in a general sense; it is behavior —decisions and actions—designed to influence other people. Anthropologists frequently find that political behavior is linked to economic behavior, "economics" being defined as the allocation of goods and services. Seekers of political power are usually also seekers of economic power. Thus in many cultures those individuals who have economic power also are seen to have political power. Kinship behavior is also seen by anthropologists to be linked to political and economic behavior through both affinal and consanguineal ties. For example, marriage—an affinal tie—may involve not only the exchange of economic goods but also may represent or create a political alliance; consanguineal ties, on the other hand, may provide one with political supporters—in the simplest cultures one can usually turn only to kinsmen for protection when homicides and blood revenge occur.

Anthropologists interested in the political aspects of any culture must concern themselves with four factors. First, they must distinguish political communities and ascertain the manner in which these political units are distributed on the earth's surface. There is always this spatial aspect. Such units may be large or small—both in population size and in amount of territory occupied. Second, they must analyze the organizational structure of the political communities in terms of their component units and the types of leaders which head these units. Special attention must be paid to the political leaders who head the political communities. Third, they must describe the means by which conflicts within the political units are resolved and the manner in which decisions made by leaders are enforced. Such a description constitutes an analysis of the legal systems of the political communities. Fourth, anthropologists must study the relationships between political communities in order to provide a complete description of the political aspects of any culture. These relationships include diplomacy and warfare (Bohannan 1963: 266–267).

POLITICAL SYSTEM

A political community is composed of local groups organized into a maximal territorial unit under the direction of a political leader, while a culture is composed of local groups whose members share the same culture and speak the same language (see "Basic Concepts," in Chapter 1). Both political communities and cultures have a spatial dimension. Since both kinds of units are composed of local groups, it is possible to find local groups of the same culture in several political communities or to find local groups of different cultures in the same political community. These two possibilities give rise to two basically different types of situations which are illustrated in Figure 2. First, one or more political communities occur within a single culture. Since each political community is composed of local groups of the same culture, each political community within the culture is culturally homogeneous. A consequence of this homogeneity is that the members of the local groups, whether they are in the same political community or not, can communicate with each other since they

Situation 1

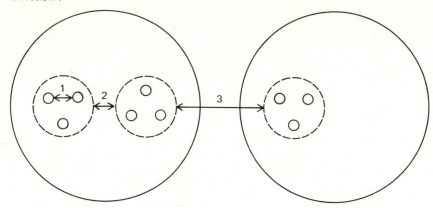

Situation 2

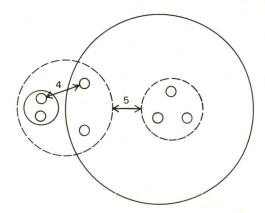

KEY:

Circles
Small circles represent local groups
Broken-line circles represent political communities
Solid-line circles represent cultures

Double-headed arrows (⟵⟶)
1 relationships between local groups within the same culture
2 relationships between political communities within the same culture
3 relationships between political communities within different cultures
4 relationships between culturally different local groups within the same
   political community
5 relationships between a culturally heterogeneous and a homogeneous political
   community

FIGURE 2   Diagram of Basic Concepts—II

speak the same language. Most of the cultures of the world, except in regions with complex political systems, are divided into several political communities. Second, a single political community includes local groups from two or more cultures. Thus the political community is culturally heterogeneous. A consequence of this heterogeneity is that the members of the local groups which are culturally different cannot communicate with each other, since they speak different languages. Bilingualism or the use of a lingua franca in most instances appears to overcome only partially the difficulty in communication. Heterogeneous political communities are usually found only in regions of complex political systems.

When two or more political communities occur within a culture and the culture is adjacent to one or more other cultures, three types of intergroup relationships can be distinguished. First, relationships will exist between the local groups within each political community. These relationships may include economic reciprocity, joint military operations, use of land in common, joint cooperation on ceremonial occasions, and membership in the same clans or phratries. These intrapolitical community relationships are overseen by the leader of the political community, and in some political communities he has the power to intercede and adjudicate disputes arising out of these relationships. Where adjudication occurs law exists. Second, relationships will exist between the political communities within the culture. Third, relationships will exist between the political communities which are within two adjacent cultures. The relationships between political communities, whether they are culturally the same or not, are different from the relationships which occur within political communities, since there is not a single political leader who can oversee the relationships. Diplomacy, warfare, and trade are the major kinds of inter-political community relationships. Members of the same culture, although they are in different political communities, have the same cultural perspective with which to deal with problems and conflicts arising out of inter-political community relationships. Members of different cultures will deal with such problems and conflicts from the perspective of their own cultures, for there is usually no commonly accepted way of handling such matters (Campbell and LeVine 1961:82–108). Thus it is important to distinguish the relationships between political communities which are culturally the same from the relationships between political communities which are culturally different.

When a single political community includes local groups from two or more cultures and the political community is adjacent to other political communities, two types of intergroup relationships can be distinguished. First, relationships will exist between local groups which are culturally the same and those which are culturally different. Since the members of culturally different local groups do not speak the same language, problems arising between such local groups are difficult for the political leader to resolve. That is, heterogeneous political communities are characterized by conflicts which develop out of "race relations." Resolution of the problems and conflicts is difficult, not only because of the communication problem, but also because the political leader is usually a member of one of the two contending cultures. Second, relationships will exist between the political community and adjacent political communities. The type of inter-political community relationships will probably be the same whether or not the neighboring political communities are culturally homogeneous or heterogeneous, since cultural differences exist between the political communities. The only situations in which cultural differences might not be of importance would be when the dominant culture in both political communities is the same.

The territorial organization of a political community may form a system consisting of a series of hierarchical levels. Although some political communities are composed of only one local group, most are composed of numerous local groups. Sometimes these local groups are organized into territorial units within the political community. These territorial units are called districts. In some political communities the districts are organized into larger territorial units called provinces. Local groups, districts, and provinces—like the political community itself—are headed by political leaders. There is one hierarchical level if the political community is composed of one local group, two levels if it is composed of two or more local groups, three levels if it is composed of districts, and four levels if it is composed of provinces. These levels form a system in that the leaders at each level, except for the head of the political community, are subordinate to a leader at a higher level. Political communities differ one from the other in terms of the number of hierarchical levels composing their political systems. The more levels there are to a political system, the more complex it is. Thus the number of levels provides a measure of political complexity. The greater the number of hierarchical levels the greater the complexity of the political community.

Two basic types of political communities were delineated above: those which are culturally homogeneous and those which are culturally heterogeneous. Homogeneous political communities are composed of local groups of the same culture. If a political community consists of only one local group, it probably will be culturally homogeneous. Thus the political systems of culturally homogeneous political communities will range in complexity from one to several hierarchical levels. Culturally heterogeneous political communities are composed of local groups of different cultures. Since there must in most cases be two or more local groups in a heterogeneous political community, in nearly every instance there will be at least two hierarchical levels present. Thus the political systems of culturally heterogeneous political communities will range in complexity from two to several hiearchical levels. Since heterogeneous political communities rarely consist of only one level, it follows on a logical basis that heterogeneous political communities in general will have complex political systems. There is also an empirical reason why the political systems of heterogeneous political communities are complex. The conquest of local groups by culturally different local groups produces, by definition, heterogeneous political communities. It also creates a series of hierarchical levels, since it is necessary for the leaders of the conquering local groups to superimpose an administrative organization upon the conquered local groups. Since a complex political system is a means of territorially organizing conquered local groups, political communities with such political systems are likely to be culturally heterogeneous. (Of course, local groups of the same culture may also be organized into a complex political system through conquest.)

Naroll's definition of a territorial team should be used to distinguish political communities (1964:268):

A group of people whose membership is defined in terms of occupancy of a common territory and who have an official with the special function of announcing group decisions—a function exercised at least once a year.

Only maximal territorial units should be distinguished initially. By maximal is meant that the unit with its political leader is not included within a larger unit. Maximal territorial units or political communities may contain subunits within them which have their own leaders. In some cultures, particularly those whose political systems are not complex, there may be a large number of political communities. The number of political communities may total in the hundreds—if each local group within the culture is a maximal territorial unit. When a culture of this type is being analyzed, it may be necessary to estimate the number of political communities, provided the ethnographer does not furnish a figure. In addition, if the information is available, the size—in terms of population—of each political community should be noted. If there are a large number of political communities in the culture, the average size can be determined by dividing the number of political communities into the population size of the culture.

In many instances it is difficult to distinguish political communities, since many cultures have been conquered and absorbed into modern nations and the leaders of the constituent political communities have been incorporated into the political structures of the nations. Schapera's definition is an attempt to deal with this problem (1956:8): "By a 'political community' I mean a group of people organized into a single unit managing its affairs independently of external control (except that exercised nowadays by European governments)." Probably the best solution to the problem, however, is to utilize information concerning the culture which pertains to a period before the culture lost its political autonomy. For some cultures, such as those of highland New Guinea, that period is now; for others it is the eighteenth or nineteenth century. This period before a culture's political communities were absorbed into the conquering nation is known as the *ethnographic present* (see "The People," in Chapter 2). If information pertaining to the ethnographic present is utilized to distinguish political communities, the date or approximate time level to which the information applies should be recorded.

20. **How many hierarchical levels are there in the political system?**

If each local group in the culture is a maximal territorial unit, there is only one level to the political system of each political community. If there are several local groups in a political community, there are two hierarchical levels to the political system. If local groups are organized into districts with district leaders, there are three hierarchical levels. A lineage and clan system—if the lineages are local groups and the clans are districts—will form a three-level political system. If districts are organized into provinces with district and province leaders, a political system with four hierarchical levels exists. A lineage, clan, and phratry system—if the lineages are local groups, the clans districts, and the provinces phratries—constitutes a four-level political system. It is also possible to find complex political systems with more than four hierarchical levels. If such a system is being analyzed the exact number of levels should be recorded.

The Bahamas, rather than Andros Island, is the political community (see Question 1, in Chapter 2). There is a "commissioner for the area," who is a government appointee (Otterbein 1966:39).

These areas or administrative districts constitute a level between the local groups and the Bahamas Government; thus, there are three hierarchical levels to the political community. However, at the time of fieldwork the Bahamas were a British possession. Newspaper pictures of the British royal family were tacked to the walls of homes (Otterbein 1966:87). If Great Britain is considered the political community, then there would be four hierarchical levels to the political community. No information is given as to the degree of homogeneity or heterogeneity of the Bahamas.

Each Yanomamö village is a political community (Chagnon 1968:101):

Whether the ties between neighboring villages will be one of blood, marriage exchange, reciprocal feasting, or casual trading depends on a large number of factors, particularly on village size, current warfare situation with respect to more distant groups, and the precise historical ties between the neighboring villages. Whatever the nature of the ties between neighbors, each strives to maintain its sovereignty and independence from the others.

The political communities are culturally homogeneous. Chagnon estimates the number of Yanomamö villages at 125 (see Question 10, in Chapter 3, for quotation). Since each Yanomamö village or local group is a maximal territorial unit, there is only one hierarchical level to the political system of each political community.

For hundreds of years (since A.D. 1300) the Qemant have been absorbed into larger political communities—first, the "medieval Abyssinian feudal state," today, the modern nation of Ethiopia (Gamst 1969:15–16). It is thus impossible to describe the Qemant political community as it existed prior to its conquest. For this reason Ethiopia has been selected as the political community. Therefore, the questions in this chapter, "Polity and Warfare," will be answered from this perspective. Where possible, however, the relationship of the Qemant to this larger political unit will be examined.

Ethiopia is a heterogeneous political community which includes seventy or more cultures (Gamst 1969:5–6):

The affinities of the Qemant to their neighbors in Ethiopia, an area of 450,000 square miles populated by an estimated 22,000,000 people divided into seventy or more language groups, are of interest. The northern and north-central part of highland Ethiopia, once called Abyssinia, is the region in which field research was conducted. It is inhabited by three major groups which together are sometimes called Abyssinians. They are: the Amhara, who number about 5,000,000 and are politically dominant; the Tegre, numbering about 1,500,000, and the Agaw. . . . These three peoples are racially one and have many common cultural roots as well, in spite of the fact that the first two groups speak Semitic languages and the third group speaks dialects belonging to the central branch of the Cushitic languages. . . .

> There are five hierarchical levels in the political system of Ethiopia (Gamst 1969:21):

Ethiopia has five levels of government administration: (1) the nation or Empire, (2) the province or Governor Generalate (*tekelay gazat*), (3) the subprovince (*awraja*), (4) the sub-subprovince (*warada*), and (5) the sub-sub-subprovince (*meketel warada*).

> The Qemant are divided between two subprovinces (Gamst 1969:21):

One-half of the Qemant are in the Gondar *awraja*, which is administered from the town of Gondar, and the other half are in the Chelga *awraja*, which is administered from the village of Aykel, near the eastern boundary of this *awraja*.

POLITICAL LEADERS

The leaders of political communities or maximal territorial units vary greatly in the tasks which they perform—whether ceremonial, economic, or political. Thus one way of classifying political leaders would be in terms of the tasks which they perform for the members of their political communities. Another way to classify leaders would be in terms of how they succeeded to political office: is succession based on hereditary principles, is there a formal election, does informal consensus occur, or is the position seized by the strongest individual? Leaders vary also in two other attributes: degree of formality and degree of power. In terms of degree of formality, a leader may be almost indistinguishable from other adult males in the culture. He may dress no differently, his demeanor may be the same, and he may not be referred to by any special name. At the other extreme, the leader may be so formal that he is believed to be a deity or an earthly incarnation of a deity. Leaders likewise vary greatly in terms of their degree of power. On one hand, a leader may be so limited in power that he has no other function except announcing group decisions; and on the other hand, a leader may have such great power that he can arbitrarily put individuals to death. These two variables or attributes—degree of formality and degree of power—can be used together to construct a typology for classifying political leaders. Such a classification will be followed here.

The above two variables are used by Leopold Pospisil to derive a scheme for classifying types of political leaders, or as he calls them, authorities (1958:260–261):

These different attributes allow the authorities to be classified as different types. For our purposes we may be interested in two attributes: formality and extent of power. . . .

To give some tentative definitions of our extremes, we may say this: by formal authority is meant an individual (or individuals) with his (or their) role, rights, duties, and activities defined by custom and/or law. . . . The informal authority, on the other hand, has no ceremonial importance and little public emphasis. . . . His rights, duties, and procedures are not defined by law or custom.

A limited authority is acquired by a procedure which is controlled by the society. Approval by the majority of the members of the society is necessary, or nomination by another person with relatively greater authority must take place. . . . An absolute authority is different in many respects. His power is not limited by someone else. The subordination of his followers is emphasized in personal contacts. . . .

By measuring the two variables discussed above, we should be able to place each authority in a definite position that indicates his qualities within the two ranges. An authority then will be defined by the following possible combination of the two measured attributes and their negatives: formal and absolute, informal and absolute, formal and limited, or informal and limited. . . .

Pospisil ends his development of the typology at this point. It is possible, however, to proceed further and to label each of his four combinations with a pertinent term. Four types of political leaders are listed in the following chart along with their defining attributes:

Types of Political Leaders	Degree of Formality	Degree of Power
King	formal	absolute
Dictator	informal	absolute
Chief	formal	limited
Headman	informal	limited

Thus a typology of four different types of political leaders has been constructed. Each type is defined in terms of the degree of formality and the degree of power of the political leader. Political communities headed by leaders with absolute power (kings and dictators) are known as *states*, and political communities headed by leaders with limited power (chiefs and headmen) are considered to be stateless (Fortes and Evans-Pritchard 1940).

Dictators will rarely be found, since in most cases a political leader who has absolute power and who is not a formal leader will rapidly attempt to formalize the position which he has just seized or created by bestowing titles upon himself, by wearing special clothing, by claiming certain social prerogatives, and possibly even by claiming to have been divinely chosen. Political scientists would say such a leader is attempting to legitimize his position.

An ethnographic example of a dictator would be Shaka, the famous warrior-king who rose from the ranks of the army and through a series of battles and conquests became undisputed ruler in 1822 of the Zulu empire—a territory of 80,000 square miles encompassing 300 tribes. He legitimized his position by declaring himself king. So tyrannical was he that his brothers assassinated him in 1828 (Otterbein 1967).

These terms—*king, dictator, chief, headman*—can be used not only to classify the leaders of political communities, but also to classify the leaders of subunits within political communities. The leaders of local groups, districts, and provinces will probably have less formality and power than the leader of the political community. Many different combinations of leaders can occur; the combinations depend in part upon the number of hierarchical levels within the maximal territorial unit. Some likely combinations are as follows: king, chiefs, chiefs, headmen; king, chiefs, headmen; chief, headmen, headmen; king and chiefs; chief and headmen.

If there is more than one hierarchical level in the political community, the type of leader of each subunit should be recorded.

21.   What type of political leader is present?
   1. king
   2. dictator
   3. chief
   4. headman

In the classification of political leaders several difficulties are likely to arise. In the first place, the definitions of formal, informal, limited, and absolute are definitions of the extreme ends of two variables or continua. If a political leader fits somewhere near the middle on either variable, it may be difficult to make a decision as to whether his position is formal or informal or whether his power is limited or absolute. If the difficulty arises, a decision should be made never-theless, and a statement describing the basis for the decision should be recorded. Another difficulty in classifying political leaders stems from the indiscrimant use in some ethnographies of two of the above terms. The terms chief and headman are sometimes applied to any leader without regard for his formality or power.

Thus, for example, the term chief may be used to describe an informal leader, while the term headman may be used to describe a formal leader. This difficulty can be avoided by ignoring the terms employed in the ethnography and by classifying the leader according to the above attributes. Once the degree of formality and power of the leader have been established, the appropriate term for the type of political leader can be ascertained from the above chart. Yet another difficulty in classifying political leaders may arise if there are several leaders or a council occupying the top position in the political community. They may be kings, dictators, chiefs, or head-men, or a council of the same. If multiple political leaders exist this should be noted.

The Bahamas at the time of fieldwork had a Governor. At the local level the only political leader is the constable-postmaster (Ot-terbein 1966:29–30), a formal position whose incumbent has limited power. Much more power lives in the hands of the commissioner, who performs a number of tasks for the residents of his district, including the drafting of legal documents like engagement letters, hiring people to build and repair local paths, and paying old-age pensions (Otterbein 1966:29, 39, 41, 100–101).

The political leader of each Yanomamö political community is a headman because he is an informal authority and has a limited degree of power (Chagnon 1968:96):

Kaobawä has definite responsibilities as the headman and is occasionally called upon by the nature of the situation to exercise his authority. He is usually distinguishable in the village as a man of some authority only for the duration of the incident that calls forth his leadership capacity. After the incident is over, he goes about his own business like the other men in the group. But even then, he sets an example for the others, particularly in his ambitions to produce large quantities of food for his family and for the guests he must entertain. Most of the time he leads only by example and the others follow if it pleases them to do so. They can ignore his example if they wish, but most of the people turn to him when a difficult situation arises.

> At the time Gamst conducted fieldwork the political leader of Ethiopia was Emperor Haile Selassie I (Gamst 1969:16). Although specific information is not given in the ethnography, it can be inferred from descriptions of the relationship of the Qemant to the central government that the political leader has great power and has formal authority (Gamst 1969:16, 20–22, 57, 119–122). He can be classified as a king.
>
> The Qemant have their own leaders, all of whom have limited power (Gamst 1969:3):

The indigenous political structure of the Qemant . . . has three levels: councils of elders on the lowest level, higher and lower priests in intermediate positions, and the *wambar*, the arch politicoreligious leader, at the apex. The wambar acknowledges the secular sovereignty of the Amhara administrators who have social positions and roles within an ascending hierarchy of authority constituting what might be termed a feudal system.

> The *wambar* and the priests are formal authorities (Gamst 1969:39–43), and thus can be classified as chiefs (see Question 26, below). Elders, on the other hand, may be either formal or informal leaders (Gamst 1969:58):

Councils of elders are the basic units of authority among the Qemant. The councils are democratic assemblies composed of males who are "old enough to have gray hair" and who usually have a moderate amount of prestige. Elders who do most of the debating and have the greatest voice in making decisions are those who have undergone the rite of *kasa*, marking transition to the esteemed status of venerable elder. This special status signifies marked closeness to Mezgana (God). Although the rite of kasa is not required for all elders, the councils of elders are closely integrated with the religion.

> Thus some elders can be classified as chiefs, others as headmen.

LEGAL SYSTEM

> In every political community there are conflicts between individual members of the same or of different local groups which create ruptures in intra-political community relationships. These conflicts be-

tween individuals are referred to as *trouble cases* by anthropologists who study "primitive law." In many political communities the political leader has the power to intercede and adjudicate disputes. Sometimes this is done by a leader of a subunit within the political community or by a special official whose function is to adjudicate trouble cases. The leaders of some political communities have so little power that they cannot intercede and settle disputes; in these political communities ruptures in intra-political community relationships persist. If the rupture is serious, such as a feud resulting from a homicide, the political community may fragment and form two political communities. Kings and dictators, by definition, have the power to intercede and adjudicate disputes. Chiefs and headmen—although their power is limited—may have sufficient power to settle disputes. Thus any type of political leader may be able to resolve conflicts between individuals.

If trouble cases are resolved by political leaders (or by authorities acting in their stead), a situation exists in which law can develop. Three elements must be present for law to exist: "official authority," "privileged force," and "regularity" (Hoebel 1954:28). The authority must be able to back his decision with physical force, and the use of this force must be deemed appropriate by the members of the political community. The decision must be applied with regularity in similar trouble cases. If an authority does not intend for his decision to be applicable to other trouble cases, nor employs decisions made earlier by himself or by other authorities in resolving the trouble case, the settlement of the trouble case is not legal. That is to say, the decision is political, not legal. If these three elements are involved in the settlement of some disputes, law is present in the political community. If authorities do not have the power to apply physical coercion to enforce decisions or do not apply decisions with regularity, law does not exist.

Two types of legal sanctions may be applied by an authority: restitutive and penal. A restitutive sanction is a requirement that one individual (the defendant) must make payment to the other individual (the plaintiff) in the dispute. Payment is usually in the form of animals, material goods, money, or some other type of wealth. If payment is not made, the authority may use physical force. The use of a restitutive sanction defines a legal case as being an example of the *law of private delicts*. Modern jurisprudence would classify such actions as cases of civil law. Actions treated as private delicts include homicide, wounding, theft, adultery, and failure to pay debts. A penal sanction, on the other hand, is a punishment inflicted upon an individual who is responsible for violating a rule of conduct. Penal sanctions include incarceration, exile, torture, and execution. These sanctions come into effect when the local group or the political community as a whole has become outraged over the behavior of an individual or when the decisions or commands of authorities have been disobeyed. Such situations are not, strictly speaking, trouble cases unless the offended local group or the authority is viewed as a party in the dispute. Nevertheless, "cases" in which penal sanctions are employed are legal since the three defining elements of law are present. The use of a penal sanction defines a legal case as being an example of the *law of public delicts*. Western law would define such actions as cases of criminal law. Actions treated as public delicts include incest, sorcery, sacrilege (Radcliffe-Brown 1959:212–219). From the point of view of judicial process it should be noted that if the defendant in a trouble case does not make restitution, he has disobeyed the decision of the authority; if such disobedience leads to the application of a penal sanction, the case becomes transferred from the realm of private law to the realm of public law. Thus penal sanctions reinforce restitutive sanctions.

22.   What types of law are present?
   1. law absent
   2. law of private delicts (based upon restitutive sanctions)
   3. law of public delicts (based upon penal sanctions)

The first task facing a person who undertakes an analysis of the legal system of a political community is to identify the political leader and any other authorities who make decisions, decisions which are often attempts to resolve trouble cases. If penal sanctions are regularly employed to punish individuals who break rules of conduct or to enforce restitutive sanctions, law exists—in particular the law of public delicts. If restitutive sanctions are used by authorities in resolving trouble cases and these sanctions are reinforced by penal sanctions, then the law of private delicts is also present. If authorities cannot enforce a restitution requirement imposed upon one of the individuals in a dispute, neither restitutive nor penal sanctions are present; and therefore law is not present. Thus a political community may be without law, it may have public law only, or it may have both public and private law. Private law alone does not occur.

The position taken here differs from that taken by some anthropologists who study "primitive law." Hoebel (1954) and Pospisil (1958), for example, interpret the key concepts—official authority, privileged force, and regularity—so broadly that at least some trouble cases in any political community are classified as legal cases.

(For a criticism of their position consult Fried [1967:90–94, 141–153].) Regularity requires that there be multiple cases involving the same decision; penal sanctions must actually be applied at times for there to be evidence of privileged force; and an authority must be an official, not a forceful individual who usurps the privilege of settling trouble cases. All three elements must be present in the settlement of some disputes for law to exist in a political community.

The *Statute Laws of the Bahama Islands* operate fully on Andros Island (Otterbein 1969:39, 41, 46–47, 49, 68). They are administered at the local level by the commissioner. Both the law of public delicts and the law of private delicts are present. The post office-courthouse in Motion Town (Otterbein 1966) is used by the commissioner to hear cases and make payments, and by the constable-postmaster to receive and dispense mail.

The Yanomamö have no law. The official authority—the headman—seemingly does not have the right of privileged force, nor is there apparently any regularity in the settling of conflicts. The following trouble case involving the ethnographer indicates that Kaobawä, the headman, was unable to adjudicate disputes (Chagnon 1968:68):

On one occasion a young man stole my flashlight and gave it to Shiimima, a younger brother to Kaobawä, but already a mature adult. I asked Kaobawä to help me get it back. After a day or so I asked him if he had gotten my flashlight back from Shiimima, whereupon he replied: "I have spoken to him about it. He will return it if he sees fit. I cannot order him to do so because he is already fierce."

In another trouble case, the headman could possibly be exercising privileged force, but there is no indication that similar trouble cases would be handled in the same manner (Chagnon 1968:120):

One of the young men took the wife of another because she was allegedly being mistreated by him. This resulted in a brutal club fight that involved almost every man in the village. The fight escalated to jabbing with the sharpened ends of the clubs when the husband of the woman in question was speared by his rival and wounded. The headman of the village . . . had been attempting to keep the fighting restricted to clubs. When the husband's rival speared his opponent, the headman went into a rage and speared him in turn, running his own sharpened club completely through the young man's body. He died when they tried to remove the weapon.

The wife was then given back to her legitimate husband, who punished her by cutting both her ears off with his machete.

The kinsmen of the dead man were then ordered to leave the village before there was further bloodshed.

The Qemant legal system is embedded in the administrative and judicial system of Ethiopia. Thus the wambar's decisions are enforced by higher Ethiopian authorities (see Question 24, below). For this reason penal sanctions can be said to be present. The wambar also has the power to impose ostracism. It is not clear, however, from the following passage whether this sanction involves physical removal from Qemantland. If it does not, ostracism is not a penal sanction (Gamst 1969:63):

The wambar preserves Qemant mores with awesome punishments that reach beyond the grave and bar the way to heaven. Curses and ostracism are the ultimate punishments handed out by a wambar, and they are ordinarily levied only if someone challenges his authority. For example, if a person does not abide by a wambar's decision, or if he violates a major religious rule, such as marrying outside Qemant religious laws, he is ostracized. Ostracism is complete and final and continues after death. An ostracized person receives no funeral and no rite of passage into heaven.

Restitutive sanctions are also present. In homicide cases blood money may be paid (see Question 24, below, for quotation). The amount of restitution may be as high as Eth. $1000 (Gamst 1969:63).

Since penal and restitutive sanctions occur, both the law of public delicts and the law of private delicts are present. This would be true for both Ethiopia and the Qemant.

MILITARY ORGANIZATIONS

A military organization is the means by which a political leader defends his political community from enemy attacks. It may also be used internally by the political leader to enforce the law and to carry out penal sanctions. Military organizations can range in size from small raiding parties composed of several warriors to large standing armies composed of hundreds of thousands of men (Mead 1964:270). Armed combat, which is fighting with weapons, is performed by military organizations. If there is more than one military organization within a political community and these military organizations engage each other in armed combat, this is considered feuding or civil war, depending upon the scope of the conflict. Warfare (excluding civil war) is defined as armed combat between political communities. When the political communities within the same culture engage in warfare, this is considered to be internal war. When warfare occurs between political communities which are not within the same culture, this is referred to as external war. These concepts relating to the activities of military organizations are discussed in this and the next two sections; the relationships among these major concepts are graphically illustrated in Figure 3. Concepts dealing with aspects of military and political organization are represented by circles, and types of armed combat between military and political organizations are shown by double-headed arrows (Otterbein 1968b).

Military organizations, which can be viewed as a particular type of social organization, engage in armed combat in order to obtain certain goals. They differ, however, from other organizations in that the goals or objectives they pursue are usually directed at military organizations in other political communities. The goals of war include subjugation and tribute, land, plunder, trophies and honors, defense, and revenge (see "Causes of War" below). All these objectives are carried out at the expense of other political communities. The military organization which is the winner of the armed combat is more likely to achieve its goals than is the defeated military organization. The outcome of an armed combat between two military organizations will depend upon the efficiency of their military practices. A victorious military organization makes a political community militarily successful and increases its likelihood of survival in inter-political community conflicts (Otterbein 1970a).

The warriors composing a military organization may be either professionals or nonprofessionals. Professionals, in contrast to nonprofessionals, devote a substantial part of their time during their early adulthood to intensive training, which may involve not only practice in the use of weapons but also practice in performing maneuvers. They may be members of age-grades, military societies, or standing armies, or they may serve as mercenaries employed for a specific purpose. Political communities with age-grades, military societies, and standing armies are considered to have military organizations composed solely of professionals. Political communities which employ mercenaries to lead, train, or assist untrained warriors are considered to have both professionals and nonprofessionals in their military organizations. If all members of a military organization are warriors who have not had intensive training in the art of war, the military organization is considered to be composed solely of nonprofessionals. If both professional and nonprofessional warriors

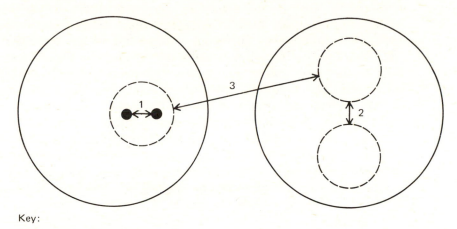

Key:

Circles
Solid circles represent military organizations
Broken-line circles represent political communities
Solid-line circles represent cultures

Double-headed arrows (⟵⟶)
1 feuding
2 internal war
3 external war

FIGURE 3   Diagram of Basic Concepts—III

are absent, there is of course no military organization. A recent cross-cultural study of war examined the military practices of fifty cultures. It was found that nine political communities had military organizations composed of professionals, thirteen had military organizations which included both professionals and nonprofessionals, twenty-four had military organizations composed of nonprofessionals, and only four had no military organizations (Otterbein 1970a). Thus one is most likely to find military organizations composed of nonprofessional warriors. On the other hand, one rarely finds a culture which does not have a military organization.

The fact that few political communities do not have military organizations raises the fundamental question: Why do most political communities have military organizations? The answer seems to be that if a political community is to have contact with other political communities and yet to remain a social entity, it needs to have the means to defend itself from the attacks of neighbors and to retaliate if the attacks have been successfully made against them. The four political communities without military organizations, mentioned above, are all found in isolated locations. Their members are descendants of groups which had been driven from other areas and had taken refuge on an island, in arctic wasteland, or on the top of a mountain. Relocated in an area where they were protected by their isolation, they no longer found it necessary to maintain a military organization. Thus a political community which does not have a military organization capable of defending it will probably be annihilated and absorbed into other political communities unless it is able to flee and protect itself, not by arms, but by hiding in an isolated area. A further indication that a military organization is a necessity, if a political community is to persist through time, is to be found in the fact that defense and revenge are universal causes of war. Several studies have shown that all known military organizations go to war at some time or another for defense and revenge (Otterbein 1970a; Naroll 1966; Wright 1942).

23. **What type of military organization is present?**
    1. a military organization is absent
    2. a military organization composed of professional warriors
    3. a military organization composed of both professional and nonprofessional warriors
    4. a military organization composed of nonprofessional warriors

If all the military personnel in the political community are either members of age-grades, military societies, standing armies, or mercenary units, the type of military organization present is composed solely of professional warriors. On the other hand, if none of the warriors has had intensive training in the art of war, the military organization is composed entirely of nonprofessional warriors. It is also possible that the political community will have a military organization composed of both professional and nonprofessional warriors.

The Andros Islanders do not have military organizations. Thus they have not been drafted nor have they volunteered for military service. Some do, however, join the police, the only quasi-military organization in the Bahamas. During World War II many men served as agricultural laborers in the United States (Otterbein 1966:31).

It is clear from Chagnon's detailed description of Yanomamö warfare that their military organizations were not composed of age-grades, military societies, standing armies, or mercenaries. As the following quotation indicates, the training of a warrior was an informal, on-the-spot process (1968:130–132):

The raiders always develop a strategy for attacking the unwary enemy. They usually split into two or more groups and agree to meet later at a predetermined location at some point between their own village and the enemy's. These smaller groups must contain at least four men, six, if possible. This is so because the raiders retreat in a pattern. While the others flee, two men will lie in ambush, shooting any pursuers that might follow. They, in turn, flee, while their comrades lie in ambush to shoot at their pursuers. If there are novices in the raiding party, the older men will councils of elders on the lowest level, higher and lower priests in interme- dummy or soft log is frequently employed in this, as was the case in the *wayu itou* held in the village the day before the raiders left. Particularly young men will be positioned in the marching party somewhere in the middle of the single file of raiders so they will not be the first ones to be exposed to danger should the raiders themselves be ambushed. These young men will also be permitted to retreat first. Damowä had a twelve- year-old son when he was killed. This boy, Matarawä, was recruited into the raiding party to give him an opportunity to avenge his father's death. The older men made sure he would be exposed to minimum danger, as this was his first raid.

Hence, it can be concluded that Yanomamö military organizations are composed of nonprofessionals.

Although explicit information is lacking, it can be inferred from Ethiopian history that the military organization is composed of fessional warriors (see Question 26 for quotation). The Qemant do not have their own military organization, but they have served with distinction in the Ethiopian army (Gamst 1969:21, 81, 105, 109).

FEUDING

Feuding is a type of armed combat within a political community in which if a homicide occurs, the kin of the deceased take revenge through killing the offender or a close relative of his. Such armed combats are usually initiated by a small group of men, relatives of the deceased, who lie in ambush and attack the unsuspecting victim who is often alone and has little chance of escape. The ambushers are of necessity sufficiently armed and organized so that the group which they form can be referred to as a military organization; that is, a sufficient degree of organization must prevail if the warriors are to arrange the ambush in secret, to remain silently in hiding, and to spring the attack at the appropriate moment. These small-scale military organizations are fraternal interest groups. They are usually composed of nonprofessionals. It has been shown by van Velzen and van Wetering (1960) that fraternal interest groups, which are power groups composed of related males, resort to aggression when the interests of their members are threatened. Such groups can come into existence either through the operation of a patrilocal (or virilocal) residence rule, since patrilocal residence produces households in which related males are living together, or through the practice of polygyny, since polygyny usually produces a situation in which men will have a number of unmarried sons living with them. If residence practices and marriage rules result in the scattering of related males over a large area, it will be difficult for them to support each other's interests.

A cross-cultural study of feuding has demonstrated that fraternal interest groups—as measured by patrilocal residence and polygyny—lead to feuding. One would think that in a complex political system the political leader would intercede and prevent the relatives of the victim from taking blood revenge, either by use of a judicial procedure or by persuading the relatives of the deceased to accept some form of compensation for their loss. Contrary to expectations the study shows that this does not necessarily occur. If fraternal interest groups were present, feuding was found to be frequent in cultures whose political communities had complex political systems consisting of more than one hierarchical level. Since the political leaders who head these political communities are likely to be kings and dictators (and perhaps chiefs with some degree of power, although it be limited), this is surprising. The study does show, however, that political communities with complex political systems do not have feuding if they frequently engage in warfare. Presumably these leaders use their power to intervene to prevent the development of feuding only when the political community is threatened by war or is engaged in war. In political communities with simple political systems consisting of only one hierarchical level, warfare does not diminish the frequency of feuding. Since the leaders of such political communities are chiefs and headmen with limited power, they are unable to intervene to prevent feuding. In other words, in a political community there is an official who can, if he has sufficient power, and will, if he perceives that the inter-political community situation demands it, intervene between the feuding fraternal interest groups. Since it is only in complex political systems that political leaders have sufficient power—power which they may choose to exercise only under demanding circumstances—to control the activities of the warriors in their political communities, it is only in complex political systems which are engaged in war that one finds that the feuding of fraternal interest groups is curtailed (Otterbein and Otterbein 1965; Otterbein 1968*b*).

In a recent cross-cultural study Kang (1976*a*) tested the theory that conflicting loyalties which arise from the practice of clan exogamy, cousin marriage, and local group exogamy create cross-cutting ties which reduce violent conflict and feuding. Contrary to the prediction of the theory, Kang found that there is no relationship between these culture traits and feuding. However, an additional feature, "dispersion of the vengeancy group," was found associated with the absence of feuding. The study concluded that "conflicting loyalties reduce feuding only if they involve a division of allegiance between residential loyalty and male agnatic kin loyalty—where residence and male agnatic kin loyalties are compatible, fraternal interest groups and feuding occur" (Kang 1976*a*:208).

Homicide cases are handled by political communities in three different ways: (1) Feuding does not occur if there is a formal judicial procedure for punishing the offender or if homicides are always settled through compensation. (Of course, feuding is not likely to arise if homicides rarely occur.) The trouble cases arising out of homicides are legally adjudicated if the political leader or an authority imposes a restitutive or penal sanction upon the party responsible for the homicide. (2) Feuding with compensation occurs if the relatives of the deceased sometimes accept compensation in lieu of blood revenge. (3) Feuding without compensation occurs if the relatives of the deceased are expected to take revenge through killing the offender or any close relative of his. If feuding invariably follows a homicide or if compensation need not be accepted by the relatives of the deceased, the trouble cases resulting from homicides are not legally adjudicated. In many cultures accidental as well as deliberate homicide can trigger feuding. In other words, the offended fraternal interest group does not take into account the intentions of the killer. However, in those cultures which have feuding with compensation, the intention of the killer may determine whether compensation is accepted. That is, if the relatives of the deceased are convinced that the homicide was accidental, they may be willing to accept compensation. On the other hand, in those cultures which have feuding without compensation, accidental homicide will probably lead to feuding.

24. Is feuding present?
1. absent
2. feuding with compensation
3. feuding without compensation

Feuding is absent if there is a formal judicial procedure for punishing killers or if the account states that homicides rarely occur. Feuding occurs if the kin of the deceased take revenge through killing the offender or a close relative of his. If restitution in the form of animals, material goods, money, or some other type of wealth is sometimes offered by the relatives of the killer and is sometimes accepted by the relatives of the deceased, feuding with compensation occurs. If restitution is never offered and never accepted, feuding without compensation occurs. If the ethnography—and it is highly unlikely—provides statistical data on homicides and how they are resolved, this information should be recorded.

The Andros Islanders do not engage in feuding. Fighting apparently does not lead to homicide (Otterbein 1966:128):

The members of a man's kindred, which of course includes all his cousins, are expected to try to prevent his becoming involved in fights. Any kinsman should stop a fight between two of his relatives. If he is related to only one of the men, he will try to stop that man. Kinsmen of the other man will try to hold their relative. However, if the two fighters are related and if their relatives want and expect to see one of the men beaten, they are likely to let the fight proceed. If the two men fighting are not related, any one of three things can happen. Relatives may pull them apart, as occurred at the fight at the wedding [previously] described . . . . Or kin of each may say, "Let them fight." If both sets of relatives are in agreement, the fight will proceed. But if only one side wants the fight, a general brawl may start, with several men involved.

Feuding without compensation may occur among the Yanomamö, and when it does it leads to village fissioning, with each segment becoming a separate political community (Chagnon 1968: 40–41):

By the time a village approaches 100 to 150 people, such fights over women are so frequent that the group elects to fission rather than attempt to keep an uneasy internal peace. Although a larger village has an advantage in terms of its capacity to raid other groups and is better able to defend itself from raids, the internal fights often lead to killings within the group. Then, there is no alternative but for one of the factions to leave. Its members may anticipate a situation like this and begin making a new garden long before the fighting becomes violent enough to lead to deaths, for a fight can develop unexpectedly and result immediately in bloodshed. The guilty faction must then seek refuge in the village of an ally until it can establish its own garden. Usually, however, the larger group fissions while its members are on relatively peaceable terms, and the two resulting villages remain in the same general area so that they can reunite when raids threaten them.

For a specific example of fissioning see Question 22 above.
When conflicts over women arise, it is usually between men of different local descent groups (see Question 16, in Chapter 4) belonging to the same patrilineage. Two or possibly more local descent groups will break away from the village, taking with them two or more local descent groups (with whom they intermarry) from another lineage (Chagnon 1968:70–71).

Although killings and counterkillings occur among the Qemant, feuding is absent. Gamst describes homicides at length (1969:63–64):

The most serious judicial matter to reach a wambar is a killing. Qemant law does not recognize accidental death or manslaughter; to take another person's life is to murder him. The dictum of "an eye for an eye" is Qemant law, and the penalty for taking another's life is for the killer to lose his own life at the hands of the dead man's kin. The killer has only one recourse: He may pay blood money to the family of the person he has killed. . . .
If the family of the killer cannot come to an agreement with the family of the deceased through councils or other intermediaries, the wambar takes up the problem. If agreement is reached by both parties on the amount of indemnity, an oral contract is made with the help of the wambar or council of elders. This contract is then presented by both parties to the Amhara officials, who levy an additional fine upon the guilty person and confiscate any weapon used in the killing. In this way the Amhara validate Qemant judgments in cases of homicide. After the contract is fulfilled and the fine is paid, the killer cannot be punished further. . . .
Today, if a judgment of blood indemnity is disputed, the case may be referred to the Amhara judges and administrators. If the Amhara officials do not settle the case, as happens occasionally, the kin of the deceased take the life of the killer. In keeping with the idea of blood vengeance, an endless chain of vendetta may then ensue, but this rarely happens. The policy of the Ethiopian government is to try to punish for killings, thus preventing vendettas.

There are three reasons for concluding that feuding is absent: (1) there is a formal judicial procedure for punishing the offender; (2) it is the killer himself who is killed, not one of his kin (elsewhere, however, Gamst [1969:70] states otherwise [see Question 17, in Chapter 4, for quotation]); and (3) vendettas "rarely" occur.

WARFARE

Warfare, which is defined as armed combat between political communities, is conducted by military organizations. If the political communities are culturally the same, the armed combat is classified as internal war. But if the political communities are culturally different, the armed combat is external war (see Figure 3 on page 139). Two types of external war can be distinguished: a political community can either attack (offensive external war) or be attacked by (defensive external war) a culturally different political community. The military organizations which carry out the armed combat are apt to be fraternal interest groups. As was pointed out in the previous section, if the members of such a military organization make an attack upon someone who is a member of their own political community, they are engaged in feuding or the initiation of a feud. If the next day these warriors ambush a member of another political community, they are engaged in war. Thus, fraternal interest groups, employing ambushing tactics, can be responsible for both feuding and warfare. It has been shown in a cross-cultural study of internal war that fraternal interest groups lead to frequent internal war. This apparently occurs because most cultures with fraternal interest groups probably contain a large number of such military organizations because of the large number of localized kinship groups in the constituent political communities. The presence of a large number of small-scale military organizations creates the strong likelihood that internal war will be frequent. Presumably because of the greater distance between most political communities which are in different cultures, fraternal interest groups do not produce either the offensive or the defensive type of external war (Otterbein 1968a; Otterbein 1968b).

The frequency of internal war can be classified as either "continual," "frequent," "infrequent," or "never." The two types of external war can also be classified in the same manner. However, for the sake of brevity, external war and its frequency will not be discussed. It is necessary to classify the frequency of internal war on a four-point scale, since it is nearly impossible—even for an ethnographer in the field—to record the number of different attacks which the political communities within a culture make upon each other in a particular period of time. Most ethnographies include only general statements concerning the frequency of war. For any particular culture and its constituent political communities, the frequency of internal war can be classified as "continual" if the ethnographic source states that warfare is or was a constant state of affairs within the culture. Constant can be interpreted to mean that warfare occurs every year. Internal war is "frequent" if the source states that although the political communities within the culture frequently fought with each other, periods of peace occasionally occurred. An indication that periods of peace occur would be a statement that warfare is not an annual affair. Internal war is "infrequent" if warfare is described as uncommon or rare. And finally, the frequency of internal war can be classified as "never" if warfare is described as nonexistent or if there are no military organizations in the culture.

25. If there is more than one political community within the culture, how frequently do they war with each other?
1. continually
2. frequently
3. infrequently
4. never

The first problem to be faced in attempting to ascertain the frequency of internal war is to make certain that there is more than one political community within the culture. If there is only one political community in the culture or the political community is culturally heterogeneous, internal war as defined in this section cannot occur. Another problem is to find sufficient information dealing with the culture before it was militarily defeated and absorbed into a conquering state, probably a European nation. Lack of sufficient information is one reason why most ethnographies contain only general statements concerning the frequency of war. Since the ethnographic present for some cultures occurred as much as 200 years ago, detailed information is often lacking on warfare.

The Andros Islanders do not engage in internal war because their culture is contained within a single political community.

Yanomamö political communities continually war with each

other. Chagnon is one of the few ethnographers who has actually witnessed warfare while undertaking fieldwork (Chagnon 1968:40):

The village of Patanowä-teri, for example, has over 200 people. It was being raided actively by about a dozen different groups while I conducted my field-work, groups that raided it about twenty-five times in a period of fifteen months.

Since Ethiopia is a heterogeneous political community (that is, there are not distinct political communities within a particular culture), this topic and question are not applicable to the situation.

CAUSES OF WAR

Wars occur when military organizations do battle in order to obtain certain goals. These goals may vary from war to war, and they may change over time. Thus for the military organizations of a political community there will probably be several goals of war. At a given period in the history of a political community—if sufficient data are available—the order of the importance of the goals can probably be ascertained. The political leader of the political community may determine the goals and send the military organizations to war in order to achieve these goals, or the leaders of the military may make the decision as to which goals will be pursued. Thus it can be argued that wars are caused by the decisions of men as members of organizations, whether they be military organizations or political systems. There are six basic reasons for going to war: subjugation and tribute, land, plunder, trophies and honors, revenge, and defense (Otterbein 1970a).

Some social scientists have argued that states, which are political communities headed by kings or dictators, go to war for subjugation and tribute. On the other hand, political communities headed by chiefs and headmen go to war for economic, social, and defensive reasons. Of the fifty cultures in a cross-cultural study of war, ten consisted of political communities which were states. The states of seven of these cultures went to war for political objectives—namely, subjugation and tribute. Only two cultures had political communities which were not states, but which nevertheless went to war for subjugation and tribute. These cultures were composed of political communities with strong leaders (Otterbein 1970a). This almost exclusive association between states and political objectives can be explained by two conditions which must exist for subjugation and tribute to occur. First, the victorious political community must have a complex political system consisting of several hierarchical levels if it is to have the capability of incorporating conquered peoples into its political system. Moreover, the political community must have a political leader with a great deal of power who can superimpose himself and the members of his political community upon vanquished peoples. Such a leader is to be found only in states and some political communities with complex political systems. Second, even though the political machinery for subordination is present, subordination must be advantageous to the victors—advantageous in the sense that the skills possessed by the conquered peoples and the products they produce are of value to the victorious political community. If the conquered peoples are coerced into contributing some of their products to the leaders of the victorious political community, tribute is being paid. Thus states, subjugation, and tribute form a complex which is found again and again throughout the world.

The other five reasons for going to war are also likely to be pursued at one time or another by the military organizations of states. They also constitute the major reasons stateless political communities go to war. An important economic reason for attacking other political communities is to capture land by defeating and driving back or killing the inhabitants. The land may be used for fields, hunting, or grazing. Another goal of war, primarily economic, is to obtain plunder. Plunder, in addition to animals, material goods, money, and other forms of wealth, includes captives for wives, slaves, hostages, adoption, or sacrifice. Trophies and honors are social or prestige goals. Military organizations and political communities often go to war, just as individual warriors do, to obtain honors. Victory in armed combat may be the sole reason for going to war. The capturing of trophies, which are cherished items usually of little economic value, is another way of obtaining prestige. Revenge—the desire to even the score—is another reason military organizations go to war. Retaliation for the killing of a member of one's political community is often a major reason for revenge. And the final reason military organizations engage in war is defense—the organized attempt by a group of armed men to defend from enemy attacks their own lives, the lives of their families, their property and homesteads, and their political community.

26. **For what reasons does the military organization go to war?**
    1. subjugation and tribute

2. land
3. plunder
4. trophies and honors
5. revenge
6. defense

If there is more than one reason for going to war, each reason should be indicated. If the ethnographer explicitly states the order of importance, his ranking should be recorded. If such a statement is not given, the student will have to judge the order of importance from the emphasis given to the various causes of war by the ethnographer. If a judgment cannot be made, the order in the ethnography in which the causes are listed or discussed can be tentatively accepted as representing the order of importance. Of course if the political community does not have a military organization, this question is irrelevant.

Since the Andros Islanders do not have military organizations, this question does not pertain.

Yanomamö military organizations go to war for revenge, defense, and plunder (in the form of women) (Chagnon 1968:123):

Most wars are merely a prolongation of earlier hostilities, stimulated by revenge motives. The first causes of hostilities are usually sorcery, murders, or club fights over women in which someone is badly injured or killed. Occasionally, food theft involving related villages also precipitates raiding. . . .
    Although few raids are initiated solely with the intention of capturing women, this is always a desired side benefit. A few wars, however, are started with the intention of abducting women.

The military organization of Ethiopia has gone to war for the following reasons: defense, revenge, land, and subjugation and tribute (Gamst 1969:16):

In the 1870s and the 1880s Emperor Johannes IV defended Abyssinia against Egypt and then against the Dervishes of the Mahdi in the Sudan. Emperor Menelik II (1889–1913) turned back European intrusion at the battle of Adwa (1896), in which the Italians were defeated and their plans for colonization were shattered. Menelik II established the capital at Addis Ababa, conquered lands to the south of Abyssinia, and introduced elements of western industrial urban technology. Under Menelik's reign, Abyssinia was transformed and expanded into a larger, more modern nation named Ethiopia.

Change in Ethiopia continues at a faster rate under the present Emperor, Haile Selassie I. Ethiopia experienced occupation by mechanized Italian military forces from 1936 to 1941, in the early years of the Emperor's reign.

STUDY GUIDE QUESTIONS

Aim of Chapter 5

This chapter illustrates the manner in which the anthropologist classifies the political behavior of the members of a culture. In addition to analyzing the particular form of political system which is embodied within a culture, the researcher must also attempt to determine the type of political leadership which is present.

It is observed that within every political community, as well as between separate political communities, conflicts which must be dealt with arise. Such situations may be handled through legal systems or via military organizations in terms of feuding or warfare. Anthropological studies thus frequently become engaged in the study of violent as well as peaceful human relations.

Introduction

1. Define the way in which anthropologists use the term *politics*, and identify the four factors which anthropologists look at when they study politics.

Political System

2. What is a political community?
3. What kinds of inter-political community relationships occur most often?
4. Why is it difficult for political communities composed of different cultures to handle problems and/or conflicts?
5. Identify the possible hierarchical levels of the political community.
6. Differentiate between a homogeneous and heterogeneous political community.

Political Leaders

7. List several of the key functions performed by political leaders and discuss the ways in which leaders may be classified.
8. What types of political leaders are found in states? In stateless political communities?
9. What problems do anthropologists frequently encounter when attempting to classify political leaders?

Legal System

10. Identify and briefly explain the three elements which are necessary for for *law* to exist.
11. Why are many trouble cases not legal cases?
12. Define the terms restitutive and penal sanction and discuss the sanctions in terms of the types of laws and social violations which are associated with each one.

Military Organizations

13. How is warfare defined? What is the difference between internal and external war?
14. Compare and contrast professional and nonprofessional warriors.
15. Why do most political communities have military organizations? Under what conditions might a political community abandon its military organization?

Feuding

16. How is *feuding* defined and under what conditions and political systems does it usually take place?
17. What are the three ways in which a political community can handle a homicide case?

Warfare

18. By what classification system do anthropologists rate the frequency of either internal or external warfare?
19. What is the difference between feuding and internal war?

Causes of War

20. Identify the six basic goals of warfare and give several of the specific reasons underlying each goal.
21. How do these goals differ from more underlying causes of war, such as overpopulation and mass migration?

Qemant priests and laymen feasting at the *tazkar*, the second funeral, of the wambar's father.

6

WORLD VIEW AND LIFE CYCLE

Supernatural Beings
Religious Practitioners
Magic
Sorcery
Post-partum Sex Taboo
Games
Initiation Rites
Art

Anthropologists who are interested in the development of individuals within a culture focus not only upon the typical life cycle of both men and women in the culture, but also upon that part of culture which is referred to as the people's world view. According to Robert Redfield (1952:30), world view is that "outlook upon the universe that is characteristic of a people. . . . It is the picture the members of a society have of the properties and characters upon their stage of action." Supernatural beings, religious practitioners, magic, and sorcery are among the more important aspects of a people's world view. They are aspects which directly impinge upon the maturing individual. Various situations and events also influence individuals from the time of birth until death. To focus upon the common practices and customs which influence individuals at different stages of their lives is to focus upon the typical life cycle of individuals within a particular culture. Birth customs (such as the post-partum sex taboo), the games children and adults play, adolescent initiation rites, and artistic pursuits are some of the practices and events which are likely to compose the life cycle.

The individual and his development, as indicated above, are influenced both by various aspects of the people's world view and by customs which occur during the life cycle of every normal member of the culture. In most cultures there is a fit between the world view and the customs closely associated with the life cycle. For example, if the world is viewed as a harsh place, then the events of a typical life cycle are harsh in nature. This hypothesis—and that is what it is—has been tested in a cross-cultural study (Lambert, Triandis, and Wolf 1959) and in a follow-up case study conducted on Andros Island (Otterbein and Otterbein 1973). The hypothesis, for which support was found, was phrased as follows: "beliefs in the *malevolence* of the supernatural world reflect punitive practices in infant and child rearing, while beliefs in the *benevolence* of the supernatural world reflect nurturant practices in infant and child training" (Lambert, Triandis, and Wolf 1959:162). In the case study it was found "that caretakers who most fear the supernatural are those who rely most on painful methods in rearing children" (Otterbein and Otterbein 1973:1679). Thus empirical research supports the notion that there is a congruence between a people's world view and life cycle customs. Furthermore, the evidence strongly suggests that individuals growing up in a particular culture will almost invariably come to believe in the various aspects of that culture's world view and will practice its customs in a way which is in conformity with the world view.

SUPERNATURAL BEINGS

Most peoples do not distinguish between the natural and the supernatural worlds. For them the beings and spirits—which anthropologists classify as belonging to the supernatural realm—are as much a part of their everyday world (i.e., the natural world) as are their own relatives and neighbors. Supernatural beings or spirits are believed to be real—real in the sense that they exist and can influence and be influenced by human beings. Supernatural beings are personified; that is, they have personal identities, and they often have names. "They have purposes and intentions of their own as

well as the power to achieve their objectives" (Swanson 1960:7).
Supernatural beings are usually immortal, may be invisible, and
reside in particular locations either on the earth or above or below
it. Although anthropologists consider supernatural beings or spirits
to be unreal (in fact, the ethnographer in the field identifies spirits
on the basis of their lack of reality), it must be emphasized again
that supernatural beings are real to the people who believe in them.
Belief in supernatural beings is called *animism*, a term introduced to
anthropology by Edward B. Tylor in his famous book *Primitive Culture* (1958; orig. 1871).

Of the various types of supernatural beings in which a people
believe, a high god, if present, is usually considered to be the most
important of their supernatural beings. A *high god* is a supernatural
being who created the universe and/or is the ultimate governor of
the universe. In some instances the high god may have created other
supernatural beings who in turn produced the universe. Some high
gods, after they created the universe, became inactive and no longer
play any part in human affairs. Other high gods play an active part in
the affairs of humans. Some active high gods give specific support to
human morality; that is, the gods reward or punish people in accordance with their treatment of relatives and neighbors. The belief in a
high god is not rare among the peoples studied by anthropologists.
In a cross-cultural study of the origins of religious beliefs, Swanson
(1960:65) found that nineteen out of thirty-nine cultures had a belief
in a high god (data were missing for eleven other cultures in the
study). Swanson did discover, however, that the belief in such a
supernatural being was associated with social and political complexity. That is, cultures with lineage and clan systems and/or with
political communities with several hierarchical levels are more likely
to have a belief in a high god than are cultures which are structurally
less complex (Swanson 1960:55–81).

Many cultures with a high god also have superior gods. These
supernatural beings are often under the direction of a high god who
on occasion may need to intercede to keep order among them.
Superior gods personify human activities such as hunting, farming,
going to war, and making love. Each god controls all individuals who
engage in any aspect of those activities associated with the god.
They are not spirits who control particular individuals or places.
Superior gods are supernatural beings "who control all phases of
one or more, but not all, human activities" (Swanson 1960:210). The
belief in superior gods is found among a majority of cultures. In the
above mentioned cross-cultural study, Swanson (1960:87) found
that twenty-nine out of forty-nine cultures had a belief in one or

more superior gods. Furthermore, he discovered—as one would expect—that superior gods were characteristic of cultures that had part-time and full-time specialists, since superior gods are the personification of human activities, including various types of specialties (Swanson 1960:82–96).

In virtually all cultures human beings are believed to have a soul or spirit which persists after death. Spirits of the dead may go to a hereafter, or they may remain somewhere on earth. In either case they may or may not play an active part in the affairs of the living. When the spirits of the dead influence their living relatives, ancestral spirits are present in the culture. Thus *ancestral spirits* are supernatural beings who are spirits of the dead and who play some role in the affairs of their living relatives. Some ancestral spirits aid or punish their descendants. This may be to enforce morality, or to force the living to pay homage or to make sacrifices to them. In some cultures nothing that the living can do will prevent ancestral spirits from inflicting hardships upon them. In other cultures individuals may invoke their deceased relatives to aid them in their earthly pursuits, such as hunting or harming an enemy. The belief in ancestral spirits is widely spread: Swanson (1960:216) found that thirty-three out of forty-nine cultures had beliefs in active ancestral spirits. Moreover, he discovered that ancestral spirits were associated with organized kinship groups. When descent groups—which are ancestor-oriented groups—such as lineages, ambilineages, clans, and phratries are present in a culture there exists an important bond between the living and the dead; that is, social relationships exist between members of the descent group and the deceased ancestral members of the group (Swanson 1960:97–108).

In addition to high gods, superior gods, and ancestral spirits, there are supernatural beings or spirits present in many cultures which are nonhuman in origin, although they may have human attributes. These *nonhuman spirits* are supernatural beings who control particular individuals or places. In some cultures an individual may through various means acquire a guardian spirit who protects him from evil or harm. The spirit may be an animal with human attributes which is the ancestor of a particular species. Many cultures have a large number of nonhuman spirits who are associated with particular geographical locations. These spirits often dwell in lakes, rivers, prominent rocks, and mountains. Sometimes they can be invoked to assist in human activities, such as hunting and fishing. At other times they must be placated or they are apt to molest passers by. They, like guardian spirits, may be animal ancestors, or they may be animal-like creatures which have both human and animal attributes.

27. In what types of supernatural beings do the people believe?

    1. a high god
    2. superior gods
    3. ancestral spirits
    4. nonhuman spirits

Since all four types of supernatural beings are commonly found in the cultures studied by anthropologists, it is to be expected that more than one type of supernatural being will be present. If there are superior gods, each should be identified and the number recorded. The number of nonhuman spirits, if there are any, will probably be so great that it would be nearly impossible to enumerate them all.

    For those interested in the classification of religious belief systems, the following scheme can be used: Monotheism is usually defined as the belief in one god. Therefore, if a high god is present, but superior gods are not, the religious belief system can be classified as *monotheistic*. On the other hand, polytheism is usually defined as the belief in more than one god. Therefore, if superior gods are present, with or without a high god being present, the religious belief system can be classified as *polytheistic*.

    The Andros Islanders believe in the Christian deity—a high god. In the descriptions of weddings and other ceremonies and events, there are several references to God (Otterbein 1966:49, 63, 65). In the villages included in the census there are four churches: two Baptist, one Anglican, and one Church of God (Otterbein 1966: 17–18). Although no information on superior gods is given, it can be tentatively concluded—since the Andros Islanders believe in God —that superior gods are not present. There is no information on ancestral spirits or nonhuman spirits, although reference is made to people seeing "spirits" and to the dried caul being used to prevent children from being "bothered by spirits" (Otterbein 1966:64).

    The supernatural belief system of the Andros Islanders is described elsewhere (Otterbein and Otterbein 1973); its three realms are Christianity, spirits of the dead, and obeah (black magic). The spirits of the dead are ancestral spirits (Otterbein and Otterbein 1973:1672–1673):

The spirit of a person who dies in Christ, or "dies right," goes to rest and can help people; however, if an ungodly person dies, his spirit wanders about frightening and hurting people. . . . However, some caretakers of children believe that God has the bad spirits under control, so that they cannot go anywhere they want to go; others believe that good spirits, especially those of one's own family, can keep the bad spirits away. . . . Some people do not go out alone at night because they are afraid of spirits, and . . . many people keep a lamp burning in their houses all night long to keep spirits away. . . .

Chagnon provides a lengthy description of Yanomamö supernatural beings. Since there is no mention of a high god when the origin of the universe is being described, it can be concluded that a high god is absent. Superior gods, however, are in abundance (Chagnon 1968:45):

The first beings cannot be accounted for. The Yanomamö simply presume that the cosmos originated with these people. Most of them, and there were many, had a specific function, such as creating a useful plant or object. They figure prominently in mythology. Many of them bear the names of plants and animals that are important to the Yanomamö economy, and the first beings are considered to be the spirits of these.

Some of these superior gods are: Bore (first to have plantains, the headman of the first things), Iwä or alligator (first to have fire), Haya or deer, Öra or jaguar, Omauwä (sends hiccups, sickness, and epidemics to the Yanomamö), Periboriwä or Spirit of the Moon (wounded, the blood changed into men as it hit the earth), and Wadawadariwä (directs the souls of the deceased to different parts of the hereafter).

When a Yanomamö dies part of his soul goes to the hereafter, another part becomes a malevolent spirit (Chagnon 1968:48–49):

Yanomamö concepts of the soul are elaborate and complicated. The true or real portion of living man is his "will" or "self" (buhii). At death, this changes into a no borebö and travels from this layer to hedu, the place above where the souls of the departed continue to exist in an ethereal state, much in the same fashion as do the people on earth: gardening, hunting, and practicing magic.

Another portion of the soul, the no uhudi or bore, is released at cremation. This part of the soul remains on earth and wanders about in the jungle. The children who die always change into this, as they do not have the no borebö portion that goes to hedu: It must be acquired. . . . Apart from this, one is born with an uhudi (bore), which is invariably released at cremation and wanders eternally in the jungle after death. Some of these wandering *uhudi* are malevolent and attack travelers in the jungle at night. When they do so, they use sticks and clubs.

Finally, each individual has a *noreshi*. This is a dual concept: One has a *noreshi* within his being, a sort of spirit or portion of the soul, and, in addition, an animal that lives in the jungle and corresponds to his soul. The *noreshi* animals are inherited patrilineally for men and matrilineally for women.

These malevolent spirits would not be classified as ancestral spirits since they do not play a role in the affairs of their living relatives. Other nonhuman spirits are the *hekura* (see Question 28, below) and Wadoriwä, the spirit of the wind, who blows leaves off the roofs of houses (Chagnon 1968:28).

The Qemant believe in all four types of supernatural beings. The high god is *Mezgana,* the sky god (Gamst 1969:34–35):

According to Qemant, their God is male and resides in the sky. He is not different in reality from the ancient Agaw Sky God and somewhat resembles the Hebrew God worshipped by the Hebrao-pagan Falasha Agaw. Belief in the ancient Sky God is one of the principal traits that distinguishes the Qemant from their neighbors, who abhor such a marked manifestation of paganism. . . .
Qemant believe Mezgana is omnipresent, omnipotent, and omniscient, and that everything was created by Him; therefore, He has the right to destroy everything. He is an anthropomorphic God; Qemant say, "Mezgana looks like man."

A superior god is Saytan (Gamst 1969:39):

Saytan is the essence of all that is evil. Qemant, Amhara, and Falasha uniformly conceive of Saytan as being very black and horrible-looking, having human or animal form, and possessing great powers, including the ability to cause thunder and lightning.

Qemant believe in deities which Gamst calls angels since they are equated with Hebrao-Christian angels (1969:37). Because their functions are not described, it is not possible to ascertain whether they control any human activities.

Ancestral spirits, each of whom has his own sacred grove, are active in human affairs (Gamst 1969:35):

Although members of the Qemant priesthood sometimes contact Mezgana directly, they usually reach Him through intermediary culture heroes called *qedus*. *Qedus* means "saint" and "holy" and applies to the spirits of dead human beings who are culture heroes. . . .

Holy culture heroes of the Qemant are, for the most part, the ancestral heads of the clans in the Keber moiety, the more important of the two Qemant moieties. Other culture heroes include ancestors of these heads and certain wives of the ancestors.

> Some of these ancestral spirits fit into a pantheon, described in mythology, which provides the Qemant with an unwritten history that they use to validate present-day claims to land and to determine their place among other peoples (Gamst 1969:35–37).
> Nonhuman spirits are in abundance (Gamst 1969:38):

They [genii loci] are minor deities who have strong control over limited areas, usually part or the whole of a single community. A genius loci is called a qole and is referred to by the name of the place where it is venerated. . . .

> Elsewhere Gamst states that (1969:28):

Sites of qole worship are in high places, almost always on hilltops or on the edge of an escarpment. They are usually marked by a single tall tree or a prominent rock or pinnacle.

> Some persons have personal spirits which may possess them (Gamst 1969:45):

Any person may have a zar as well as other personal spirits, although most people do not have a zar, and those who do sometimes find that the spirit might not be present for months or years. Zars may be either male or female and are often of the same sex as the human beings with whom they are associated. Although usually benevolent or neutral, when "neglected," zars may become malevolent, causing disease or other misfortune. A zar can possess a person, causing uncontrolled motion and speech.

> On the other hand, all persons have guardian spirits (Gamst 1969: 49):

Although not everyone has a zar, everyone is said to have a guardian spirit, generally referred to as *yeqole* [my (guardian) spirit]. . . . Personal qoles rarely possess people, but should they turn malevolent or otherwise become bothersome, a shaman may be consulted to handle them.

There are also disease spirits (Gamst 1969:51):

While personal spirits may bring illness to a person, specific spirits of disease may cause illness of epidemic proportions to befall an entire community. These spirits of disease apparently have no other function.

RELIGIOUS PRACTITIONERS

Religious practitioners are intermediaries between men and supernatural beings. In some cultures each individual may be able to deal directly with some or all the supernatural beings. In other cultures there are specialists who serve as intermediaries for individuals, local groups, or political communities. These specialists, in their role as intermediaries, perform certain tasks or functions for both men and supernatural beings. On one hand, they may communicate the wishes of the members of their local group or political community to certain powerful gods, and on the other hand, they may interpret the wishes of the gods to the local group or political community. Different techniques are employed in performing these functions. Divination may be used to ascertain the unknown and to foretell future events; ceremonies, rituals, and offerings may be made to please the supernatural beings; prayer may be used to cajole gods and spirits; and magic may be practiced to manipulate and coerce them. Because these functions are important to both the beings who are part of the supernatural world and to the men who live on earth, religious practitioners are usually important members of the local group. In small political communities they may even be headmen. In larger political communities they may exercise more influence than the political leader. It is because religious practitioners are often important members of local groups and political communities that there are strong links between the belief and political systems, as well as the economic system. Knowledge about control of supernatural beings confers political and economic power upon religious practitioners.

Two types of religious practitioners are distinguished by anthropologists: shamans and priests. Both are specialists, the former part-time, the latter full-time. The *shaman*, who may earn his subsistence like every other man, devotes part of his time to serving as an intermediary, usually for individuals. He often works alone, since he is not usually a member of an organization composed of shamans.

He may have learned to be a shaman from an older shaman, or he may have gained his abilities from direct contact with supernatural beings. Sometimes he has a guardian spirit which visits him while he is in a trance state. One of the most common reasons individuals employ shamans—who are often expensive—is to determine the cause of an illness and to cure it. Divination may be used to seek the cause, and magic may be used to cure it. Since many peoples do not distinguish between illnesses of natural origin and those of super-natural origin (caused perhaps by sorcery or malevolent ancestral or nonhuman spirits), shamans frequently serve as medicine men for all kinds of illnesses.

The *priest*, who normally is supported by the community, de-votes nearly all of his time to serving as an intermediary, usually for his local group or political community. He is often a member of a religious organization, which has provided him with special training. Years of training may be necessary before full-fledged membership in the priesthood is granted. Such religious hierarchies are found often in association with social and political complexity. Membership in the priesthood legitimizes his position as a religious practitioner. On important occasions he and other priests may participate in cere-monies and rituals which are believed to be vital by the members of the local group or political community. These ceremonies, which express group sentiments and beliefs and which are performed in the presence of most members of the local group, are known as *rites of intensification* (Chapple and Coon 1942:397–415). In carrying out his duties, the priest may serve as an interpreter for the gods, who, if they are satisfied that their wishes are being carried out, will assist men in their daily activities. Sometimes the priest attempts to persuade important supernatural beings to help. Prayers, offerings, and sacrifices are the means which he uses (Honigmann 1959:636–638; Lessa and Vogt 1958:410–411).

28. **What types of religious practitioners are present?**
    1. absent
    2. shamans
    3. priests

Religious practitioners may not be present, but if they are, then it is necessary to determine whether they are shamans or priests. Both types, however, may be present. Although shamans and priests differ in a number of respects, the difference which should be used to dis-tinguish between these two types of religious practitioners is their degree of specialization. If they are part-time specialists, they are shamans; if they are full-time specialists, they are priests.

———

The Andros Islanders have priests, ministers, and preachers. The priests and ministers, who come from outside of Long Bay Cays (Otterbein 1966:52), are full-time religious practitioners. They can be classified as priests whether they are Anglican or Roman Catholic priests, or Protestant ministers. The preachers are part-time (Otterbein 1966:30), and hence they can be classified as shamans.

Shamans, but not priests, are the Yanomamö religious practitioners (Chagnon 1968:52):

The nature of the relationship between man and spirit is largely one of hostility. The shamans, by and large, spend most of their time casting charms on enemies and enjoining their own personal demons to prevent harm from befalling the local people. Magic and curing are intimately bound up in shamanism, the practitioner devoting his efforts to causing and curing sickness.

The demons that the shamans contact are *hekura*, very tiny humanoid beings that dwell on rocks and mountains. Particularly successful shamans can control these demons to such an extent that the *hekura* will come and live inside the chest of the shaman. Each shaman solicits the aid of numerous *hekura* and attempts to lure them into his body.

Men who want to become shamans (*shabori*) go through a simple rite of fasting and chastity. They sit before their houses, use only a few trails, eat very little, and spend most of their time in a contemplative stupor brought about by hunger and drugs. After several days of this, the initiate has entered the world of the *shabori*, and can practice his skill. Each village has as many *shabori* as there are men who wish to enter this status: probably half of the men in each village are shamans.

The Qemant have both shamans and priests. Gamst describes a particular shaman (1969:44):

Ayo, who is Erada's brother and fifty-four years of age, is like most Qemant a plowman, but he also serves as a part-time religious practitioner. Ayo deals with zars and other personal spirits, performing the role of *balazar* (master of the zar), usually in a special house of his homestead about 1000 feet from that of Erada. . . . In anthropological classification, the balazar is a shaman, one who acquires his supernatural power and his social position from his ability to contact directly animistic (spiritual) beings. These are usually minor spirits for whom the shaman serves as a medium or "mouth-piece" when the spirit takes possession of him. Shamans of the Qemant and neighboring peoples are additionally often leaders of cults addressed to personal spirits.

The priesthood is described at length (Gamst 1969:39–40, 43):

Priests . . . are organized into a hierarchy and must learn formalized ritual patterns in order to act as middlemen for communication between humans and the beings of their animistic world. . . .

He [the wambar] officiates at major ceremonies where priests perform rituals attempting to manipulate nature through supplication of members of the pantheon. The wambar makes life secure for the Qemant by praying to regulate the weather, to end disease or other personal misfortune, to eradicate dangerous wild animals, and to punish transgressors of laws. His most important act is praying for the dead during the rite of passage which follows funerals, to assure their entry into heaven. . . .

Under the wambar are two levels of priests. The higher, called *kamazana*, is elected from the Keber moiety, and the lower, *abayegariya*, is elected from the Yetanti moiety. Like the wambar, the priests must come from certain lineages in certain clans that have traditionally supplied the personnel for these religious positions. After a man has been elected to priesthood by the community, he is taken by the people to the wambar, who blesses him and confirms his appointment. . . .

Each community has at least one higher priest and one lower priest who work together in all ceremonies. . . .

Priests are remunerated with bars of salt for their services in performing the ritual in various rites of passage, rain-regulating ceremonies, and curing ceremonies such as the one with the livestock. The major source of priestly income, however, comes from labor which adult males in each community must supply to the local priests.

MAGIC

The practice of magic involves three elements: the practitioner (who may or may not be a shaman or priest), the practical aim or end to be achieved, and the magical formula itself. When an individual has an objective to achieve which cannot be coped with by ordinary means or which requires the assistance of a supernatural being, he may either practice magic himself or employ someone, possibly a shaman, to perform the magic. The practical ends for which magic is often used cover a wide range of objectives. They include objectives which can be classified as protective in that they prevent harm to the individual or cure him of illness. Other objectives can be classified as productive; they include the desire for a successful hunt, an abundant crop, ample rains, and even success in courtship and love making. Still other objectives are destructive; they include the desire to harm or destroy one's rivals or enemies. When the end to be achieved is destructive, it is said that the practitioner is performing black magic (see "Sorcery," below).

There are three aspects to the magical formula itself. First, the things used—the instruments or *medicines*. The ingredients used in magic are often difficult to obtain and to prepare. They may be difficult to obtain because they are rare or because they must be taken from or have been in contact with the being—either human or supernatural—which one wishes to influence. Second, the things done—the *rite*. The preparation of the medicines, the manner in which medicines are combined, and the placement of the medicines either on or near that which is to be influenced constitutes the rite. Third, the things spoken—the *spell*. The verbal element in magic may consist of a series of words and phrases which are fixed and invariable, or it may be simply an overt expression of the practitioner's desires. The medicines, the rite, and the spell are almost always present in any magical formula. Their relative importance, however, may vary from formula to formula and from culture to culture. For example, most cultures which are located on the African continent south of the Sahara Desert or which originated in that part of Africa place major importance on the medicines employed. On the other hand, many cultures in the Pacific Ocean region place great emphasis on the spell (Firth 1958:125–128).

Although the belief in magic appears irrational to the rational mind, there are a number of positive functions or effects which may stem from the practice of magic. In cultures in which magic is extensively practiced, most individuals are fearful that any suspicious or harmful act attributed to them will result in the threatened individual attempting to harm them, possibly through magic. Thus magic functions to promote social control by deterring many people from cheating and stealing (Otterbein 1965a). Moreover, the belief in magic may in itself deter individuals from practicing magic, since magic can be considered a suspicious or harmful act if its occurrence is discovered. The practice of magic may play an important role in technological and subsistence pursuits. It provides positive and negative sanctions, thus insuring that tasks are properly performed. Furthermore, magic creates confidence in the face of uncertainty. The belief in magic provides a theory about the nature of the world. Failure, misfortune, and death can be attributed to the practice of harmful magic. The practice of magic may also provide emotional relief for an individual who believes that he has been wronged, if he himself practices countermagic. The practitioner can vent his rage and satisfy his desire for revenge.

James George Frazer, in his famous twelve-volume work *The Golden Bough,* distinguished between two types of magic (1911:52):

If we analyze the principles of thought on which magic is based, they will probably be found to resolve themselves into two: first, that like produces like, or that an effect resembles its cause; and, second, that things which have once been in contact with each other continue to act on each other at a distance after the physical contact has been severed. The former principle may be called the "Law of Similarity," the latter the "Law of Contact or Contagion." From the first of these principles, namely the Law of Similarity, the magician [practitioner] infers that he can produce any effect he desires merely by imitating it; from the second he infers that whatever he does to a material object will affect equally the person with whom the object was once in contact, whether it formed part of his body or not.

Magic based on the law of similarity is called *homeopathic magic* (sometimes called imitative magic), and magic based on the law of contagion is called *contagious magic.*

29. **What types of magic are practiced?**
     1. homeopathic magic
     2. contagious magic

Since magic is almost universally found among the peoples of the world, it is unlikely that any culture studied by an anthropologist will be found not to have magic. In order to classify the magic practiced by the members of a culture, it is necessary to analyze a series of magical formulae. Particular attention should be given to the medicines. If they resemble that which is to be influenced, the law of similarity is being employed. Two common examples are the sticking of needles into a doll in order to injure or kill the individual which the doll resembles and the pouring of water onto the ground in order to produce rain. If the medicine has been in contact with a person, such as his clothing, or was once a part of the person's body, such as hair or nail clippings, the law of contagion is being employed. On occasion, both the law of similarity and the law of contagion may be present in the magical formula; for example, the victim's nail clippings are placed inside the doll with the needles stuck in it. In fact, rarely will the law of contagion be found to be solely present in a magical formula. Thus of the magical formulae analyzed, some may be classifiable as examples of homeopathic magic and others may be classifiable as examples of both homeopathic and contagious magic. If only formulae which can be classified as homeopathic magic are found in the culture, the only type of magic practiced is homeopathic. If homeopathic magic is present and some other formulae can be classified as both homeopathic and contagious magic, then both homeopathic and contagious magic are practiced by the members of a culture.

The Andros Islanders use homeopathic magic in various practices surrounding childbirth (Otterbein 1966:62–63):

The piece of cord extending beyond the tied string is folded back and twisted; next baby powder is put on the navel, and a large bandage is wrapped around the waist and abdomen. Every morning the navel is redressed by sprinkling it with powder. In about eight days the remainder of the umbilical cord drops off. The bandage should be kept on six to nine months just to make sure no "wind" gets into the navel, since this will cause the baby to cry and the navel to swell. To remove the band early permits wind in the navel and also weakens the back. If the navel should swell, it will remain big and long and people will consider it unsightly. As an extra precaution to prevent swelling, a flattened lead fishing sinker may be placed in the bandage over the top of the navel. A large navel can be caused not only by a careless midwife but also by being "passed by the blood," for large navels are said to run in some families.

After dressing the navel, the midwife sterilizes her fingers by dipping them in rum before continuing her duties. In order to ensure that the baby will talk correctly, she shapes the baby's mouth by pulling its cheeks and "sets up the jawbone" by pushing up on the roof of the mouth. In order not to cut the mouth with a fingernail, the midwife trims her nails very short and as an extra precaution wraps her thumb with cloth. If she should cut the baby with a fingernail, a "pimple" (infection) is apt to form. Following the shaping of the face, the sides, front, and back of the baby's head are pushed together and upward with the hands, to prevent the head from becoming long and, according to local notions, ugly. This measure is also an attempt to close the veins and the fontanelle, for if the veins should remain open, wind might get into them. (I was never told what the wind would do.)

When a woman is giving birth she is partly covered by her nightgown so that wind does not get into her veins through her vagina. If her nightgown becomes soiled, it is changed. The woman is "put back together" again by pushing the arms and legs up and back. The upper ribs are also pushed, but not the lower waist. Next the woman is rolled over on her abdomen and pressure is applied to her back. Since the veins of the head are believed to be wide open, the scalp is manipulated in the same manner as the baby's head. The midwife blows into one of her hands and slaps it down on the other hand before straightening the woman's toes and fingers. These are pulled until the sockets crack in order to "put back the joints," which are open. The midwife's breath also helps to do this. Next she washes the breasts and lets the child nurse.

> Homeopathic magic, using plant medicines, is practiced by all Yanomamö (Chagnon 1968:37–38):

Most of the magical plants are associated with benevolent or at least non-mischievous functions. "Female charms" (*sua härö*), for example, are used by men to make women more receptive to sexual advances. . . . Another magical plant is cultivated by the women. Its leaves are thrown on the men when they have club fights because it allegedly keeps their tempers under control and prevents the fight from escalating to shooting. Still other plants are cultivated to insure that male or female children grow up to be healthy adults, a different plant being associated with each sex.

Some of the plants are cultivated for malevolent purposes, such as causing the women in enemy villages to have miscarriages or pains in the back when they are pregnant, while other plants allegedly cure the same evils.

> Homeopathic magic is also practiced by shamans. As the following account indicates, medicines are not a part of the formula (Chagnon 1968:52):

If he is curing someone, he chants before the house of the patient, rubs him, massages him, and draws the evil spirit causing the sickness to some extremity, such as an arm or leg. Then he sucks or pulls the spirit out and carries it away from the sick person, either vomiting it out or throwing it away, depending on how he extracted it originally. The Yanomamö do not employ medicines made from plants or animals. Consequently, they rely exclusively on the cures that the *shabori* effect, fighting supernatural ills with supernatural medicine.

> Contagious magic appears to be absent. No direct evidence is provided. Moreover, *hekura*—not magic—are used by shamans to harm others.

> Although Gamst describes Qemant magic, none of his exam-

ples can be analyzed as either homeopathic or contagious magic. Some magic is used to protect animals and crops (Gamst 1969:54):

To protect cattle, the trailing edges of their ears are notched while the cattle are young; to protect crops, skulls of cattle on poles, or several poles made from limbs or small trees from which the bark has been peeled, are placed upright in the fields. No reason could be found for these actions except that they were "known to be effective."

Magic is employed to protect oneself (Gamst 1969:54):

To safeguard oneself against black magic, Qemant, Falasha, and Amhara wear amulets as protection against malevolent spirits and other forms of evil. Amulets are charms with protective functions and are made by magicians. In the Qemant area, amulets consist of small pieces of inscribed parchment placed in a small leather case that is worn around the neck on a cord.

Magic is also used to injure people (Gamst 1969:54–55):

When sorcerers (black magicians) practice their dark arts, they may at times use empirical means, such as drugs or physical acts of destruction, but usually they rely upon their incantatory spells, to which objects of medicine have been adroitly added. This latter method has been used against Erada. For example, when one antagonist wishes misfortune to befall Erada, he purchases some "medicine" eggs from a sorcerer. Chanting and gesturing over the eggs, the sorcerer guarantees to bring misfortune to anyone upon whose premises the foul eggs are buried. When darkness falls and Erada's dogs are asleep, the antagonist buries the eggs near Erada's homestead.

One must conclude that magic is present even though the examples given cannot be analyzed in terms of the principles of thought on which they are based.

SORCERY

The use of magic, supernatural beings, or other supernatural powers to deliberately attempt to harm or destroy another person is known as *sorcery*. An individual who uses these supernatural means to destroy others is known as a *sorcerer*. As pointed out in the previous section, one means of injuring or killing another person is through the practice of contagious magic. The presence of contagious magic in a culture, although in itself not evidence that sorcery is practiced, nevertheless provides a strong indication that sorcery occurs. Another means of practicing sorcery is to invoke a supernatural being, such as a guardian spirit or an ancestral spirit, to assist one in harming an enemy. Sometimes an individual has the ability to utilize unseen supernatural powers to bring about the destruction of another individual. The sorcerer accomplishes this by willing or performing a psychic act. In less formal terms, he is said to put a curse or an evil eye upon a person. Since magic, malevolent spirits, and unseen supernatural powers can be used to cause injury, illness, or death to individuals, there are many cultures in which sicknesses and misfortunes are attributed to the practice of sorcery. In such cultures an individual who has become ill or who has had a series of tragedies employs a shaman to diagnose and cure his illness or difficulties. The shaman may be able to not only identify the sorcerer, but also to practice magic which will counteract the malevolent attack. If the shaman is a man of great ability, he may be able —usually for a handsome reward—to use magic or other supernatural means to inflict harm upon the sorcerer. In other words, he becomes a sorcerer himself. Battles or duels between sorcerers are sometimes described in ethnographic accounts.

Sorcery, like magic, functions to promote social control by deterring many individuals from cheating, stealing, and harming others (see "Magic," above). In cultures in which sorcery is practiced an individual believes that any harmful act which he does may be discovered, perhaps through divination or other magical means. Once the acts are discovered he believes that he himself will be in danger of bodily harm—often in the form of a sorcerer's attack. Thus individuals are deterred from harmful acts and even from practicing sorcery itself. Those cultures whose political communities are headed by political leaders with little power (that is, headmen and chiefs) and whose legal systems are poorly developed (possibly penal sanctions are absent) are deficient in formal mechanisms of social control. Such political communities must rely upon informal mechanisms of social control such as sorcery. B. B. Whiting (1950) in a cross-cultural study of sorcery tested the theory that sorcery can serve to maintain order in cultures which lack formal mechanisms of social control. She discovered that sorcery was important—that is, it was given as a cause of illness in the ethnographic accounts— in those cultures in which no authority or political leader possessed sufficient power to settle disputes or punish offenses. In her terminology "superordinate control" was absent. On the other hand, sorcery was found to be unimportant in those cultures whose political communities were characterized by superordinate control.

In many cultures in which sorcery is practiced the social control aspect may, during times of great misfortunes, cease to function in a manner which stabilizes interpersonal relationships. Normally the belief in the practice of sorcery prevents many individuals from engaging in acts harmful to others. When crises arise and misfortunes occur to the local group, those members most affected seek explanations for what has happened or is happening. If these individuals believe in sorcery, they may conclude that their misfortunes are the result of an increase in sorcerers or an increase in the activities of known sorcerers. The individuals suffering the mishaps may become so infuriated that they will attack and kill people known as sorcerers or attribute sorcery to members of their own local group and then kill them. Thus scapegoats for the misfortunes are found. Some anthropologists have argued that the identification and killing of real or putative sorcerers is a means by which a local group can rid itself of undesirable members. In their view the killing of sorcerers is beneficial to the local group. It seems more reasonable, however, to interpret the killing of sorcerers as a breakdown in social control. If sorcery promotes social control by deterring individuals from harming each other, and this is viewed as socially beneficial, it cannot be logically argued that the killing of sorcerers is likewise beneficial. In fact, when a substantial number of individuals "take the law into their own hands" this undermines and threatens the authority and power of the political leaders. If the leader has the power and wishes to assert it, he will intercede and prevent the killing of sorcerers. He may also deem it against the law for unauthorized members of the local group to kill reputed sorcerers. Furthermore, the practice of sorcery itself may be outlawed. If Whiting's analysis is correct, namely that sorcery does not occur in cultures with superordinate control, the above argument provides an explanation for the relationship.

Many anthropologists, both in ethnographies and textbooks, distinguish between sorcery and witchcraft. Just as sorcery requires sorcerers, witchcraft requires witches. But witches, in contrast to sorcerers, are not people who have practiced or employed supernatural means to destroy others. Witches are individuals who have evil intentions and activities attributed to them. Thus the practice of sorcery actually occurs, but the practice of witchcraft is imaginary. (For a detailed discussion of the difference between sorcery and witchcraft, a discussion which recognizes the analytic limitations of the sorcery-witchcraft dichotomy, see Fogelson 1975:117–119.) Although many anthropologists make this distinction, analysis of actual cultures reveals that this distinction is often difficult to apply. There are some ethnographers who after months of fieldwork are unable to determine whether sorcery is practiced. In these cultures individuals attribute the practice of sorcery to others in the local group, but no one in the local group will ever admit having practiced sorcery. If the ethnographer concludes that witchcraft is present (that is, people believe in sorcery but no one practices it)—but individuals practice sorcery and will not admit it—then he has reached an erroneous conclusion. If he concludes that sorcery is present, his decision is based upon insufficient evidence. Since it is difficult, if not impossible, in some cultures to ascertain whether sorcery is practiced, it seems best not to attempt to distinguish between sorcery and witchcraft, unless the distinction is made by the people themselves. Hence, the question asks only if sorcery is present.

30. Is sorcery practiced?
    1. no
    2. yes

Sorcery is present if members of the culture deliberately use magic, supernatural beings, or other supernatural powers to attempt to harm or kill others. A problem in classification arises if the ethnographer describes sorcery practices, but states that sorcery is not actually practiced or that he has been unable to find evidence that it is practiced. Although perhaps not a fully satisfactory solution, one way of dealing with the problem is to classify all cultures whose members believe that sorcery is practiced, whether or not there are sorcerers, as being cultures in which sorcery is practiced. If the people, however, believe in both sorcerers and witches, this dual belief system should be recorded. In addition, if there is no evidence that sorcery is practiced or there is evidence that it is not practiced, this should be noted.

Except for the reference to "obeah (black magic)" (Otterbein 1966:64) there is no indication that the Andros Islanders practice sorcery. However, at the time of fieldwork there was an obeah man living in Long Bay Cays—what he told me he had done and what he taught me would be classified as sorcery.

Sorcery is practiced by Yanomamö shamans (Chagnon 1968: 49):

The *noreshi* is the vulnerable portion of the complete being, the part that is the target of witchcraft and harmful magic. The shamans (*shabori*) wage constant war against the evil demons (*hekura*) of enemy groups who have been sent to capture the *noreshi* parts of children. They, in turn, send their own *hekura* to capture the *noreshi* of enemy children. . . .

The vulnerability of the *noreshi* to magical spells is best exemplified by the fact that the shamans of every village spend most of their time chanting to the *hekura* (demons) with the intention of persuading them either to attack the *noreshi* of other (enemy) children or to drive off the *hekura* sent by enemy shamans.

The Qemant believe in and practice sorcery. Magic is used deliberately to harm others (see Question 29 for quotation). One way in which the power to injure others can be obtained is to become a Ganel *sabi* (Gamst 1969:39):

A person may acquire evil powers by entering into a league with Saytan. Such a person is called Ganel *sabi* (Ganel puller). One can also become a Ganel sabi by defecating and urinating at the outer of the three concentric walls of a circular Ethiopian church. As in the tale of Dr. Faustus, the Ganel sabi must pay for his evil powers with his immortal soul. A Ganel sabi can kill people, burn houses from a distance, cure people with Saytan's advice, and cause other fortune or misfortune. The services of a Ganel sabi may be purchased for goods or money.

The Qemant also believe in witches (Gamst 1969:52–53):

It is difficult to find a witch in Qemantland. Few people, Qemant or otherwise, consciously play the role of a witch as they do the roles of shaman, magicians, and diviner. However, the role of a witch is part of the reference group that Qemant and others relate to for guides to behavior; that is, people act and think as though witches do exist. People suspect others of being witches and believe they have felt the effects of witchcraft, even though no one admits to being a witch or perpetrating the associated blight on men, animals, plants, and events.

Gamst's cautious phrasing implies that there may be practitioners of witchcraft. Although the Qemant believe in magicians, Ganel sabi, and witches (conceived as different categories of persons), all three types of practitioners use supernatural means to destroy others; hence, they can be classified as sorcerers.

POST-PARTUM SEX TABOO

The post-partum sex taboo is a rule which prohibits a woman from having sexual intercourse with her husband, or any man, after she has given birth to a child. In the vast majority of cultures such a rule is followed, at least until after the woman's wounds have healed and she has regained her regular menstrual cycle. It was discovered by J. W. M. Whiting, Kluchkhohn, and Anthony (1958) in a cross-cultural study of fifty-six cultures that approximately half of the cultures (twenty-seven) had a post-partum sex taboo which lasted for at least a year or more after the woman gave birth. The remaining twenty-nine cultures had a post-partum sex taboo which lasted one year or less. The decision to use one year or twelve months as the dividing line between those cultures with a long and those with a short post-partum sex taboo was based upon the fact that—for some unknown reason —"the duration of the taboo is rarely in the neighborhood of one year" (Stephens 1962:4). Cultures with a long post-partum sex taboo may be divided into two groups. First, there are those cultures located in the disease-ridden tropics whose members often believe that sexual intercourse will sour the mother's milk and whose post-partum sex taboo as a consequence lasts as long as the mother nurses her child, usually two or three years. Second, there are nomadic hunting groups, located primarily in North America, whose women cannot carry two children on a long march; and as a consequence they deliberately do not have a second child until the first is old enough to walk, which may be as long as four years or more. Thus it appears that a long post-partum sex taboo results, in many cultures, from a conscious realization that the intentional spacing of children is beneficial for the health of young children and their mothers (J. W. M. Whiting 1959:176–177).

Several factors have been given credit for producing a long post-partum sex taboo. First, general polygyny has been shown to be highly related to the taboo (Stephens 1962:179). In polygynous cultures mothers and children often occupy their own living quarters and husbands occupy separate sleeping quarters or rotate their time among the living quarters of their wives. When a child is born, the separation of spouses which is already built into the domestic system is accentuated. Since the husbands have other wives, a long post-partum sex taboo does not deny them sexual gratification. Thus it is simpler and more likely for a polygynous, rather than a monogamous, culture to adopt a long taboo. Second, clan organization is likewise highly related to the post-partum sex taboo (Young 1965:

118–119). It is argued that the spacing of children is important in cultures where women must work regularly in horticultural activities and must contribute to a group larger than a household, such as a clan. Third, a protein deficiency in the diet, which often occurs in tropical climates, has also been shown to be highly related to the taboo (J. W. M. Whiting 1964). Women in such regions must avoid becoming pregnant in order that their milk will remain rich in protein. Actually, polygyny, clan organization, and protein deficiency are highly related to each other, and probably all three factors are instrumental in producing a long post-partum sex taboo.

A recent cross-cultural study of the correlates of the long post-partum sex taboo found a number of culture traits associated with a sex taboo which lasted for a year or more (Saucier 1972); the traits include agriculture, supervision of female labor, bridewealth and sister-exchange, polygyny, lineages and clans, localized kin groups, primogeniture and ultimogeniture, hereditary headmanship at the community level, customary genital mutilation, high god, cross-cousin marriage, segregation of adolescent boys, and physical isolation of the wife from her husband and the rest of the household. The study concluded (Saucier 1972:249):

A long postpartum taboo imposes a heavy burden on women and also on unmarried or monogamous young men. The successful maintenance of this taboo seems to require a community organization in which the elders are in firm control and the married women are considered "outsiders" (because of village exogamy).

Anthropologists originally became interested in the postpartum sex taboo because of its influence upon the Oedipal situation. In psychoanalytic theory the Oedipus complex refers to the sexual attraction of a boy for his mother. This results in a feeling of rivalry and hostility towards his father, which has a lasting effect on his personality and may manifest itself in unconscious fantasies, sexual fears and inhibitions, moral standards and guilt, and mental illness. Anthropologists undertaking research on the postpartum sex taboo have argued—although there are slightly different versions of the theory—that a long taboo creates dependency upon the mother, arouses the sexual desire of the male child for his mother, engenders father-son rivalry, and leads to sexual anxiety. Thus cultures with a long post-partum sex taboo will develop beliefs which reflect the psychological conflicts of adult males, and they will develop customs which serve to resolve these conflicts. Several of the beliefs and customs which are supposedly produced by a long post-partum sex taboo are as follows: the adolescent male initiation ceremony is an institution which breaks the dependency upon the mother and resolves the father-son rivalry (J. W. M. Whiting, Kluckhohn, and Anthony 1958). The importance of sorcery as an explanation for illness, which is a manifestation of paranoia, is a defense against sexual anxiety (J. W. M. Whiting 1959). The elaboration of menstrual taboos is determined by the high level of male castration anxiety which is created by the sexual desire of the child for his mother (Stephens 1962). The avoidance of female in-laws and sisters stems from the fear of sexual contact between the avoiding individuals, the genesis of which lies in the desire for sexual intercourse with the mother (Stephens 1962). Since psychoanalytic theory is not accepted as a valid explanatory system by many anthropologists, it is advisable to only tentatively accept the above theory at the present time.

31. How long is the post-partum sex taboo?
    1. absent
    2. short
    3. long

If there is no rule which prohibits a woman from having sexual intercourse within a month after the birth of a child, the post-partum sex taboo is absent. A month is chosen as the dividing line since it takes nearly a month for a woman's wounds to heal. If there is a rule and it is observed for less than twelve months, the post-partum sex taboo is classified as short. If the post-partum sex taboo is observed for twelve months or more, it is classified as long. Many ethnographies contain detailed information on this topic because the long post-partum sex taboo, although not labeled by this term, has been viewed as one of the unusual customs of primitive cultures. If the exact duration of the taboo is given in months, it should be recorded.

The Andros Islanders have a short post-partum sex taboo (Otterbein 1966:66):

In the "old days" women stayed in the house and avoided hard work for three to six months after the baby was born. They did no cooking or washing, but they might do light chores like sweeping, sewing, and getting out food. But not all women could follow this rule; some had to go out and work in fields in order to earn a livelihood. Today women resume all their duties about one month after delivery. Although the midwife will tell the mother not to have intercourse for three months, the husband will often insist on resuming coitus after two months.

> For the Yanomamö the post-partum sex taboo is long. However, the taboo is not always observed. When an unwanted child is born, infanticide is practiced (Chagnon 1968:74, 75):

The Yanomamö have taboos against intercourse when a woman is pregnant or is nursing a child. The taboo is by no means followed to the strict letter, since children are nursed for three years or more—some men sheepishly admit having coitus with a lactating wife. Rerebawä, whose youngest child is about a year old, told me that he recently tried to persuade his wife to make love. He added: "She told me to go take some drugs and chant to my forest spirits; she is still 'stingy' with her vagina."
A child is killed at birth, irrespective of its sex, if the mother already has a nursing baby. They rationalize the practice by asserting that the new infant would probably die anyway, since its older sibling would drink most of the milk. They are most reluctant to jeopardize the health and safety of a nursing child by weaning it before it is three years old or so, preferring to kill the competitor instead.

> Although Gamst provides a substantial section on Qemant childbirth (1969:99–102), no information is provided on the post-partum sex taboo. There probably is a short taboo, since it is unlikely that the taboo is absent and since it is likely that the ethnographer would have noted a long taboo (much information on childbirth is given) if it had been present. Nevertheless, one should record that no data are available for answering this question.

GAMES

> Games have always been of interest to anthropologists. Lewis H. Morgan, who along with Edward B. Tylor was one of the two major founders of anthropology, devoted an entire chapter to the discussion of games in his famous ethnography, *League of the Iroquois*, first published in 1851. Many regard this classic work, which describes the customs and way of life of the Iroquois Indians of New York State, as the first ethnography. Morgan discovered that "there were but six principal games among the Iroquois, and these are divisible into athletic games, and games of chance" (1962:291). Athletic games included lacrosse, javelins (spears thrown at rolling hoops),

snow snake (a stick thrown across the snow for distance), and archery; games of chance included the game of deer buttons and the peach stone game (both games used lots blackened on one side). Tylor was also interested in games, particularly complex games of strategy such as the nearly identical games of parcheesi (played in India) and patolli (played in Mexico), which could be used to demonstrate that distant cultures had once been in contact (1879).

Not all types of recreational activities or amusements can be considered games. For an activity to be classified as a game it must be "characterized by: (1) organized play, (2) competition, (3) two or more sides, (4) criteria for determining the winner, and (5) agreed-upon rules" (Roberts, Arth, and Bush 1959:597). Games can be classified into the three basic types delineated by such nineteenth-century anthropologists as Morgan and Tylor: "(1) games of *physical skill*, in which the outcome is determined by the players' motor activities; (2) games of *strategy*, in which the outcome is determined by rational choices among possible courses of action; and (3) games of *chance*, in which the outcome is determined by guesses or by some uncontrolled artifact such as a die or a wheel" (Roberts and Sutton-Smith 1962:166). All three types of games are played by both children and adults.

Games may serve a number of functions in any particular culture. The most obvious function, of course, is recreation. Games, for both participants and onlookers, are usually a pleasant form of entertainment. If betting occurs, valuable goods may be redistributed. Gambling—for winners—can be a profitable way of using one's time. Some anthropologists have viewed games of physical skill as being "safety-valve" mechanisms for releasing pent-up frustrations in harmless ways. Without some controlled means of releasing frustrations, so the argument goes, adult males are likely to engage in warfare, the only available outlet for their hostilities and aggression. If the argument were correct, cultures with games involving physical skill would engage in warfare less frequently than cultures without such games. In a cross-cultural study Sipes (1973) found that not only did the relationship not hold, but that warfare and combative sports were highly likely to be found in association. Rather, there is evidence that many games involving physical skill, such as the Iroquois games of lacrosse, javelins, and archery, provide training in the art of war. Games of physical skill are explicitly recognized by the members of some cultures as providing training for war.

Games are "expressive models"; that is, they are models of various cultural activities and at the same time they serve to express the needs of the players. Since games are models in the sense of being simplified representations of what actually occurs in the world of adults, they are used to teach children (usually indirectly) cultural values, social rules, and techniques for coping with the adult world without subjecting the children to the real consequences of being an adult. But not only do games serve a socialization function, they also provide therapy of sorts for individuals with psychological conflicts. Individuals with particular types of emotional conflicts are attracted to games—the type they prefer depending upon the nature of their conflict—because games provide a simplified version of the conflict situation. The individual is therefore able to cope with his problems on a reduced scale. Thus the needs of the individual are, at least while the game is being played, satisfied and expressed through the game.

This "expressive models" approach is supported by a series of empirical relationships. Games of physical skill are more likely to be played by peoples living in temperate rather than tropical climates, and those peoples with games of physical skill emphasize rewards for achievement. Presumably individuals who have difficulty in obtaining success in these achievement-oriented cultures find relief in participating in games of physical skill. Since games of strategy appear to be models of complex social interactive systems, it is not surprising to find games of strategy in cultures with complex social and political systems. Since the giving and taking of orders is characteristic of these hierarchically organized political communities, it is likewise not surprising to find pressure for obedience present. Presumably individuals who are unsure of their position in the social system but remain obedient to it, resolve their ambivalence by winning games of strategy. The sweetest victories are over parents or superiors. Games of chance are found in cultures in which the supernatural beings are benevolent and can be coerced. Reward for responsibility characterizes these cultures. Presumably individuals who perform routine tasks in these responsibility-oriented cultures can express feelings of irresponsibility by playing games of chance—such games often involve betting. Both winning and losing may satisfy the emotional conflict (Roberts, Arth, and Bush 1959; Roberts and Sutton-Smith 1962). Although these empirical results support the "expressive models" approach or theory in its general form, the specific theories which purport to explain the relationships between different types of games and different psychological conflict situations are still tentative.

Thus far only the three basic types of games have been discussed. Many games, however, contain elements of two or three of the basic principles: physical skill, strategy, and chance. For example, lacrosse, considered by Morgan to be a game of physical skill, also contains an element of strategy. Logically, in addition to the three basic types, there are three types of games composed of two basic principles and one type of game composed of all three principles. Any of these seven types of games may be played by the members of a culture. It is also possible to discover cultures which do not have games.

The American notion of "luck" is not the same thing as chance, since chance involves the use of a die, a wheel, or drawing lots, and "luck" encompasses many features of a game, including intrusion of the weather, a careless mistake of an opponent, and intervention of a supernatural being. Thus a sport such as basketball, baseball, or football involves physical skill and strategy, but not chance. (The flip of a coin to determine sides or who starts seems a minor part of these games; and thus they should not be classified as containing an element of chance.)

32. **What types of games are played?**
     1. games are absent
     2. physical skill
     3. physical skill and strategy
     4. physical skill and chance
     5. physical skill, strategy, and chance
     6. strategy
     7. strategy and chance
     8. chance

The procedure to be followed in determining what types of games are played is to analyze each game described in the ethnography in terms of the three basic principles. After each game is analyzed it should be recorded by name after one of the seven types. When all games have been analyzed and recorded, not only is it possible to mark (in the left margin) which types are played, but it is also possible to count the number of games per type. Thus a measure of the relative importance of each type of game can be determined. For some cultures a student may wish to list a game which is the only example of its type with several games listed for another type. In cross-cultural studies Roberts and his collaborators often combined games of physical skill and chance with games of physical skill, and games of strategy and chance with games of strategy. They found no examples of games of physical skill, strategy, and chance (Roberts and Sutton-Smith 1962:169).

Games are not described in *The Andros Islanders*.

Games are not described in the Yanomamö ethnography. Young boys shoot arrows at captured lizards, but this is an amusement, not a game (Chagnon 1968:90–91). An intervillage feast lasting several days is described in detail, but nowhere in the lengthy account of drug taking, dancing, eating, chanting, and dueling are games mentioned or described (Chagnon 1968:105–117).

Chest-pounding duels, side-slapping contests, and club fights do not qualify as games. Although organization, competition, sides, and agreed-upon rules are present, there is no criterion for determining the winner. The side which is taking the worse beating often escalates the fighting to a more violent form of armed combat, such as an axe or machete duel, a spear fight, or a battle with bows and arrows in which men are killed (Chagnon 1968:113–114):

There were about sixty adult men on each side in the fight, divided into two arenas, each comprised of hosts and guests. Two men, one from each side, would step into the center of the milling, belligerent crowd of weapon-wielding partisans, urged on by their comrades. One would step up, spread his legs apart, bare his chest, and hold his arms behind his back, daring the other to hit him. The opponent would size him up, adjust the man's chest or arms so as to give himself the greatest advantage when he struck, and then step back to deliver his close-fisted blow. The striker would painstakingly adjust his own distance from his victim by measuring his arm length to the man's chest, taking several dry runs before delivering his blow. He would then wind up like a baseball pitcher, but keeping both feet on the ground, and deliver a tremendous wallop with his fist to the man's left pectoral muscle, putting all of his weight into the blow.

Fighters take turns throughout the duel (Chagnon 1968:115):

At one point Kaobawä's men, sore from the punishment they had taken and worried that they would ultimately lose the fight, wanted to escalate the contest to an axe duel. Kaobawä was vigorously opposed to this, as he knew it would lead to bloodshed. . . . The fight had still not been decided, although Kaobawä's group seemed to be getting the worst of it. They then insisted on escalating the fighting to side slapping, partly because their chests were too sore to continue in that fashion, and partly because their opponents seemed to have an edge on them.

The side slapping duel is nearly identical in form to chest pounding, except that the blow is delivered with an open hand across the flanks of the opponent, between his rib-cage and pelvis bone. It is a little more severe than chest pounding because casualties are more frequent and tempers grow hotter more rapidly when a group's champion falls to the ground, gasping for wind, and faints.

The duel ended with the guests backing out of the village with arrows drawn in their bows.

Club fights, which result from arguments, may also escalate into brawls in which men are killed (Chagnon 1968:119):

Most duels start between two men, usually after one of them has been caught *en flagrante* trysting with the other's wife. The enraged husband challenges his opponent to strike him on the head with a club. He holds his own club vertically, leans against it and exposes his head for his opponent to strike. After he has sustained a blow on the head, he can then deliver one on the culprit's skull. But as soon as blood starts to flow, almost everybody rips a pole out of the house frame and joins in the fighting, supporting one or the other of the contestants.

For a specific case in which one man died, see Question 20, in Chapter 5.

Since neither side will admit defeat, there is no criterion for determining the winner. Hence, chest-pounding duels, side-slapping contests, and club fights are not games.

No data on the types of games played are furnished in the Qemant ethnography.

INITIATION RITES

Initiation rites are ceremonies, supervised in part by the adults of a culture, which are mandatory for all adolescents of one sex only (Young 1965:12). If the ceremony is mandatory for all boys of a given culture, it is a *male initiation rite*; if it is mandatory for all girls of a given culture, it is a *female initiation rite.* A culture may have both male and female initiation rites. Since initiation rites occur periodically, usually when there are a sufficient number of boys or girls in the local group to be initiated, the adolescents undergoing initiation may range from approximately ten to twenty years of age. Thus for many members of a culture initiation does not occur precisely at puberty. Most anthropologists view initiation rites as ceremonies which mark the passage of an individual from the social status of child to the social status of adult. Thus an initiate goes through a period of social transition in which he gives up one identification for another. Since it is a crisis period for him, the public nature of the ceremony enhances his self-esteem and assists him in assuming a new identification. During the ceremonies the boys or girls are often given instruction in customs which are supposedly known only to adults.

The classic analysis of initiation rites is Arnold van Gennep's treatise on *The Rites of Passage* (1960; orig. 1909). In addition to initiation ceremonies, other rites of passage are those rites related to birth, marriage, and death. For van Gennep a rite of passage was a ceremony of regeneration, a rite of death and rebirth, a transition from the profane to the sacred. He showed that rites of passage can be divided into three consecutive major phases which he called separation, transition, and incorporation. Although recent theories have modified van Gennep's analysis, it nevertheless still provides the basis for all contemporary discussions of initiation ceremonies.

Initiation rites vary in their degree of elaborateness from one culture to another. Young (1965:14–17) has developed a four-step scale of "sex-role dramatization" for measuring the degree of elaborateness of both male and female initiation ceremonies. Each step of the scale represents an increase in dramatization and social participation. The steps are as follows: (1) customary minimal social recognition (gift, party, change of name, and so forth), (2) personal dramatization (initiate is ceremonially dressed or adorned), (3) organized social response (group dresses up and/or performs), and (4) affective social response (beating or severe hazing of initiates). The steps are cumulative. This means, for example, that if male initiation rites in a culture can be classified as "affective social response" (step 4), all three lower items on the scale (steps 1, 2, and 3) are present also. Although Young states that "initiation ceremonies proper begin with step 1" (1965:15), many anthropologists probably would prefer to restrict the definition of initiation rites to include only rites which can be classified as step 3 or step 4, for only those rites involve the active participation of members of the local group. Rites which can be classified as either step 1 or step 2 would not be considered initiation rites since they focus upon individuals and not groups of initiates.

Although initiation rites perform the important function of symbolizing the transition from childhood to adulthood, many cultures do not have any type of initiation ceremonies. In a cross-cultural study of fifty-four cultures Young found that 60 percent of the cultures did not have any male initiation rites and 43 percent did not have any female initiation rites (1965:15). Moreover, Young found that male initiation rites are more likely than female initiation rites to occur at step 4 on the scale of sex-role dramatization. He thus concludes that "male initiation rites are generally more elaborate or intense than those for females" (1965:16).

Why do some cultures have initiation rites, while others do not? This is a question which anthropologists have been attempting to answer since the time of van Gennep. In the past fifteen years two major explanations have been offered for male initiation rites and two for female rites. J. W. M. Whiting, Kluckhohn, and Anthony (1958) argue that male initiation rites are produced by a long postpartum sex taboo and by a long (over one year) exclusive mother-son sleeping arrangement. These two customs supposedly develop in boys dependence upon their mothers and hostility toward their fathers. According to the theory, male initiation rites break this dependence and resolve the hostility toward the father. Young (1965), who disagrees with Whiting, Kluckhohn, and Anthony, argues that male solidarity—not childhood customs—is responsible for male initiation rites. By male solidarity Young means that there is cooperation in work and war among the men of the local group. The greater the degree of male solidarity, the higher the male initiation rite will rank on the scale of sex-role dramatization. "The dramatization of sex role—initiation rites—is functionally necessary for maintaining the solidarity of men" (1965:41). Anthropologists are undecided as to which theory, if either, is correct.

The solidarity theory has also been used by Young (1965) to explain the presence of female initiation rites. He argues that female solidarity is great if there are female work groups and institutionalized household unity present in the culture. The need to maintain female solidarity accounts for female initiation rites. Brown (1963), who has developed a similar theory, argues that in those cultures in which girls continue to reside in the homes of their mothers after marriage (that is, matrilocal residence), the rites represent an announcement of the girls' changed status. This symbolization of adulthood is necessary because the women spend their adult lives in the same households in which they had been children. Brown also shows that female initiation rites are likely to occur in cultures in which women make an important contribution to subsistence activities. These theories have also received only tentative acceptance.

33. **What types of initiation rites are present?**
     1. initiation rites absent
     2. male initiation rites, step_____
     3. female initiation rites, step_____

As Young has shown, initiation ceremonies, both for boys or for girls, can be ranked on a four-step scale of sex-role dramatization. In addition to determining whether male or female initiation rites are present in the culture, the student should determine at what step of the scale the rites occur. The scale score should be recorded for each type of initiation rite. A zero (0) can be used to indicate an absence of either type of rite.

The Andros Islanders do not have initiation rites. The transition from childhood to adulthood is achieved through procreation (Otterbein 1966:67, 56–57):

A double standard of sexual morality regulates the behavior of men and women. In order to claim adult status a man must have premarital as well as extramarital sex relations, for Andros Islanders believe that the biological nature of the male compels him to have sexual intercourse with as many women as possible. This drive is expected to manifest itself in adolescent males. If a boy does not begin to have coitus by his late teens, people will begin to wonder if he is a "sissy" (homosexual). Most young men, however, live up to community expectations—behavior which is expressed in the saying: "Boys are like dogs." On the other hand, the girl is expected to remain a virgin until the time she has intercourse with her fiancé, and after her marriage to remain faithful to her husband.

Manhood and womanhood are established in Long Bay Cays by having a child, an event expected by the community shortly after the first year of marriage. If a child is not born to a newly married couple, people will call each spouse a "beau-stag" (my spelling), a term of derision which indicates not only sterility but also inability to achieve complete adulthood. In such circumstances, the man will try to have a child by another woman; if he is successful, people will drop the uncomplimentary term. Subsequently, the husband is likely to give part of his earnings to the mother of his child rather than to his wife, undoubtedly causing resentment and therefore producing a situation which may lead to a separation. Since the wife does not have a child that needs support, no economic barriers prevent her from leaving her husband. If after a separation the wife has a child by another man, the community will stop calling her a beau-stag.

On the other hand, a man who fathers a child every year is called a "double-luck," a term of praise. Men believe that siring several children is a sign of their masculinity; in contrast, many women are content to have just one child.

Among the Yanomamö, male initiation rites do not occur.

However, female initiation rites, which can be ranked on step two of the scale of sex-role dramatization, do occur (Chagnon 1968:85):

A girl's transition to womanhood is obvious because of its physiological manifestations. At first menses (*yobömou*) Yanomamö girls are confined to their houses and hidden behind a screen of leaves. Their old cotton garments are discarded and replaced by new ones manufactured by their mothers or by older female friends. During this week of confinement, the girl is fed by her relatives: her food must be eaten by means of a stick, as she is not allowed to come into contact with it in any other fashion. She must also scratch herself with another set of sticks. . . . After her puberty confinement, a girl is eligible to begin life as a wife and take up residence with her husband.

Males, on the other hand, do not have their transition into manhood marked by a ceremony. Nevertheless, one can usually tell when a boy is attempting to enter the world of men. The most conspicuous sign is his anger when others call him by his name.

Gamst explicitly states that for the Qemant initiation rites are absent (1969:106):

Marriage (*fahu yewinat*), and the marriage ceremony (*senaw*), constitute a rite of passage from adolescence to young adulthood for Qemant males. This is not always the case for females because of their youth. There is no other coming-of-age ceremony for males or females.

Marriage of course is a rite of passage, but it has not been considered an initiation rite by anthropologists.

ART

Every culture has decorative patterns which may adorn baskets and pottery vessels, tools and weapons, fabrics and clothing, furniture and houses. Sometimes even the human body is decorated—with paint, tattooing, or scarification. In some cultures nonutilitarian objects are produced which can be classified as art objects if they are considered to be beautiful by members of the culture. Both ornamentation and objects of art have been considered to be art. In his 1927 book *Primitive Art*—the classic and probably still most authoritative work on the art of nonliterate peoples—Franz Boas divided the "arts of space" into "graphic arts" and "plastic arts." Graphic or two-dimensional art includes painting, drawing, tattooing, and embroidering; plastic or three-dimensional art includes sculpture and ceramics. Boas classified poetry, music, and dance as "arts of time." Although many of the same principles and conclusions developed in the study of graphic and plastic art apply to the study of poetry, music, and dance, the "arts of time" will not be discussed. The focus of this section will be upon graphic art.

Art may serve a number of different functions both for the artist and for the viewer. First, it affords enjoyment for the artist through "the joy engendered by the mastery of technique and also by the pleasure produced by the perfection of form" (Boas 1955:349). For the viewer it provides enjoyment through an aesthetic reaction. Second, art is informative since it permits the artist to express his emotions and thoughts, and it permits the viewer to receive a message. Sometimes an object of art purposely tells a story, as in a wall mural. Third, art is religious. Often the artist produces representations of supernatural beings which may be used in religious ceremonies, and the viewer has a material representation through which he can communicate with the supernatural beings. Fourth, art objects are a sign of status and wealth. Through their production the outstanding artist gains renown, and the viewer, provided he is the owner, has a means of displaying his good taste and his success in the material world. Sometimes art objects are treasures which symbolize the importance of the political community and its leader.

Three types of graphic art can be distinguished. *Abstract* art depends upon formal elements such as lines, triangles, diamonds, squares, circles, with the pattern formed from these elements showing such properties as symmetry, repetition, balance, and rhythm. The pattern is based upon a conscious arrangement of parts. The repetition of motifs produces a simple, and often geometric, pattern. Arbitrary meaning can be assigned to the elements by the artist and other members of his culture if the elements symbolize things in the real or supernatural world, or if natural forms are incorporated into the pattern. Meaning is attached to the individual elements, not the overall pattern. *Representational-expressionistic* art depicts people, animals, or natural phenomena, but the treatment of the figures is exaggerated. The representation is based upon a deliberate overemphasis of certain parts of the figures depicted. Geometric patterns may be used to produce the exaggeration. Since individual, nonrepetitive motifs are employed, the pattern formed is more complex than the pattern in abstract art. In contrast to abstract art, meaning is attached to the overall pattern, not to the individual elements (although certain elements or figures in the design may have meaning). *Representational-naturalistic* art depicts people, animals, or natural phenomena in a realistic manner. The representation is based upon a deliberate attempt to portray things as they appear. Formal elements and geometric patterns are not employed. The pattern formed is in most instances more complex than the pattern in representational-expressionistic art. In naturalistic art, as well as in expressionistic art, meaning is attached to the overall pattern (Hays 1958:147–160).

Nineteenth-century anthropologists were interested in the evolution of art. Some viewed art as evolving from geometric or abstract to naturalistic patterns; others viewed it as evolving from naturalistic to geometric or abstract patterns. Boas (1955) demonstrated the futility of such approaches by showing that abstract and naturalistic art are often found in the same culture. For example, one type of art will be used on certain utilitarian objects, while the other type of art will be employed in the construction of nonutilitarian objects. In some cultures the men produce naturalistic art and the women abstract art. Boas concluded that the types of art, and their particular manifestations, developed by a culture were the outcome of the stimulus of forms in the physical environment, the limitations of the materials used, the motor habits of the artists, the historical contacts which the culture had with other peoples, and the beliefs and values of the members of the culture.

Two cross-cultural studies, both using the same sample of thirty cultures, have shown the relationship of the complexity of design to both child training practices and social stratification. Since expressionistic art is more complex than abstract art and since naturalistic art is more complex than expressionistic art, it is possible to translate the three types of graphic art into a single measure of design complexity which corresponds to the variable or attribute employed in the two cross-cultural studies. This variable "was defined at the upper extreme as a design with many unrepeated figures to form a complex organization of design; the lower extreme of this variable was defined as a design with few figures or repetition of figures to form a simple organization of design" (Barry 1957:380). In the first of these studies, Barry (1957) found that severity of socialization, particularly severe pressures for independence rather than obedience, was characteristic of cultures with complex or naturalistic design patterns. In the other study, Fischer (1961) tested and found support for the theory that cultures with a well-developed social hierarchy will have complex designs, and cultures with an egalitarian social and political system will have simple designs. Underlying his theory is the notion that on a psychological level the elements in a design are "unconscious representations of persons in the society" (1961:81). Since persons are equal in an egalitarian culture, the repetition of the same design elements represents a number of equal comrades; since persons are unequal in a hierarchical culture, they are represented by a variety of distinct elements in the design. These psychological theories, just as the psychological theories described in the three previous sections, have received only tentative acceptance by anthropologists.

34. What types of graphic art are present?
1. abstract
2. representational-expressionistic
3. representational-naturalistic

Since the three types of graphic art vary in design complexity from simple to complex, distinguishing criteria related to complexity should be employed to differentiate the types. Representational art can be distinguished from abstract art by examining the formal elements in the design: if the elements are repeated, it is abstract art; if they are not repeated (that is, the formal elements are different or formal elements are absent), it is representational art. Expressionistic art can be distinguished from naturalistic art by examining the "picture" in the design: if parts of the figures depicted are exaggerated (that is, out of proportion to other parts of the figures), it is expressionistic art; if it appears that the picture is a more or less accurate representation of reality, it is naturalistic art. Since there are conventional ways of handling certain design problems—such as depth perception—in naturalistic art, a picture which does not look like a photograph should not necessarily be classified as expressionistic. For example, American primitive paintings or the paintings of children in the United States should be classified as naturalistic even though they lack perspective. They are naturalistic because the artist attempted to depict reality. If the ethnography contains statements that artists in the culture deliberately distort their figures or that they attempt to accurately depict what they see, more substantial evidence is available for classifying examples according to the two types of representational art.

In classifying types of graphic art, photographs or line drawings in the ethnography may be used. More than one type of graphic art may be present in the culture. All illustrative materials should be examined—including pictures of pottery, weapons, clothing, and houses—for examples of graphic art. In addition to noting the different types of graphic art present, the objects on which the designs occur should be listed. If men produce one type of art, and women another type, this should be recorded. It is worth noting whether three-dimensional art is present.

––––––––––

The Andros Island ethnography does not provide information on graphic art. However, since there is a detailed analysis of the division of labor by age and sex and there is no mention of doing art work in a long list of activities, it can be concluded that graphic art is absent.

The Yanomamö ethnography provides little information on art. Nevertheless, two photographs show circles and wavy lines painted on men's bodies and faces (Chagnon 1968:25,112), Apparently both men and women paint their bodies when intervillage feasts are held (Chagnon 1968:109):

The men of the host group had finished their preparations for the feast; they were all painted in red and black, bearing colorful feathers. . . .
While the men were taking their drugs, the women were busy painting and decorating themselves with feathers and red pigment.

In another photograph a woman is wearing a woven belt decorated with diamonds and circles (Chagnon 1968:38). On the basis of these examples, Yanomamö art can be classified as abstract.

Almost no information on Qemant art is available in the monograph. What little information there is permits one to classify their graphic art as abstract (Gamst 1969:54, 105):

As a neck pendant, the case [of the amulet] is regarded as decorative. The parchment is inscribed in Geez or Arabic with mixed characters or with phrases from the Bible or Koran. Figures and geometric designs may be included.

Tattooing is a common form of adornment and is done on the upper gums, neck, chest, forehead, hand, lower forearm, and ankles. Nug oil and soot are heated together to make a dark blue dye for the tattoos, which are done by puncturing the skin repeatedly with the thorns of a variety of acacia tree dipped into the pigment. In addition to being decorative, tattoos serve therapeutic and protective functions.

STUDY GUIDE QUESTIONS

Aim of Chapter 6

This chapter examines several elements of the belief system which mutually serve to structure behavior within a culture. Anthropologists have found that an understanding of the world view of a people is essential to an appreciation of their motivations, their child rearing practices, and even their personality development.

The analysis of the belief system takes the anthropologist into the area of classifying religion, religious practitioners, and religious practices, including various forms of magic.

The belief system also sets up standards for other forms of human behavior, and anthropologists typically look for expressions of these standards in such areas as sex taboos, initiation rites, and even games and forms of art.

Introduction

1. How is *world view* defined?
2. Explain how the world view of a culture can influence the development and behavior of its members.

Supernatural Beings

3. What is *animism*?
4. Define the terms *high god* and *superior god,* and contrast their functions.
5. What are *ancestral spirits*, and how do they relate to the living?
6. How do *nonhuman spirits* differ from high and superior gods and ancestral spirits? What is the function of nonhuman spirits?
7. Contrast monotheistic and polytheistic religious belief systems in terms of the belief in a god or gods.

Religious Practitioners

8. What are the functions of religious practitioners?
9. In what way do supernatural beings differ from religious practitioners?
10. Contrast the role of the *shaman* and the *priest*.

Magic

11. Identify the three elements which are involved in the practice of magic, as well as the three aspects associated with the magical formula itself.
12. What are several common objectives of magical acts?
13. Discuss magic in terms of the positive functions or effects which may stem from the practice of magic.

14. Distinguish between the law of similarity and the law of contagion.

Sorcery

15. Define the term *sorcery*, explain how it is performed, and discuss it in terms of its social functions.
16. Distinguish between *sorcery* and *witchcraft*. Is the distinction analytically useful?

Post-Partum Sex Taboo

17. What is the *post-partum sex taboo*? Identify the factors/reasons which are associated with a long post-partum sex taboo.

Games

18. For an anthropologist to classify an activity as a game, what five criteria are required?
19. Identify the three basic types of games. What are some of the main social functions served by games?

Initiation Rites

20. What are initiation rites? Who is involved? When do the rites occur? How are the rites associated with social status?
21. Contrast *rites of intensification* with *rites of passage*.
22. Based upon the theories presented in the text, discuss why some cultures have initiation rites while others do not.

Art

23. Distinguish between graphic and plastic arts.
24. What are the functions of art?
25. Identify and contrast the various forms of graphic art.
26. In what kind of culture would you expect to find representational-naturalistic art?

(Left) Qemant grandparents with their grandchildren.
(Right) A family on Andros Island.
(Below) A Yanomamö father relaxing with his son.

7

CONCLUSION

Comparison of Cultures and Culture Traits
Linkages and Hypotheses
Testing of Hypotheses

The sections of this volume have dealt with thirty-four topics. Each section has described one or more of the important concepts used by anthropologists, concepts which make up the basic vocabulary of cultural anthropology. They are used as guidelines in collecting data in a field situation and in gleaning information from published accounts. If the concepts are used to summarize the way of life of a culture, they become the vehicle by which an ethnographer communicates with his reader—the concepts represent the reality which was observed. They are also used by anthropologists in comparative research. Any attempt to compare two or more cultures in terms of their similarities or differences will employ these important concepts, as will any discussion which purports to explain why certain beliefs and practices occur. For example: Why are the Yanomamö polygynous? Why are some peoples polygynous and not others? Why are a majority of the world's cultures polygynous? Anthropologists cannot have a discussion—orally or in print—without using many of the concepts defined in the previous chapters.

Within each section a question was stated. The answers to the questions were concepts. Each question asked: For the particular culture which I am now studying, which concepts represent culture traits present? The answers of course also provided information on which concepts were not represented by culture traits. The thirty-four topics are listed on the following table, and the questions are listed exactly as they appear in the text on a data sheet at the end of this chapter. At the end of each section there was a discussion and usually a quotation from my study of the Andros Islanders (1966), from Chagnon's ethnographic account of the Yanomamö (1968), and from Gamst's study of the Qemant (1969). These discussions provided information on culture traits which were present in Andros culture, in Yanomamö culture, and in Qemant culture. This information is summarized on the following table—after each topic is listed the concept which represents the culture trait which is characteristic of either the Andros Islanders, the Yanomamö, or the Qemant. A perusal of the first column of the table provides a "thumbnail" or brief ethnographic sketch of Andros culture; the second column, an ethnographic sketch of Yanomamö culture; the third column, a sketch of Qemant culture. The sketches are presented almost entirely in terms of anthropological concepts.

COMPARISON OF CULTURES AND CULTURE TRAITS

The table titled "Summary Analysis of Cultures" can be used to compare cultures and culture traits. Space for one blank column is provided on the table. After a culture has been analyzed and the information recorded on a data sheet containing the thirty-four questions, the culture traits present in that culture can be listed in the blank column; that is, the concepts which represent the culture traits. (If more than one culture is analyzed, a new table can be made on which to list the culture traits present in each culture.)

When information on two or more cultures has been gathered using a set of questions such as those on the data sheet, the cultures

TABLE 3   Summary Analysis of Cultures

Topics	Cultures		
	Andros Islanders	Yanomamö	Qemant
1. the people	a fishing and farming community within a modern nation	primitive culture	peasants, dependent native people
2. language	one spoken	one spoken	multilingual
3. physical environment	tropical forest	tropical forest, mountains	mountains, desert, grassland, temperate forest
4. history	recent migrants	recent migrants	original inhabitants
5. subsistence technology	fishing, horticulture	horticulture	agriculture
6. population density	4.46 persons per square mile	.25 persons per square mile	15 persons per square mile
7. division of labor	part-time and full-time specialists	part-time specialists	part-time and full-time specialists
8. house form	single household dwellings	multihousehold dwelling	compounds
9. settlement pattern	dispersed homesteads	compact villages	dispersed homesteads
10. settlement size	337 persons	250 persons	2640 persons
11. economy	market exchange	balanced reciprocity	market exchange
12. stratification	classes	absent	feudal
13. residence	virilocal, uxorilocal, commonlocal, neolocal	commonlocal, virilocal	patrilocal, matrilocal, commonlocal, virilocal
14. marriage	monogamy	general polygyny	monogamy
15. household type	independent nuclear family, grandparent, female-headed, and male-headed households	independent nuclear and polygamous family households	independent nuclear and extended family households
16. descent groups	unrestricted descent groups	patrilineages	patrilineages, clans, moieties

TABLE 3   Summary Analysis of Cultures (Cont.)

Topics	Cultures		
	Andros Islanders	Yanomamö	Qemant
17. kindreds	kindreds present	kindreds absent	kindreds present
18. cousin marriage	first cousin marriage absent	matrilateral and patrilateral cross-cousin marriage	first cousin marriage absent
19. kinship terminology	Eskimo	Iroquois	Eskimo
20. political system	three levels	one level	five levels
21. political leaders	chiefs	headmen	king, chiefs, headmen
22. legal system	law of public delicts, law of private delicts	law absent	law of public delicts, law of private delicts
23. military organizations	absent	composed of non-professional warriors	composed of professional warriors
24. feuding	feuding absent	feuding without compensation	feuding absent
25. warfare	not applicable	continually	not applicable
26. causes of war	not applicable	revenge, defense, and plunder	defense, revenge, land, subjugation and tribute
27. supernatural beings	a high god, ancestral spirits	superior gods, nonhuman spirits	a high god, superior gods, ancestral and nonhuman spirits
28. religious practitioners	shamans and priests	shamans	shamans and priests
29. magic	homeopathic magic	homeopathic magic	magic present—unclassifiable
30. sorcery	sorcery present	sorcery present	sorcery present
31. post-partum sex taboo	short	long	no data
32. games	no data	games are absent	no data
33. initiation rites	initiation rites absent	female initiation rites, step 2	initiation rites absent
34. art	graphic art absent	abstract	abstract

can be compared and contrasted. The use of the same questions permits systematic comparison of the cultures. The table is useful in conducting such a comparison—it is a simple matter to count the number of culture traits which are the same and the number which are different. Generally speaking, the greater the number of culture traits which are the same, the more similar are the cultures. And conversely, the greater the number of culture traits which are different, the less alike are the cultures. Moreover, this method of comparison can be applied to the study of a single culture if two different ethnographic accounts—done at two points in time—are available. It is thus possible to compare the culture at two time periods in the same manner that one would compare two cultures. Any differences can be attributed to changes which have occurred in the culture since it was first studied. And, if a culture has been studied at three points in time—a rare event—the same method of comparison can be used to analyze changes which have occurred over the time span encompassed by the three studies. The study of a culture over a period of time is known as a *diachronic* (cross-time) study. In contrast, the study of a culture in a single period of time is termed *synchronic*.

The following example focuses on changes in household types within the same culture, at three points in time. In order to keep the example simple, changes in other culture traits are not considered. In 1959 and 1961 I conducted an ethnographic study of several small villages on Andros Island. Using census forms, I collected data from every household in four villages. From the census reports I was able to compute the frequency of household types. In 1961, 38 percent of the households were independent nuclear family households and 18 percent were grandparent households. The remaining households were headed by either single females or single males (Otterbein 1963). In 1968 I returned to the villages and again took a census of every household. Computation of the frequency of household types revealed that the percentages had changed. Thirty percent of the households were independent nuclear family households, a decline of 8 percent, and 27 percent were grandparent households, an increase of 9 percent. Single parent households remained nearly the same at 43 percent (Otterbein 1970*b*). In 1975 I returned to the villages and took a census for the third time. The trends noted in 1968 had not continued. Thirty-six percent of the households were occupied by independent nuclear families, an increase of 6 percent, and grandparent households had decreased by 3 percent—so had single person households. The data for all three time periods are shown in Table 4.

TABLE 4   Changes in Percentages of Household Types in Long Bay Cays from 1961 to 1975

Household Type	Time Periods		
	1961	1968	1975
Nuclear family households	38	30	36
Grandparent households	18	27	24
Single person households	44	43	40
Percent	100	100	100

Until the data on household types were analyzed schematically, the changes and trends could not be ascertained. The reason for these changes is complex—it involves rates of migration from the villages, as well as the location of economic opportunities within the Bahamas (Otterbein 1970*b*, n.d.).

If one question from the data sheet is used to collect information from a substantial number of cultures, perhaps thirty or more, it is possible to compute the frequency with which different culture traits occur. The cultures may be from a restricted geographical region such as the American South West, from a continental area such as North America, or they may be chosen to represent all parts of the world. Computation of frequencies, in percentages, makes it possible for the anthropologist to reach a conclusion regarding the rarity or prevalence of certain culture traits, either on a regional or worldwide basis. A number of examples are provided in the text: A study of 554 cultures showed that 24 percent of the world's cultures were monogamous, 75 percent were polygynous, and 1 percent were polyandrous. This study demonstrated the rarity of polyandry and the common occurrence of polygyny. A much smaller study of thirty-three cultures which practiced either matrilateral or patrilateral cross-cousin marriage revealed that only seven cultures (21 percent) practiced patrilateral cross-cousin marriage. Thus it was demonstrated that this form of cross-cousin marriage was more rare than the matrilateral form. Another study, this time of fifty cultures, provided evidence that most cultures have military organizations by showing that only four cultures (8 percent) did not have military organizations. A study of supernatural beings found that nineteen (49 percent) out of thirty-nine cultures had a belief in a high god, twenty-nine (55 percent) out of forty-nine cultures had a belief in one or more superior gods, and thirty-three (67 percent) out of forty-nine cultures had a belief in active ancestral spirits. Thus it is to be expected that many cultures will have more than one type of supernatural being. The long post-partum sex taboo—a custom which one might think would be rare—was found present in twenty-seven (49 percent) out of fifty-six cultures. And in a study of initiation rites in fifty-four cultures it was shown that 40 percent of the cultures had male initiation rites and 57 percent had female initiation rites. Thus initiation rites for both sexes commonly occur.

Given a substantial number of cultures, it is also possible for an anthropologist to locate, geographically, cultures which are characterized by a particular culture trait. The cultures can be from a region, from a continent, or from the world as a whole. Once the cultures are plotted on a map, it is readily apparent if these culture traits cluster geographically. That is, some culture traits, rather than being evenly distributed over the earth's surface, may be concentrated in specific geographic regions. This concentration may be due to the influence of the physical environment, or a process known as diffusion may be operating. *Diffusion* is the geographic spread of culture traits; it occurs through the acceptance of culture traits from one culture by the members of another culture. Only one example of geographically locating those cultures which have a particular trait is given in the text. A long post-partum sex taboo is found primarily in the disease-ridden tropics and in regions of North America inhabited by nomadic hunting groups. This geographical distribution led J. W. M. Whiting (1959) to conclude that a long post-partum sex taboo results from a conscious realization that the intentional spacing of children is beneficial for the health of young children. The physical environment is chiefly responsible for the poor health of children that necessitates their spacing.

LINKAGES AND HYPOTHESES

Ethnographies, in addition to being descriptions of the cultures of particular groups of people, are also descriptions of how particular cultures are integrated. The basic technique employed by ethnographers to demonstrate the integration of cultures consists of describing *linkages* between culture traits. An example of such a linkage would be the statement that the members of such-and-such culture have a nomadic settlement pattern because their hunting and gathering mode of subsistence prevents the formation of year-round settlements. Thus a linkage connects two culture traits. If

the culture traits are designated as *a* and *b*, the linkage can be diagrammed as follows:

Culture traits can be linked in more complex ways. For example, three traits can be connected, producing three linkages. This can
be diagrammed as follows:

Four interconnected culture traits, as shown in the following diagram, produce six linkages:

Each culture trait is shown related to each of the other culture traits.
On the other hand, several culture traits can be connected to a
single culture trait while not being linked to each other, as the
following diagram shows:

Although an ethnographer may have "seen" certain linkages
and combinations of linkages while he was conducting fieldwork, it
is not until he analyzes his field data that these linkages become
crystallized in his mind. That is, they become apparent to him at
that stage in the analysis when he is reading and rereading his information and is organizing and reorganizing his topical outline. Once

the linkages have been formulated, the ethnographer can proceed with the writing of the report. These linkages become the focal points around which the ethnography is written. Thus an ethnography is not only a description of the culture of a particular group of people, but also a description of how the culture is integrated.

Linkages are of three different types. It should be clear from the above discussion of the procedure followed by an ethnographer in delineating linkages that they are inferences made by the ethnographer. They are not ethnographic data. Since they are inferences, they must be examined for their validity. The first type of linkage— and it is the only type of valid linkage—is the functional relationship. In a functional relationship two culture traits are linked such that they are both mutually dependent; that is, a change in one trait produces a change in the other. Mathematicians show this relationship as follows: $x = y$ (x is a function of y, and y is a function of x; that is, a change in x produces a change in y, and vice versa). When a functional relationship is found to exist, it can be stated that the linkage is a valid one. In other words, a true or real relationship is being described by the linkage. The second type of linkage—and it is not a valid linkage—is the nonfunctional or concomitant relationship. The two traits are found together, but a change in one does not produce a change in the other, since they are not mutually dependent. In fact, it is more precise not to speak of this type of linkage as being a relationship, since it is a linkage based upon an inferred, but invalid, relationship. The ethnographer has put together two or more culture traits which are not functionally related. The third type of linkage is the tautological relationship. A relationship exists between the two traits, or rather the concepts representing the traits, but it results from overlapping definitions. For example, there is a relationship between monogamy and independent nuclear family households. By definition, an independent nuclear family household is a domestic group consisting of a married couple (that is, one man married to one woman) and their children; monogamy, by definition, is the marriage of one man to one woman. Thus the presence of monoamy is one part of the definition of an independent nuclear family household. Therefore, overlapping definitions create a relationship. In the language of logic the linkage is said to be tautological.

Linkages of either the functional or nonfunctional type are hypotheses. The only difference between linkages and hypotheses is that linkages usually purport to be valid, true, or real relationships, while hypotheses are usually considered to be statements of relationships which need to be tested to determine their validity. Linkages and hypotheses are thus the same in terms of their basic structure. Although tautological linkages can be considered hypotheses, they should not be so treated, since the relationships between their concepts are derived only from overlapping definitions. As was indicated in the preceding paragraph, some linkages are valid and others are invalid. A hypothesis is a linkage which an anthropologist wishes to test; that is, he wishes to determine the validity of the linkage. If the relationship described by the linkage is precisely stated in the ethnography, it is an explicit hypothesis and is ready for testing. If the relationship is only implied or vaguely described, the linkage is an implicit hypothesis, and should be rephrased in a more explicit fashion before testing; that is, it should be converted into an explicit hypothesis. This process of converting vaguely described linkages into explicit hypotheses is known as deriving hypotheses. It is only through the testing of a hypothesis and the determination of its validity that one can establish whether the linkage described is functional or nonfunctional. If a hypothesis is tested and found to be valid, then, the linkage from which it was derived is a description of a functional relationship. If the hypothesis is tested and found to be invalid, then the linkage from which it was derived is a description of a nonfunctional or concomitant relationship. Thus the classification of linkages by type can only be accomplished if the linkages are treated as hypotheses and subjected to testing.

TESTING OF HYPOTHESES

A *hypothesis* is a statement of a precise relationship between that which is to be explained and that which is to do the explaining—a relationship between two variables. When an anthropologist attempts to explain why a certain culture trait occurs, he formulates a hypothesis. Hypotheses usually take one of the following forms: (1) An invariable relationship: if A, then B. (2) A direct relationship: the greater (or higher, or larger) A, the greater (or higher, or larger) B. (3) An inverse relationshp: the greater (or higher, or larger) A, the less (or lower, or smaller) B.

In order to test a hypothesis, the variables stated in the hypothesis must be indexed. To index a variable is to establish a series of values for the variable. Variables may have two or more values, and each value must be defined. In deriving a hypothesis some of the thirty-four questions on the data sheet may be used directly as variables. They are the questions for which there is only one "answer." (Questions for which there can be several "answers" can be used as variables if they are separated into more than one question, each question having a single "answer.") The "answers" or concepts which accompany these questions correspond to values, and the definition of each concept corresponds to the definition of each value. Sometimes the values or concepts are referred to as points or categories on the variable. Hypotheses which state the conditions under which certain things will occur—invariable relationships—usually employ two-valued variables, while hypotheses which state either direct or inverse relationships often employ variables which have more than two values. Thus the type of variables used will depend to a great extent upon the manner in which the hypotheses have been formulated.

If an anthropologist is interested only in whether a particular culture trait is to be found or not found in a culture, he employs a two-valued or dichotomous variable. The presence or absence of the culture trait—or rather the concept which represents it—constitutes such a variable, since "present" is one value and "absent" is the other value. A definition of the concept is attached to the "present" value, and the definition of the "absent" value is simply the statement that the phenomenon is not found in the culture. The presence or absence of sorcery (Question 30, in Chapter 6) is an example of a dichotomous variable. Other questions on the data sheet can be converted into dichotomous variables by placing any concept that appears on the data sheet in a question which has the following form:

Is (or are) _____ practiced (or present)?
    1. no
    2. yes

Many of the questions on the data sheet may be used as multivalued variables. They are questions for which three or more possible, mutually exclusive "answers" are listed or, in the case of computed numerical answers, can be derived. The classification of the occurrence of internal warfare as continual, frequent, infrequent, or never (Question 25, in Chapter 5) is an example of a multivalued variable. Many of these more complicated variables require a definition for each of the values of the variable. However, some variables—such as population size of largest settlement (Question 10, in Chapter 3) or number of hierarchical levels in the political system (Question 20, in Chapter 5)—do not require a definition for each possible value. Other variables which make use of a formula—such as population density (Question 6, in Chapter 3)—require a definition for each component of the formula.

The basic way in which a hypothesis is tested is to examine a culture for the purpose of determining whether the culture conforms to the hypothesis. If both the culture trait which is to be explained and the culture trait which is presumed responsible for that culture trait are present in the culture, the hypothesis is confirmed. If either culture trait is absent, the hypothesis is disconfirmed. If both culture traits are absent, the hypothesis is neither confirmed nor disconfirmed. The logic of hypothesis testing is set forth in the following paradigm. A and B represent two culture traits in a hypothesis which has the form: if A, then B (i.e., an invariable relationship).

Hypothesis:	If (A) ,	then (B) .
Confirmed	A present	B present
Disconfirmed	A present	B absent
Disconfirmed	A absent	B present
Neither confirmed nor disconfirmed	A absent	B absent

(The same basic logic applies to statements which hypothesize either a direct or indirect relationship.)

Although the presence of both culture traits in a particular culture confirms the hypothesis, this confirmation is only tentative. When an anthropologist examines one culture, or one culture at a time, he cannot be certain that some unconsidered variable other than the variable given in the hypothesis may better explain the culture trait. In order to demonstrate that other factors (such as the physical environment) or culture traits are not influencing the culture trait which he wishes to explain, it is necessary for the anthropologist to "control" these factors by special techniques. One technique is known as the method of *controlled comparison*. This technique requires that the anthropologist examine two similar cultures simultaneously. The cultures are compared in terms of a series of culture traits. The cultures must be so similar that all the culture traits compared must be the same except for the two culture traits which are stated in the hypothesis. These two culture traits must be present in one of the cultures and absent in the other. Although it is often difficult to find two cultures which meet these requirements, the finding of two such cultures not only confirms the hypothesis, but also rules out as influencing factors those culture traits which are the same in both cultures. (Since local groups within the same culture often differ slightly from each other, such groups can sometimes be used in controlled comparisons.) This technique still does not control or rule out culture traits which are not compared. The thirty-four topics discussed in this book provide an excellent list of culture traits which can be used in controlled comparisons.

The following example of a controlled comparison tests the hypothesis that ambilineages and ambilineal descent are the result of a scarcity of land. The argument underlying this hypothesis is that in cultures where land is plentiful and controlled by unrestricted descent groups based on multilineal descent, an increase in population will lead to a shortage of land, which in turn will result in some of the members being excluded from the unrestricted descent groups. Those excluded will be those members not living on the land. Once certain lines of descent are excluded from the unrestricted descent groups, they become converted into ambilineages. Thus an increase in population density will result in the formation of ambilineages. For the hypothesis to be confirmed a culture must be found in which the population density is high and ambilineages are present. Jamaica is such a culture. The population density of Jamaica is 230 persons per square mile, and Jamaica has ambilineages. To control for factors other than population density, a culture similar to Jamaica must be found, but it must have a low population density and unrestricted descent groups must be present. A culture meeting these requirements is the Bahamas. The population density of the Bahamas is 15 persons per square mile, and the Bahamas has unrestricted descent groups. In the actual controlled comparison which was conducted, thirteen culture traits, excluding the two stated in the hypothesis, were compared. The culture traits controlled included kindreds, ambilocal residence, ancestor worship, and a number of factors specific only to the two cultures and the British West Indies. Thus the hypothesis is confirmed, and thirteen culture traits have been ruled out as possible explanatory factors (Otterbein 1964).

Another technique for testing hypotheses is the *cross-cultural survey*. This technique requires that the anthropologist examine a large number of cultures simultaneously. The cultures should be chosen to represent all parts of the world, and they all should be chosen before any of the data is collected. The cultures are analyzed in terms of the two concepts which are stated in the hypothesis. For analyzing the cultures a table, known as a 2 × 2 contingency table, is constructed. The following table, which has four empty cells designated by Roman numerals, is based upon the paradigm presented to illustrate the logic of hypothesis testing. As in the paradigm, A and B represent two culture traits in a hypothesis which has the form: if A, then B.

	B absent	B present
A present	I	II
A absent	III	IV

After the data on both culture traits have been collected for each culture in the study, cultures which have A present and B absent should be placed in cell I, cultures which have A present and B present should be placed in cell II, cultures which have A absent and B absent should be placed in cell III, and cultures which have A absent and B present should be placed in cell IV. The names of the cultures shoud actually be recorded in the appropriate cells of the table. It is the cultures in cell II which confirm the hypothesis (cultures in cell III serve to support the hypothesis by not disconfirming it). The cultures in cells I and IV disconfirm the hypothesis. Thus if the majority of cultures in the study are placed in cells II and III, the hypothesis is tentatively confirmed. However, if the majority of cultures are in cells I and IV, the hypothesis is disconfirmed. The number of cultures in each cell can be counted, and percentages can be computed. There are statistical tests which measure the degree of association between the two variables and which determine whether chance could have produced the distribution of cultures in the cells. Any introductory statistics textbook will provide the procedures and formulae to be used. A more technical discussion of the procedure is given in my article titled "Basic Steps in Conducting a Cross-Cultural Study" (Otterbein 1969).

The results of a number of cross-cultural studies have been discussed in the text. In one study reviewed (Otterbein and Otterbein 1965:1473) the following hypothesis was tested: patrilocal residence produces feuding. (The explanation for this relationship is described in the section dealing with feuding.) Fifty cultures, twenty-five with patrilocal residence and twenty-five with other types of residence, were examined for the presence of feuding. Twenty-two of the cultures had either feuding with compensation or feuding without compensation. The frequencies are shown in the following table. Thirty-three of the cultures confirm the hypothesis; seventeen

	Feuding absent	Feuding present
Patrilocal residence present	10	15
Patrilocal residence absent	18	7

disconfirm the hypothesis. Thus the hypothesis was tentatively confirmed. Appropriate statistical tests added further support (Otterbein and Otterbein 1965:1473).

This book has laid out in systematic fashion the conceptual order of anthropology. Many of the important topics and most of the basic concepts of cultural anthropology have been set forth in the preceding chapters. Mastery of this conceptual order is a prerequisite to obtaining competence as a professional anthropologist. Whether or not he has the time or desire to become a professional anthropologist and undertake fieldwork, the beginning student of anthropology can—with the aid of the questions and concepts in this book—simulate the methods of the ethnographer by analyzing the detailed descriptions of various customs or culture traits which are contained within ethnographies. This book presents a way of learning about a culture that is like that of the anthropologist's as he studies a people, organizes the data, and writes his ethnography. Thus the book has provided a framework for students to use in studying the way of life of a particular people, as that way of life is described by an anthropologist in an ethnography. This conceptual framework permeates every stage of the anthropological enterprise, from fieldwork, to writing the ethnography, to conducting comparative research.

STUDY GUIDE QUESTIONS

Aim of Chapter 7

At the turn of this century, when anthropology was in its infancy, ethnographers were primarily concerned with compiling long lists of culture traits of particular cultures. As the field of anthropology developed, however, it became more complex in both its goals and its methods.

Modern ethnographers are concerned with discovering the interrelationships among various culture traits; thus the development of means for the testing of anthropological knowledge has arisen. This chapter discusses a variety of the ways in which the anthropologist tests the data which he has collected.

Introduction
1. How and why do ethnographers use anthropological concepts?

Comparison of Cultures and Culture Traits
2. What is the anthropological value in using the data sheet and the Summary Analysis of Cultures which appear in the text?
3. Compare the study of cultures by the *diachronic* and *synchronic* methods.
4. In what ways can questions from the data sheet be used for cross-cultural surveys?

Linkages and Hypotheses
5. Explain what is meant by the statement "culture traits may be linked together."
6. What forms may culture trait lineages take?
7. Why is the study of lineages of importance to the anthropologist?
8. In an earlier chapter it was suggested that a culture may be analyzed into economic, political, social, and belief subsystems. Can you now give several examples illustrating the linkage of culture traits both within and among these subsystems? (answer not in text)

Testing of Hypotheses
9. Define the term *hypothesis*.
10. Identify the three forms which a hypothesis generally takes. Can you develop an example for each form? (answer not in text)
11. Explain the basic procedure for testing a hypothesis.
12. Discuss the value to the anthropologist of using *controlled comparisons* and *cross-cultural surveys*.

Conclusion
13. How useful have you found this text to be in terms of (1) basic topics and concepts covered; (2) as a tool for analytical culture studies; and (3) to your understanding of anthropology as a field of study? (answer not in text)

APPENDIX

DATA SHEET

Name of Culture _____ Ethnographer _____

Title of Ethnography _____

Location _____ Time _____

Name of Local Group _____ Language _____

1. What did the ethnographer study?
   1. a state
   2. a primitive culture
   3. a dependent native people
   4. a peasant community
   5. an ethnic group
   6. other: _____

2. Is more than one language spoken by the members of the culture?
   1. no
   2. yes, the culture is multilingual
   3. yes, a trade language or pidgin

3. In what type of physical environment is the culture located?
   1. desert
   2. tropical forest
   3. Mediterranean scrub forest
   4. temperate forest
   5. grassland
   6. boreal forest
   7. polar land
   8. mountains

4. When did the members of the culture enter the region where they are now living?
   1. original inhabitants
   2. ancient migrants (over 500 years ago)
   3. recent migrants (within past 500 years)

5. What subsistence technology is dominant (or codominant)?
   1. hunting and gathering
   2. animal husbandry
   3. horticulture
   4. agriculture
   5. Industrialism

6. What is the population density of the culture? _____

7. What is the division of labor?
    1. age and sex only
    2. part-time specialists
    3. full-time specialists

8. What house form is present?
    1. compounds
    2. single household dwellings
    3. multihousehold dwellings

9. What is the settlement pattern?
    1. nomadic
    2. seminomadic
    3. dispersed homesteads
    4. hamlets and/or compact villages
    5. towns and/or cities

10. What is the population of the largest settlement? _____

11. Which principle of exchange is dominant?
    1. balanced reciprocity
    2. generalized reciprocity
    3. redistribution
    4. market exchange

12. What types of stratification are present?
    1. absent
    2. castes
    3. classes
    4. slavery

13. What type of marital residence is practiced?
    1. ambilocal
    2. patrilocal
    3. matrilocal
    4. avunculocal
    5. neolocal
    6. virilocal
    7. uxorilocal
    8. commonlocal
    9. matri-patrilocal
    10. other: _____

14. What type of marriage is practiced?
    1. monogamy
    2. limited polygyny
    3. general polygyny
    4. polyandry

15. What types of households are present?
    1. independent nuclear family
    2. independent polygamous family
    3. extended family
    4. stem family

16. What types of descent groups are present?
    1. descent groups absent
    2. patrilineages
    3. matrilineages
    4. ambilineages
    5. unrestricted descent groups
    6. clans
    7. phratries
    8. moieties

17. Are kindreds present?
    1. absent
    2. present

18. What types of first cousin marriage are practiced?
    1. first cousin marriage absent
    2. matrilateral cross-cousin marriage
    3. patrilateral cross-cousin marriage
    4. parallel cousin marriage

19. What type of kinship terminology for first cousins is employed?
    1. Hawaiian
    2. Eskimo
    3. Sudanese
    4. Iroquois
    5. Crow
    6. Omaha

20. How many hierarchical levels are there in the political system? _____

21. What type of political leader is present?
    1. king

    2. dictator
    3. chief
    4. headman

22. What types of law are present?
    1. law absent
    2. law of private delicts (based upon restitutive sanctions)
    3. law of public delicts (based upon penal sanctions)

23. What type of military organization is present?
    1. a military organization is absent
    2. a military organization composed of professional warriors
    3. a military organization composed of both professional and nonprofessional warriors
    4. a military organization composed of nonprofessional warriors

24. Is feuding present?
    1. absent
    2. feuding with compensation
    3. feuding without compensation

25. If there is more than one political community within the culture, how frequently do they war with each other?
    1. continually
    2. frequently
    3. infrequently
    4. never

26. For what reasons does the military organization go to war?
    1. subjugation and tribute
    2. land
    3. plunder
    4. trophies and honors
    5. revenge
    6. defense

27. In what types of supernatural beings do the people believe?
    1. a high god
    2. superior gods
    3. ancestral spirits
    4. nonhuman spirits

28. What types of religious practitioners are present?
    1. absent

   2. shamans
   3. priests

29. What types of magic are practiced?
   1. homeopathic magic
   2. contagious magic

30. Is sorcery practiced?
   1. no
   2. yes

31. How long is the post-partum sex taboo?
   1. absent
   2. short
   3. long

32. What types of games are played?
   1. games absent
   2. physical skill
   3. physical skill and strategy
   4. physical skill and chance
   5. physical skill, strategy, and chance
   6. strategy
   7. strategy and chance
   8. chance

33. What types of initiation rites are present?
   1. initiation rites absent
   2. male initiation rites, step _____
   3. female initiation rites, step _____

34. What types of graphic art are present?
   1. abstract
   2. representational–expressionistic
   3. representational–naturalistic

CASE STUDY QUESTIONS FOR SEVEN CASES

James F. Downs, *The Navajo*

Forward and Introduction

1. Identify the particular topics and areas of focus which the author has chosen to study in this book. (iii–iv, 2)
2. Where is the Navajo Indian Reservation located, what is its size, and how many people are members of the Navajo tribe? (1)
3. Identify the several sources of information which the author has drawn upon for his study of the Navajo. (3)

Chapter 1

4. Who are the Navajo and where are they thought to have come from? (5–8)
5. Compare and contrast the culture traits of the Navajo Apache and their Apache neighbors. (9–11)
6. Contrast the influence which the Spanish had on the Navajo and the Pueblos. (11)
7. Describe the subsistence patterns of the Navajo. (12)
8. Discuss the importance of trade and raiding to the Navajo. (12–13)
9. How was Navajo leadership determined? (12)
10. Summarize the history and changes in Navajo culture from the 1860s to the 1930s. (14–16)

Chapter 2

11. What is the Navajo Reservation and how is it governed? (17–18)

12. Describe the land of the Navajo in terms of its sacred meaning to the tribe as well as its geographical appearance. (19–20)

Chapter 3
13. Explain why the trading post is important in Navajo life. (21)
14. Discuss the importance of the following four themes in Navajo culture —the female principle, individualism, the primacy of age, and debt payment. (22–26)

Chapter 4
15. How is the term *family* used by the Navajo, and what are the key functions of this social group? (28–30)
16. Contrast the definitions of the Navajo *outfit* and *homestead group*, and specify the main functions and social composition of the homestead group. (31–32)
17. What is a *clan*, and how does it operate in Navajo society? (36–37)
18. Compare and contrast the behavior among various Navajo kinsmen and in particular that involving parents, siblings, in-laws, mother's brother, and cross-cousins. (37–41)

Chapter 5
19. Describe the Navajo mobility patterns, specify the primary reasons for moving, and identify the variety of factors which determine the location of the Navajo homestead. (42–48)
20. Describe the various forms of the Navajo hogan and discuss its several functions in their cultural life. (48)

Chapter 6
21. Why did the Navajo, rather than other Apache groups or the Puebloan peoples, make herding their life goal? (49)
22. Compare and contrast the ownership of horses and dogs. (50–56)
23. Compare and contrast the work involved in herding sheep, goats, and cattle. (57–69)
24. Identify the tools used by the Navajo in dealing with sheep and goats, cattle, and horses. (69–80)
25. Contrast the past and present hunting behavior of the Navajo. (80–83)
26. How do Navajo children learn the techniques of herding and riding? (83–86)
27. Identify the similarities and differences in the ownership, benefits, and responsibilities of caring for sheep, goats, horses, and cattle. (86–88)
28. Describe the relationship of the Navajo family to their sheep herd. (89–90)

Chapter 7

29. Discuss the farming complex of the Navajo in terms of the crops grown, the techniques required, the division of labor, and the ownership of the crop. (91–93)
30. Contrast farming and herding in terms of the interpersonal relations which exist. (93–94)

Chapter 8

31. Describe the Navajo outlook on the universe. (95–96)
32. Identify some of the key Navajo mythological characters and specify their supposed functions. (96–98)
33. How does the daily life of the Navajo illustrate their belief system? (98–100)
34. Discuss the Navajo sing and singers in terms of structure and function. (101–102)
35. Identify the two key public ceremonies of the Navajo and compare and contrast them in terms of their functions, elaborateness, and participation requirements. (102–108)
36. How do the Navajo approach death and the dead? (108–109)
37. How does the Navajo belief in witches and witchcraft serve to give greater unity to the homestead group? (109–112)

Chapter 9

38. Identify the various items which represent wealth to the Navajo. (114–119)
39. Discuss the role of the trader and the trading post in terms of their social and economic importance in Navajo life. (115–116, 119–121)

Chapter 10

40. Identify the various individuals and groups who have held a position of political influence in Navajo society, and specify the basis for the political power in each case. (122–128)
41. Trace the development of Navajo political life from pre-reservation days up to the present. (122–128)
42. What do each of the following have to do with Navajo political behavior: the governmental chapter, the tribal police, the Grazing Committee, and the rodeo? (125–128)

Chapter 11

43. Identify the key cultural changes and sources of change which have occurred in Navajo society during the past few decades. (129–133)
44. What elements have allowed the Navajo to retain their distinct cultural identity in the face of social and cultural change? (130–131, 133)

James F. Downs, *Two Worlds of the Washo: An Indian Tribe of California and Nevada*

Chapter 1

1. Identify the particular topics and areas of focus which the author has chosen to study in this book. (2–3)
2. Discuss the several sources of information which the author has drawn upon for this study of the Washo. (3)
3. What does Lake Tahoe mean to the Washo? (1–2)
4. Identify at least five culture traits of the Washo which are presented in this chapter. (1–3)

Chapter 2

5. In what geographical areas did the Washo live? Which part of their territory was most strongly defended from the intrusion of neighboring tribes? (4–5; also review p. 1)
6. What was the population size and density of the Washo? (4)
7. Describe the settlement patterns of the Washo. What does this suggest concerning their "tribal" unity? (4–5)
8. With what other cultures did the Washo frequently come in contact? What was the nature of the contacts? (4–5)
9. What does the language of the Washo tell us about their possible past history? (6–7)

Chapter 3

10. Describe the land of the Washo in terms of life zones and animal and plant life. (8-11) Which three areas within their territory did they primarily draw upon for subsistence? (9–11)

Chapter 4

11. How did the environment act as a restrictive element on the culture of the Washo? (12)
12. Describe the fishing year and the fishing complex of the Washo. Include in your answer the techniques of fishing, the division of labor associated with fishing, and discuss how fishing was linked to social cooperation among the Washo. (13–17)
13. Describe the gathering year of the Washo. Who did the gathering? What plant foods were gathered? (17–22)
14. Identify and describe the elements which make up the piñon nut complex. What technology was used to gather the nuts. Discuss the importance of ritual to the piñon nut harvest. (20–26)
15. What was the importance of the "Big Time"? (22–24)

16. Discuss the Girl's Dance ceremony in terms of its social importance. (24–25)
17. What activities did the Washo engage in during the winter? (25)
18. Describe the hunting year of the Washo. Who did the hunting and how were the skills learned? (26)
19. How was the jack rabbit hunted? (27)
20. Discuss the manner in which the Washo hunted deer, and the rituals which were associated with the hunt. (27–30)
21. Describe the antelope complex. What was the role of the antelope shaman? How does this illustrate culture trait diffusion? (30–32)
22. Of what importance were the bear and sheep to the Washo? (32–33)
23. How did the Washo hunt birds and water fowl? (33–34)
24. What other animals, insects, and reptiles did the Washo take? (34–35)
25. Describe the culture of hunting, and its relationship to the coming of age of a young man. (35–36)
26. Describe Washo trade relations. (36–37)

Chapter 5

27. Discuss the structure and functions of the Washo family unit. (38–42)
28. How did the Washo take care of their aged? (41, 48) (also see 59)
29. Describe the birth complex, including the taboos and rituals associated with childbirth. (42–44)
30. What was the "bunch," and how did it operate? (44–46)
31. How did the Washo reckon kinship? What was the obligation of kinship? (46–48)
32. Describe the Washo moiety system. (49–50)
33. Why did individuals tend to stay in the area in which they grew up? (50)
34. Discuss Washo feuding and warfare and explain their relationship to Washo tribal unity. (51–54)

Chapter 6

35. Describe the shaman complex. (56–59)
36. How did ghosts enter into the Washo belief system? In what ways did the belief in ghosts influence their behavior? (59–60)
37. Discuss the manner in which the Washo handled death and disposal of the dead. (59–60)
38. What was the world view of the Washo? (creation, power figures, etc.) How might they have come to these conclusions? (60–64) (also review Chap. 1)

Chapter 7

39. Compare the Washo and Great Basin cultures to the typical California Indian culture in terms of the following:

a. life zones (65)
b. village structure (66)
c. population (66)
d. warfare (66, 68–69)
e. culture elaboration (66–67)
f. religious life (67, 69)
g. death complex (67, 69)
h. world renewal ceremonies (68)
i. horticulture (68)
j. subsistence patterns (69)
k. technology (70)

Chapter 8

40. Describe Washo contacts with the Spanish and the Americans. (73–74)
41. Compare and contrast the effects of ranching, farming, and mining on the traditional Washo culture. (74–76)
42. Compare how the whites and the Washo viewed each other. (77–78)
43. Define the term *acculturation*, and discuss Washo acculturation (pages 78–88) in terms of subsistence practices. (72, 78–88)
44. What was the social role of the Washo "captain"? (90–92)
45. Discuss the origin and function of the "Ghost Dance." (93–94)
46. Briefly review the relationship between the Washo and the federal government. (94–96)
47. What was happening to the Washo and their culture in the early 1900s? (97–98)

Chapter 9

48. What culture changes have affected the Washo during the twentieth century? (Include the following in your answer—leadership, the tribe, peyote, economics, residence, society, ceremonies, etc.) (99–110)
49. What does the future probably hold for the Washo culture? (110)

C. W. M. Hart and Arnold R. Pilling, *The Tiwi of North Australia*

Introduction

1. Trace the known and inferred history of the native Australian. What evidence suggests that they have long been an isolated cultural and breeding population? (1-7)
2. What was the population size and density of the Australians prior to the arrival of the Europeans? (5–6)
3. Discuss the diversification of Australian languages and the probable population size of the linguistic groups. (6)

4. List the key culture traits of the Australians which are given in this chapter. (1–7)
5. Identify the main study objectives of this ethnography. (7) (also see "About the Book" on p. v)

Chapter 1

6. Explain Tiwi cultural isolation in terms of their geographical location and behavior toward outsiders. (9–11)
7. What evidence is available which suggests that the Tiwi and mainland Australians maintained cultural isolation from one another? (9–11)
8. Compare and contrast the Tiwi orientation toward band and tribe. What is the size of each grouping? (11–13)
9. Describe the land of the Tiwi and discuss their conception of *territory*. (11–13)
10. Describe the Tiwi *household*. (13–14)
11. Analyze the customs of Tiwi marriage by betrothal. (14–18)
12. How did a man accumulate many wives? (14–21)
13. Explain the way in which widows were remarried in Tiwi society. (18–21)
14. Discuss the naming rules of the Tiwi and explain how the right of naming gave power and social position to Tiwi males. (21–25)
15. Define the terms *levirate*, *sororate*, and *cross-cousin* marriage and explain how each practice fits into the Tiwi culture pattern. (25–28)
16. Review the section "The Household: An Overview."

Chapter 2

17. Define the Tiwi concept of *band* and *household*. Why is the household the important social unit in Tiwi society? (31–33) (also review 11–13)
18. Discuss the Tiwi division of labor in terms of food production. (33–36)
19. How did the Tiwi view the sharing of food? (36)
20. Comment on the Tiwi ideal of marital faithfulness in contrast to social reality. How did husbands react toward unfaithful wives and their lovers? (37–40)
21. Identify the main joint activities which bring the Tiwi together. Analyze the opportunity of engaging in ceremonies on the basis of age, sex, social position, and household size. (40–46)
22. What types of artifacts were produced by the Tiwi? Who were the skilled craftsmen? How was the food supply and household size related to manufacturing and artistic production? (46–50)
23. Discuss the means by which Tiwi youths learned the skills required in adulthood. (49)
24. If you were a Tiwi man, what combination of economic factors would allow you to enjoy a life of wealth and social importance? (31–50)

Chapter 3

25. What formed the basis of Tiwi status and social power? (51–53)
26. Briefly outline the road to career success in Tiwi society. In contrast, what factors are associated with failure among the Tiwi? (54–63)
27. What anthropological value is attached to the in-depth study of families such as that of Ki-in-kumi? (63–65)
28. Discuss the importance of the information presented in Table III "The Food Production Units of Malau." What does it suggest concerning Tiwi career patterns? (65–66)
29. Analyze the politics of widow remarriage in terms of the political struggles engaged in and identify the individuals possessing the greatest amount of influence in this area. (67–71)
30. How did fathers use their daughters to forward their own social careers? (71–77)

Chapter 4

31. Why was elopement (wife stealing) rare among the Tiwi? (79–80)
32. Discuss the structure and function of the "duel." (80–83)
33. Describe Tiwi warfare. (83–87)
34. For what reasons did the Tiwi go to war? (83–87)
35. What reasons are given for the lack of positive magic in Tiwi culture? (87–88)
36. Define the term *pukimani*. When do the Tiwi engage in this form of behavior, and how do they feel about it? (88–90)
37. What was the Tiwi reaction to death? Why is mourning a time of both religious and political behavior? (90–93)
38. Describe the male initiation cycle. Why were the Tiwi able to conduct such prolonged initiation rites? (93–95)

Chapter 5

39. Briefly outline the period from 1600 to 1900 in terms of culture contact with the Tiwi. (97–100)
40. What was the nature of most contacts with outsiders? (97–100)
41. Identify the new objects which were thrust into the Tiwi world during the 1600–1900 period. How did the Tiwi react to these objects? (99)
42. Discuss the reasons behind the Tiwi decline in hostility during the 1900–1928 period. (100–103)
43. Compare and contrast the effects which the Japanese pearlers and Catholic missionaries had on the Tiwi culture. (100–103)

Chapter 6

44. How did the Tiwi life style change after 1930? What factors were responsible for the change? (105–107)

45. Discuss the influence of the Catholic church on traditional Tiwi marriage patterns. What general changes in marriage patterns occurred? (107–109)
46. Review the changes in Tiwi residence patterns. Have the functions of the household also changed? Explain your answer. (109–111)
47. Explain how the Tiwi changed from a patrilineal emphasis to basically a matrilineal organization. (111–112)
48. Discuss some of the new social roles which are being made available to the Tiwi. (112–113)

General Discussion Questions

49. Reflecting back over the entire ethnography, do you feel that contact with outsiders has been helpful or harmful to the Tiwi?
50. What do you think the future holds for the Tiwi people and culture?

E. Adamson Hoebel, *The Cheyennes: Indians of the Great Plains*

Introduction

1. What does the author set down as his major concern in writing *The Cheyennes*? On what time period does his research focus? (1–2)
2. Discuss the history of the Cheyennes for the last few hundred years. (1–3)
3. Where are the Cheyennes located today? What kind of work are they engaged in? Identify the elements of their past culture which have survived to today. (3)
4. Discuss the several sources of information which the author has drawn upon for his study of the Cheyennes. (3)
5. What additional culture traits can you identify from the Introduction? (1–3)

Chapter 1

6. Describe the structure and function of the Renewal of the Sacred Arrows ceremony. (6–11)
7. Analyze the structure and function of the Sun Dance. (11–16)
8. How does the Animal Dance differ from the above two dances? (16–17)
9. Regardless of the dance or dances performed in a particular year, what was the end psychological result for the Cheyennes? (17)

Chapter 2

10. Define the concept *social structure* and identify the most significant social groups among the Cheyennes. (20)

11. Describe Cheyenne courtship and marriage. (20–22)
12. What type of economic exchange occurs with a marriage? (21)
13. What form of residence is usually practiced after marriage? (22)
14. Describe the Cheyennes kindred structure. (22–30)
15. How would you characterize the psychological outlook of the Cheyenne male and female? (26)
16. Compare and contrast the behavior among various Cheyenne kinsmen and in particular that involving brother and sister, parents, grandparents, in-laws, brothers/sisters-in-law, etc. (26–29)
17. How does divorce take place? (27)
18. What is the place of the levirate and sororate in Cheyenne culture? (28)
19. Compare the importance of the kindred to the nuclear family for the Cheyennes. (30)
20. What is the composition and function of the *band* in Cheyenne society? (31–32)

Chapter 3
21. Discuss the structure and functions of the military societies. (33–36)

Chapter 4
22. What is the Council of Forty-four? its functions? (37, 46–47)
23. What is the ideal Cheyenne personality? (37)
24. Describe Cheyenne government. (46)
25. How are chiefs chosen? (37, 45–46) What characteristics should the chief have? (37–38)
26. Briefly review the origin myth of the Cheyennes Council of Forty-four. What are the main aspects of the myth? (38–44)

Chapter 5
27. Describe the aspects of Cheyenne law as associated with the following:
    a. focus (49, 53)
    b. juristic skill (50)
    c. greatest achievement (50)
    d. murder (51)
    e. worst aggressions (51, 53)
    f. purpose (51)
    g. public and private law (49)
28. How do the Cheyennes view suicide? (53)

Chapter 6
29. Describe the land of the Cheyennes. (58–59)

30. Contrast the economic activities of men and women. (59–68)
31. What implements does a woman use to do her tasks? (61–62)
32. Describe Cheyenne clothing. (63)
33. What methods do the men use to take game? (66–67)

Chapter 7

34. What is the place of warfare in Cheyenne life? (69–70)
35. Describe the types of warfare engaged in by the Cheyennes. (70–74)
36. What weapons and equipment did the Cheyennes use in warfare? (74–76)
37. Describe the structure and function of the Scalp Dance. (77–79)

Chapter 8

38. How does the Cheyenne view his universe? (82–85)
39. What types of spirits does the Cheyenne believe in? (83–87)
40. What is the Cheyennes attitude toward sex? (84)
41. Describe the role of the Cheyenne medicine man. (85)
42. Describe the reaction of the Cheyennes to death, i.e., what they do and how they feel. (86–88)
43. Contrast the two forms of Cheyenne healing, i.e., medical practices. (88–89)

Chapter 9

44. What additional factors can you add to the ideal Cheyennes personality over those given on page 37? (90)
45. Describe the Cheyenne birth complex and child-rearing practices. (90–93)
46. Discuss the Cheyennes attitude toward wealth. (94)
47. Describe male and female puberty rites. (94–95)
48. What are the social roles of the Contraries and the Halfmen-Half-women? Comment on each role from a psychological point of view. (96–97)
49. Review the author's summary on pages 97–99.

William Lessa, *Ulithi: A Micronesian Design for Living*

Chapter 1

1. Describe the Ulithi Atoll in terms of its location, geography, climate, soil and water conditions, and wildlife. (1–5)
2. Briefly outline the history of Ulithi contact with outsiders from the sixteenth through twentieth centuries. (5–8)

3. Discuss the people of Ulithi in terms of their probable origin, language, physical characteristics, and health. (8–10)
4. Identify the main demographic characteristics of the Ulithians. Discuss the anthropological value of collecting such information. (10–11)
5. What are the main psychological traits of the Ulithians? Can you suggest any reasons why anthropologists are frequently concerned with the psychological make-up of their subjects? (11–12)
6. Identify the main sources of food for the Ulithians. What techniques do they use in growing or collecting foods? (12–15)

Chapter 2

7. What social units compose the Ulithian community? (16)
8. Describe the physical structure of the village. (16–19)
9. Discuss the forms of social behavior which occur within and between Ulithian villages. (19–21)
10. Identify the functions of the nuclear family. In what ways does the Ulithian nuclear family vary from the norm? (21–22)
11. Compare the *ideal* and *real* forms of descent and residence patterns practiced by the Ulithi. (22)
12. How do kinship terms influence Ulithi behavior? Give several examples. (23–26)
13. Define the term *lineage* and identify the characteristics of Ulithi lineages. (26–29)
14. What are the duties of the lineage headman, or *mal*? The duties of the head female, or *fefel*? (27–28)
15. What is an Ulithian's *ieremat*? Identify several of its functions. (29–30)

Chapter 3

16. Discuss the structure and functions of the *village council* and *district*. (31–33)
17. What is the job of the Ulithi paramount chief (king), how is he chosen, and how is he supposed to act? (33–35)
18. Analyze the relationship which exists between the Ulithi and Yap in terms of political and social behavior. (35–39)

Chapter 4

19. Does law exist on the Ulithi Atoll? Explain your answer. (40–44)
20. Identify the informal pressures which encourage most people to behave in accordance with the social norms of Ulithi. (40–44, 46–47)
21. How does the leaf distraint, or *harmechung*, act to prevent severe conflicts and feuds? (45–47)
22. Analyze the Ulithian view of liability in terms of antisocial acts committed by children, psychotics, and animals. (47–48)

Chapter 5

23. What is ancestor worship? How does the belief in lineage ghosts affect Ulithian behavior? (49–54)
24. What reasons does the author give for the Ulithian practice of ancestor worship? (49–54)
25. How does the belief in demons serve to explain human misfortunes and the unknown, as well as to give the Ulithians some peace of mind? (54–55)
26. Identify the main gods of the sky and earth. Explain their importance to the Ulithians. (56–60)

Chapter 6

27. Describe Ulithi magic in terms of the desired ends, the techniques employed, and the observance of taboos. (61–64)
28. Contrast amateur and part-time magicians in terms of their knowledge and practices. (63–66)
29. What is the source of a magician's power? How does one attain this power? (64–66)
30. Identify the variety of events which are guarded over by the use of magic. (66–71)
31. Define the term *sorcery*. How does the belief in sorcery affect the behavior of the Ulithi? (71–74)
32. What is the purpose of an *amulet*? (73–74)
33. Analyze Ulithi magic in terms of the positive social effects which it provides. (74–76)

Chapter 7

34. What ideas do the Ulithi hold regarding decency and decorum? (78–80)
35. In what ways do the Ulithi project themselves in the area of erotic expression and stimulation? (81–86)
36. Discuss Ulithian sexuality in terms of sexual pleasure and guilt, sexual taboos, premarital and extramarital sexual activities, heterosexual and homosexual behavior, and sexual deviency. (86–92)
37. Do you consider that the Ulithians have a healthy or unhealthy approach to sex? Explain your answer. (86–92)

Chapter 8

38. Identify the five epochs in the lifetime of a Ulithian. (93)
39. How do the Ulithi feel about their children? (93–101)
40. Describe the Ulithi child-rearing practices. (93–101)
41. Discuss the socialization process of Ulithian children. (93–101)
42. The author suggests that the basic personality is determined during

childhood. Can you suggest what some of the personality traits of the Ulithian might be? (94–101)

43. Describe the male and female coming-of-age ceremonies. (101–104)
44. What changes in status and behavior are associated with attaining adulthood? (101–104)
45. Briefly outline Ulithian marriage and divorce practices. What are the main reasons underlying marriage and divorce? (104–108)
46. Describe the birth complex of the Ulithi. (105–107)
47. Compare and contrast the characteristics of the ideal man and woman in Ulithian society. Do these characteristics adequately describe the ideal American as well? If not, what changes in the description should be made? (109)
48. Describe the death complex of the Ulithi. (111–114)

R. Lincoln Keiser, *The Vice Lords: Warriors of the Streets*

Preface

1. Why did the author choose the Vice Lords as a subject group, and what is the major purpose of this book? (vii)
2. How did the author collect his data and on what time period does his research focus? (vii)

Chapter 1

3. Outline the historical development of the Vice Lord organization. (1–11)
4. Discuss the variety of ways in which the Vice Lords gained members. (2–5) (*also see* 20–21)
5. Define the term *institutionalization* and summarize the ways in which it took place in the Vice Lord organization. (6–7)

Chapter 2

6. Explain what a Vice Lord "branch" is and identify the three ways in which branches are formed. (12–13)
7. Discuss the basis behind interbranch alliances and conflicts. (13–14)
8. How did "feuds" among Vice Lord branches differ from "wars" between clubs? (14)
9. Briefly analyze the composition of the Vice Lord organization in terms of branches, sections, age groups, cliques, and offices. (12–18)
10. Describe the relationship between the Vice Lords and the Vice Ladies. (16–17)
11. Analyze the Vice Lord concept of "territory." Why did the author have difficulty in understanding what this spatial unit represented? (22–27)

Chapter 3

12. Compare and contrast the Vice Lord social groups which are involved in gang fights stemming from the following: accidental encounters, defense of territory, and offensive raids on enemy territory. (29–34)
13. What factors determine whether or not the Vice Lords will retaliate if a member is "jumped on"? (33–34)
14. Identify the typical group members who are involved in the following activities: hustling, wolf packing, pulling jive, attending club meetings, and shooting craps. (34–36)

Chapter 4

15. Discuss the social role which the author calls "Vice Lord–Vice Lord" in terms of activities engaged in and the ideal and real behavior patterns involved. (38–42)
16. Describe the "Street Man" social role. (42–44)
17. What forms of behavior are typically engaged in when a "Vice Lord–Enemy" encounter occurs? (44–45)
18. Explain what "situational leadership" is and give an example from the text. (45–48)
19. Analyze Vice Lord leadership in terms of the following: definition, power, context, and following. (45–48)

Chapter 5

20. Identify the four ideological sets which the author gives as representative of Vice Lord culture. (49)
21. Summarize the "heart" ideology of the Vice Lords. On what grounds does this qualify as culture? (49–52)
22. What is *soul*? How is it judged? Give several examples of "showing soul." (52–53)
23. Analyze wine drinking in terms of the ideology of "brotherhood." (53–54)
24. In what way does the "game" ideology represent the development of Vice Lord culture? (54–55)

Chapter 6

25. Analyze Cupid's autobiography in terms of the culture features which he describes. Look specifically for culture traits, social roles, social systems, ideology patterns, attitudes, etc., in his presentation. (56–80)

Conclusion

26. In what areas does the author feel that this ethnography is lacking? Do you feel that there are any additional areas which need further study? (81)

Hilda Kuper, *The Swazi: A South African Kingdom*

Introduction

1. Briefly describe the people who are to be studied in this ethnography. (1–6)
2. Identify the particular topics and areas of focus which the author has chosen to study in this book. On what time period does her research focus? (1–6)
3. Describe the anthropological approach and techniques used by the author. What problems was she confronted with while conducting her research? (4–6)
4. Describe the land of the Swazi. (2)
5. List the key culture traits of the Swazi which are given in this chapter. (1–6)

Chapter 1

6. Briefly trace the historical development of the Swazi over the past several centuries. (7–15)
7. What was the "paper conquest" of the Swazi? (9–13)

Chapter 2

8. On what basis are Swazi clans graded? How many levels of clans are there? What are the functions of clans? (16–18)
9. What are the rights of fatherhood and how are they acquired? (18)
10. Explain what a *homestead* is, and identify the key functions of this residential unit. (18–22)
11. Describe the physical layout and social organization of the typical Swazi homestead. (19–22)
12. How does the homestead of the king differ from that of the average Swazi headman? (19–22)
13. What factors guide a Swazi in selecting a location for a new homestead? (22)
14. Discuss the types of marriage engaged in by the Swazi. (22–25)
15. What is the function and importance of the *lobola* practice in Swazi culture? (18, 23–24)
16. Analyze the traditional Swazi marriage ceremony in terms of the intergroup relations which are involved. (24–25)
17. Review the following key relationships within the Swazi homestead: ego to patrilineal kinsmen; ego to matrilineal kinsmen; husband-wife; father-children; mother-children; sibling-sibling; ego to in-laws; grandparents-grandchildren. (25–28),

Chapter 3

18. Describe the relationship of the king to the queen mother. How does

this relationship function to minimize conflict and abuse of power? (30–31)

19. How do Swazi rulers maintain their position of authority? (31)
20. Who are the *tinsila* and what functions do they perform for the king? (31–32)
21. Briefly outline the structure and functions of the Swazi political structure from the king and queen mother to the homestead headman. (30–35)
22. How are chiefs and subjects supposed to behave toward each other? (34–36)
23. Describe the traditional legal system of the Swazi. In addition, identify the two primary forms of wrong doings and give examples of each as well as the punishments involved. (36–37)
24. Discuss in general terms the changes which have come about in the Swazi political structure as a result of British colonialization. (38–40)

Chapter 4

25. Discuss the "agricultural complex" of the Swazi in terms of its main characteristics. (41–43)
26. Describe and analyze the importance of the "cattle complex" for the Swazi. (43–45)
27. Compare and contrast the Swazi division of labor on the basis of sex, age, and pedigree. (45–46)
28. What forms of economic specialization have arisen among the Swazi? (46–48)
29. What is the Swazi outlook on wealth, begging, and sharing? How is witchcraft related to the accumulation of wealth? (48–49)

Chapter 5

30. Identify the eight recognized periods of individual growth from birth to "almost an ancestor." (50–52)
31. How and when are male age classes created? What are the functions of the age classes for the individual and the society? (52–56)
32. Describe Swazi warfare. (54–55)
33. Discuss the female age classes in terms of membership, formality, and functions. (57)

Chapter 6

34. What is an *ancestral cult*? How do the Swazi view their ancestors? (58–60)
35. In what ways does the ancestral cult influence the lives of the Swazi? (58–60)
36. Explain how forces of nature fit into the Swazi belief system. (61)

37. Compare and contrast the practices of the Swazi medicine men and diviners. (62–65)
38. Who practices Swazi witchcraft and sorcery and for what reasons? (65–67)
39. What has been the influence of Christianity on traditional Swazi religion? (67–68)
40. Identify the purposes served by the *Incwala* ceremony. (68–72)

Chapter 7

41. Discuss the advantages and disadvantages which are associated with the economic changes in modern Swaziland. (73–76)
42. Identify the sources of economic change in Swaziland and suggest what the economic future looks like for the Swazi. (73–76)
43. Describe the effects which internal migration plus the immigration of foreigners are having on Swazi society. Can you forecast possible future developments based on such movements? (76–78)
44. Discuss the key changes in the traditional Swazi political system. (78–82)
45. Identify both the main agents causing the political changes in Swaziland and the primary supporters of such change. (78–82)
46. What values do the Swazi place on formal education and health services? (82–83)
47. What do you think the future holds for the Swazi people and nation? (answer not in text)

GLOSSARY

GLOSSARY

ABSTRACT ART: Graphic art which depends upon formal elements, such as lines, triangles, diamonds, squares, and circles, with the pattern formed from these elements showing such properties as symmetry, repetition, balance, and rhythm.

AFFINAL: Relationship by marriage.

AGRICULTURE: The technology of farming or raising crops with the use of a plow and draft animal.

AMBILINEAGE: A descent group whose membership is based upon a rule of ambilineal descent. Also called RAMAGE.

AMBILINEAL DESCENT: A cultural principle which filiates an individual through either his father or mother to a descent group that consists of only some of his kinsmen.

AMBILOCAL: This form of marital residence pertains to the frequency of both patrilocal and matrilocal residence in a local group or in the culture as a whole. Ambilocal residence occurs if neither patrilocal nor matrilocal residence exceeds the other in actual frequency by a ratio of greater than two to one. Also called BILOCAL.

ANCESTRAL SPIRIT: A supernatural being who is a spirit of a dead person and who plays some role in the affairs of his living relatives.

ANCIENT MIGRANTS: A culture whose members entered the region over 500 years ago.

ANIMAL HUSBANDRY: The practice of breeding and raising domesticated animals.

ANIMISM: Belief in supernatural beings.

AVUNCULOCAL: Marital residence in which the newly wed couple lives with or near a maternal uncle of the groom; that is, the couple joins the household of the husband's mother's brother.

BALANCED RECIPROCITY: Direct exchange in which goods and services of commensurate worth are traded within a finite period.

BILINGUAL: Speaking only two languages. Cultures, as well as individuals, can be bilingual.

BOREAL FORESTS: Forests, consisting primarily of conifers, which are characterized by cold, swampy tracts, in which the temperature is usually below 50° Fahrenheit throughout the year and rainfall is slight.

CASTES: An ascriptive occupational role system found in preindustrial state systems. Caste members frequently have the same occupation.

CHANCE, GAME OF: A game in which the outcome is determined by guesses or by some uncontrolled artifact such as a die or a wheel.

CHIEF: A formal political leader with limited power.

CITIES: See TOWNS or CITIES.

CLAN: A descent group composed of two or more lineages. Clans are nonlocalized, are named, and are based upon the same rule of descent as the lineages which compose them.

CLASSES: An achieved occupational role system found in modern nations with industrialism. Class members typically have similar occupations.

COMMONLOCAL: Marital residence in which the newly wed couple establishes their household in the same local group in which the parental homes of both the man and the woman are located.

COMMUNITY: The maximal group of persons who normally reside together in face-to-face association. When a local group becomes so large that each adult member does not know every other member of the local group, it ceases to be a community.

COMPOUNDS: Several buildings, usually adjacent, occupied by a single household.

CONSANGUINEAL: Descended from a common ancestor.

CONTAGIOUS MAGIC: Based on the "law of contact or contagion"; that is, the principle of thought that things which have once been in contact with each other continue to act on each other at a distance after the physical contact has been severed. The practitioner of this type of magic infers that whatever he does to a material object will affect equally the person with whom the object was once in contact.

CONTROLLED COMPARISON: A research technique used to demonstrate that factors or culture traits not stated in the hypothesis are not influencing the culture trait which the anthropologist wishes to explain. The technique requires that two highly similar cultures be compared simultaneously.

CREOLE LANGUAGE: A language which is viewed by anthropologists and linguists as having originated in a pidgin. Unlike a pidgin, its vocabulary is extensive and its grammar and pronunciation assumes the more elaborate and regular patterns that all people seem to invest in their native languages.

CROSS-COUSIN: An individual's mother's brother's child or his father's sister's child. Cross-cousins are the children of a brother and a sister; that is, the children of opposite sex siblings.

CROSS-COUSIN MARRIAGE: The marriage of a man to either his mother's brother's daughter or to his father's sister's daughter.

CROSS-CULTURAL SURVEY: A research technique which tests hypotheses by comparing simultaneously information from a large number of cultures. Research reports emanating from this method are known as cross-cultural studies.

CROW KINSHIP TERMINOLOGY: Parallel cousins are referred to by the same terms used to refer to brother and sister; father's sister's son is referred to by the term used to refer to father, and father's sister's daughter is referred to by the term used to refer to father's sister; mother's brother's son is referred to as son or brother's son, and mother's brother's daughter is referred to as daughter or brother's daughter.

CULTURE: The way of life of a particular group of people. Culture includes everything that a group of people thinks, and says, and does, and makes.

CULTURE, A: A particular group of people who share the same way of life. Two criteria are used to distinguish one group of people from another: language distinctness and geographic separation.

CULTURE TRAIT: Although it has been defined as the smallest identifiable unit in a given culture, the term in actual practice is applied to any aspect of a people's way of life.

DEPENDENT NATIVE PEOPLE: A primitive culture which has been conquered and incorporated into a state.

DESCENT: A cultural principle whereby an individual is socially allocated to a specific group of consanguineal kinsmen.

DESCENT GROUP: A group of consanguineal kinsmen, membership in which is determined by a rule of descent. Descent groups are multigenerational, ancestor-oriented, and include in their membership only descendants of the ancestor.

DESERTS: Dry lands which are characterized by an annual rainfall of less than ten inches.

DICTATOR: An informal political leader with absolute power.

DIFFUSION: The geographic spread of culture traits. It occurs through the acceptance of culture traits from one culture by the members of another culture.

DISPERSED HOMESTEADS: Settlement pattern in which the members of the culture reside in permanent homesteads with fields between the homesteads. Homesteads may be from several hundred feet to several hundred yards from each other.

DISTRICT: A territorial unit within a political community which is composed of local groups.

DOUBLE DESCENT: Not a rule of descent per se, but a designation used by anthropologists for a culture which has both patrilineages and matrilineages (and hence both patrilineal and matrilineal descent are present).

EGO: The particular individual from which the relationships between kinsmen (including affinals) are reckoned. This technical term is often found on kinship diagrams.

ENDOGAMY: The practice of marrying a member of one's descent group. It is marriage within either a lineage, clan, or phratry. May also refer to marrying within one's caste or local group.

ENVIRONMENTAL POSSIBILISM: That point of view which looks upon the physical environment as providing both opportunities and limitations for the way of life of a people living in that environment.

ESKIMO KINSHIP TERMINOLOGY: Cousins are referred to by a distinctive term which is different from the terms used to refer to brother and sister.

ETHNIC GROUP: A people, usually residing in a large urban center, whose cultural background distinguishes them from their neighbors.

ETHNOGRAPHER: An anthropologist who conducts research on the culture of a particular people and who writes a descriptive account of their culture.

ETHNOGRAPHIC PRESENT: The period between the time when Europeans first discovered and observed a culture and the time when the culture's political communities were absorbed into a conquering nation.

ETHNOGRAPHY: A descriptive account of a people's culture. Usually an ethnography describes the culture of a particular local group within the culture.

ETHNOHISTORICAL STUDY: An ethnography which describes a people's culture as it was several centuries ago; since fieldwork is not conducted, information must be gleaned from historical documents and archaeological investigations.

ETHNOLOGY: The comparative study of cultures.

EXOGAMY: The practice of marrying an individual who is not a member of one's descent group. It is marriage outside either a lineage, clan, phratry, or moiety. May also refer to marrying outside of one's caste or local group. (Note: It is possible to have lineage exogamy and clan endogamy or to have lineage and clan exogamy and phratry endogamy.)

EXTENDED FAMILY HOUSEHOLD: A domestic group consisting of three (or possibly more) generations of related individuals, including one or more marital groups in each of two adjacent generations.

EXTERNAL WAR: Warfare between culturally different political communities; that is, political communities which are not within the same culture.

FEMALE HEADED HOUSEHOLD: *See* MOTHER-CHILD HOUSEHOLD.

FEUDING: Armed combat within a political community, in which, if a homicide occurs, the kin of the deceased take revenge through killing the offender or a close relative of his.

FEUDING WITH COMPENSATION: Feuding which occurs if the relatives of the deceased sometimes accept compensation in lieu of blood revenge.

FEUDING WITHOUT COMPENSATION: Feuding which occurs if the relatives of the deceased are expected to take revenge through killing the offender or any close relative of his. The possibility of paying compensation does not exist.

FILIATION: Allocation of an individual, through either his father or his mother, to a descent group. (The term may be used more generally to refer to the basis of membership in other than descent groups.)

FRATERNAL JOINT FAMILY HOUSEHOLD: A domestic group composed of two or more brothers, their wives, and their children.

FRATERNAL POLYANDRY: The marriage of one woman to two or more brothers at one time.

FULL-TIME SPECIALISTS: Specialists who devote nearly all of their working time to their specialized tasks.

GAME: An activity which is characterized by organized play, competition, two or more sides, criteria for determining the winner, and agreed-upon rules.

GENERAL POLYGYNY: This type of polygyny exists if the percentage of polygynous marital groups in a culture ranges between 20 and 100 percent of all marital groups.

GENERALIZED RECIPROCITY: Exchange in which goods and services flow predominantly one-way, with appreciation and respect flowing from the recipient.

GRAPHIC ART: Two-dimensional art which includes painting, drawing, tattooing, and embroidering.

GRASSLANDS: Savannas, prairies, and steppes are classified as grasslands. Grasslands are characterized by rich subsoil, covered with grasses.

GROUP MARRIAGE: The marriage of two or more men to two or more women at one time.

HAMLETS OR COMPACT VILLAGES: Settlement pattern in which the members of a culture reside in permanent homesteads or houses that are close to each other. The population of a hamlet or compact village is not more than 5,000 persons. In some cultures there are compact villages with outlying satellite hamlets.

HAWAIIAN KINSHIP TERMINOLOGY: All male cousins are referred to by the same term which an individual uses to refer to his brother and all female cousins are referred to by the same term which he uses to refer to his sister.

HEADMAN: An informal political leader with limited power.

HETEROGENEOUS POLITICAL COMMUNITY: The local groups composing the political community are from two or more cultures.

HIERARCHICAL LEVEL: An administrative level within a political community. Local groups constitute one level; if local groups are organized into districts this is another level; if districts are organized into provinces this is a third level.

HIGH GOD: A supernatural being who created the universe and/or is the ultimate governor of the universe.

HOMEOPATHIC MAGIC: Based on the "law of similarity"; that is, the principle of thought that like produces like, or that an effect resembles its cause. The practitioner of this type of magic infers that he can produce any effect he desires merely by imitating it.

HOMOGENEOUS POLITICAL COMMUNITY: The local groups composing the political community share the same culture.

HORTICULTURE: The technology of farming or raising crops with the use of hand tools, such as a digging stick or hoe.

HOUSEHOLD: One or more persons who live together in the same dwelling and cooperate in a variety of domestic affairs. Members of a household are said to share a common hearth.

HUNTING AND GATHERING: Includes fishing. Consists of techniques of obtaining natural foodstuffs—animal and vegetable—from the environment.

HYPOTHESIS: A statement of a precise relationship between that which is to be explained and that which is to do the explaining. The relationship is a linkage between two culture traits or two concepts which the anthropologist wishes to test in order to determine the validity of the relationship.

INDUSTRIALISM: The technology of producing foodstuffs and goods in large quantity at a manufacturing site.

INFORMANT: The individual from whom an anthropologist obtains his information about the way of life of that individual's culture.

INITIATION RITES: Ceremonies, supervised in part by the adults of a culture, which are mandatory for all adolescents of one sex only. If the ceremony is mandatory for all boys, it is a "male initiation rite"; if it is mandatory for all girls, it is a "female initiation rite."

INTERNAL WAR: Warfare between political communities within the same culture.

IROQUOIS KINSHIP TERMINOLOGY: Parallel cousins are referred to by the same terms used to refer to brother and sister, while cross-cousins are referred to by a different term.

KINDRED: An ego-oriented category of kinsmen. A kindred is a social category rather than a social group because its membership is composed of individuals who define their respective membership in the category in terms of their relationship to a particular individual.

KING: A formal political leader with absolute power.

KINSHIP TERMINOLOGY: The terms used to refer to relatives, either consanguineal or affinal.

LAW: A "case" is legal (that is, law exists) if three elements are present:
official authority, privileged force, and regularity.

LAW OF PRIVATE DELICTS: The settlement of a legal case by means of a restitutive sanction.

LAW OF PUBLIC DELICTS: The settlement of a legal case by means of a penal
sanction.

LEVIRATE: The marriage of a man to the widow of his deceased brother.

LIMITED POLYGYNY: This type of polygyny exists if the percentage of polygynous marital groups in a culture ranges between 1 and 19 percent of all
marital groups.

LINEAGE: Either a patrilineage or a matrilineage.

LINGUA FRANCA: *See* PIDGIN

LINKAGE: A presumed relationship between two culture traits.

LOCAL GROUP: A spatially distinguishable aggregate of people. It may be as
small as a single family or as large as a city.

MAGIC, THE PRACTICE OF: Involves three elements: the practitioner, the practical aim or end to be achieved, and the magical formula itself.

MAGICAL FORMULA: The traditional procedures followed by a practitioner (of
magic) in carrying out his aims. The formula usually consists of three
aspects: the things used—the instruments or medicines; the things done
—the rite; and, the things spoken—the spell.

MARITAL GROUP: The group formed when individual men and women enter into
one or more marital unions. Marital groups can be either monogamous,
polygynous, or polyandrous.

MARITAL RESIDENCE: The location where a couple lives.

MARITAL RESIDENCE RULE: An explicit cultural rule which states where a
couple should live.

MARRIAGE: A sexual relationship between a man and a woman who share a
common residence. Also called MARITAL UNION.

MARKET EXCHANGE: The exchange of goods and services according to the law
of supply and demand.

MATRILATERAL CROSS-COUSIN: A individual's mother's brother's child.

MATRILATERAL CROSS-COUSIN MARRIAGE: A marriage between a man and
his mother's brother's daughter.

MATRILINEAGE: A descent group whose membership is based upon a rule of
matrilineal descent.

MATRILINEAL DESCENT: A cultural principle which automatically filiates a child
at birth through his mother to a descent group that consists of all kinsmen
who are related to him through his female ancestors.

MATRILOCAL: Marital residence in which the groom leaves his parental home and lives with his bride, either in the house of her parents or in a dwelling nearby; that is, he joins the household of his wife's parents.

MATRI-PATRILOCAL: Marital residence in which there is an initial period, usually for a year or until the birth of the first child, of matrilocal residence followed by permanent patrilocal residence.

MAXIMAL TERRITORIAL UNIT: An alternate term for political community.

MEDITERRANEAN SCRUB FORESTS: Scrub forests characterized by broadleaf evergreens and oaks, with mild, rainy winters and hot, dry summers prevailing.

MILITARY ORGANIZATIONS: A particular type of social organization which engages in armed combat with other similar organizations in order to obtain certain goals.

MOIETY: One of two clans or two phratries. A culture has moieties if it has only two clans or two phratries, and every individual is a member of one or the other.

MONEY, GENERAL PURPOSE: Money which serves all three of the following functions: a medium of exchange, a standard of value, and a means of discharging obligations.

MONEY, LIMITED PURPOSE: Money which serves only one or two of the following functions: a medium of exchange, a standard of value, and a means of discharging obligations.

MONOGAMY: The marriage of one man to one woman.

MONOLINGUAL: Speaking only one language. Cultures, as well as individuals, can be monolingual.

MONOTHEISM: Belief in one god. If a high god is present, but superior gods are not, the religious belief system can be classified as monotheistic.

MOTHER-CHILD HOUSEHOLD: A domestic group composed of a woman, who is either unmarried, widowed, separated, or divorced, and her children, and sometimes her grandchildren. Also called FEMALE HEADED HOUSEHOLD.

MOUNTAINS: A land mass which rises conspicuously above the surrounding region. All seven of the other types of physical environments described in the text may be found on mountains if they are located near the equator.

MULTIHOUSEHOLD DWELLING: A house occupied by more than one household or domestic group. Each household resides within a separate section of the structure.

MULTILINEAL DESCENT: A cultural principle which automatically filiates a child at birth through his father and his mother (and through his four grandparents, and through his eight great grandparents, and so on) to every descent group founded by one of his ancestors.

MULTILINGUAL: Speaking two or more languages. Cultures, as well as individuals, can be multilingual.

NEOLOCAL: Marital residence in which the couple establishes a household independent of the location of the parental home of either partner. Specifically this means that they establish their household in a local group other than the local group or groups where their parental homes are located.

NOMADIC: Settlement pattern in which the members of the culture are grouped into small bands which shift from one section of their territory to another throughout the year.

NONHUMAN SPIRIT: A supernatural being who controls a particular individual or place. He may be a guardian spirit, an animal ancestor, or an animal-like creature who has both human and animal attributes.

NUCLEAR FAMILY HOUSEHOLD, INDEPENDENT: A domestic group consisting of a married couple and their children who occupy a dwelling which is not part of any other household.

OEDIPUS COMPLEX: A key term in psychoanalytic theory which refers to the sexual attraction of a boy for his mother, which results in feelings of rivalry and hostility towards his father.

OMAHA KINSHIP TERMINOLOGY: Parallel cousins are referred to by the same terms used to refer to brother and sister; father's sister's son is referred to by the term used to refer to son or sister's son, and father's sister's daughter is referred to by the term used to refer to daughter or sister's daughter; mother's brother's son is referred to as mother's brother and mother's brother's daughter is referred to as mother.

ORIGINAL INHABITANTS: A culture whose members have always been located in the same region or have been there over 2000 years.

PARALLEL COUSIN: An individual's father's brother's child or his mother's sister's child. Parallel cousins are the children of two brothers or two sisters; that is, the children of same sex siblings.

PARALLEL COUSIN MARRIAGE: The marriage of a man to his father's brother's daughter.

PART-TIME SPECIALISTS: Specialists who devote only a part of their time, either daily or seasonally, to their specialized task.

PATRILATERAL CROSS-COUSIN: An individual's father's sister's child.

PATRILATERAL CROSS-COUSIN MARRIAGE: A marriage between a man and his father's sister's daughter.

PATRILINEAGE: A descent group whose membership is based upon a rule of patrilineal descent.

PATRILINEAL DESCENT: A cultural principle which automatically filiates a child at birth through his father to a descent group that consists of all kinsmen who are related to him through his male ancestors.

PATRILOCAL: Marital residence in which the bride leaves her parental home and lives with her husband, either in the house of his parents or in a dwelling nearby; that is, she joins the household of her husband's parents.

PEASANT COMMUNITY: A local group of rural cultivators which is incorporated into a state—either a modern nation or a primitive state.

PENAL SANCTION: A punishment inflicted upon an individual who is responsible for violating a rule of conduct.

PHRATRY: A descent group composed of two or more clans. Like clans, phratries are nonlocalized, they are named, and they are based upon the same rule of descent as the clans which compose them.

PHYSICAL SKILL, GAME OF: A game in which the outcome is determined by the players' motor activities.

PIDGIN: A simplified language used to facilitate trade and other forms of inter-group relations.

PLASTIC ART: Three-dimensional art which includes sculpture and ceramics.

POLAR LANDS: Tundra, polar deserts, and permanent ice caps are classified as polar lands. Polar lands are characterized by little snowfall and no forests except for scrub vegetation and dwarf trees.

POLITICAL COMMUNITY: A group of people whose membership is defined in terms of occupancy of a common territory and who have an official with the special function of announcing group decisions—a function exercised at least once a year.

POLITICAL LEADER: The leader, official, or head of a political community.

POLITICAL SYSTEM: The organization of hierarchical levels within a political community.

POLYGYNY: The marriage of one man to two or more women at one time.

POLYGAMOUS FAMILY HOUSEHOLD, INDEPENDENT: A domestic group consisting of either a polgynous or a polyandrous marital group and its children who occupy a dwelling which is not part of any other household.

POLYGAMY: A term which refers to either polygyny or polyandry: multiple mates.

POLYGYNY: The marriage of one man to two or more women at one time.

POLYTHEISM: Belief in more than one god. If superior gods are present, with or without a high god being present, the religious belief system can be classified as polytheistic.

POPULATION DENSITY: The number of persons per square mile (or kilometers). The formula for computing is as follows:

$$\text{Population Density} = \frac{\text{Population Size}}{\text{Square Miles (or Kilometers)}}$$

POST-PARTUM SEX TABOO: A rule which prohibits a woman from having sexual intercourse with her husband, or any man, after she has given birth to a child. The post-partum sex taboo is considered "long" if it is observed for twelve months or more; it is considered "short" if it is observed for less than twelve months.

PRIEST: A religious practitioner who devotes nearly all of his time to serving as an intermediary, usually for his local group or political community. He is regarded as a full-time specialist.

PRIMITIVE CULTURE: A culture whose members speak an unwritten language.

PROVINCE: A territorial unit within a political community which is composed of districts.

RAMAGE: *See* AMBILINEAGE.

RECENT MIGRANTS: A culture whose members entered the region within the past 500 years.

RECIPROCITY: The exchange of goods and services between units of the same kind, such as individuals, households, kinship groups, or local groups. *See also* BALANCED RECIPROCITY and GENERALIZED RECIPROCITY.

REDISTRIBUTION: The systematic movement of goods and services toward an administrative center and their reallocation by the authorities.

RELIGIOUS PRACTITIONERS: Intermediaries between men and supernatural beings.

REPRESENTATIONAL-EXPRESSIONISTIC ART: Graphic art which depicts people, animals, or natural phenomena, but the treatment of the figures is exaggerated.

REPRESENTATIONAL-NATURALISTIC ART: Graphic art which depicts people, animals, or natural phenomena in a realistic manner.

RESTITUTIVE SANCTION: A requirement that one individual (the defendant) must make payment to the other individual (the plaintiff) in a dispute.

RITES OF INTENSIFICATION: Ceremonies or rituals which express group sentiments and beliefs and which are performed in the presence of most members of the local group.

RITES OF PASSAGE: Ceremonies signifying death and rebirth—the end of one stage of life and the beginning of another. They can be divided into three consecutive major phases: separation, transition, and incorporation. Rites of passage often occur at birth, initiation, marriage, and death.

SEMINOMADIC: Settlement pattern in which the members of the culture spend part of the year in permanent settlements and the remainder of the year migrating as bands.

SHAMAN: A religious practitioner who devotes part of his time to serving as an intermediary, usually for individuals. He is regarded as a part-time specialist.

SHIFTING CULTIVATION: A type of horticulture in which fields are allowed to return to fallow, either bush or jungle. Shifting cultivation is often found in conjunction with slash-and-burn agriculture.

SINGLE HOUSEHOLD DWELLING: A house occupied by a single household or domestic group. The house and household are coterminous.

SLASH-AND-BURN AGRICULTURE: A type of horticulture in which the vegetation removed from the land is heaped and burned, and the ash used to fertilize the soil. Slash-and-burn agriculture is often found in conjunction with shifting cultivation.

SLAVERY: A form of servility in which one individual has legal rights in another, if these rights are held to the exclusion of other persons and are not derived from either contractual or kinship obligations.

SORCERY: The use of magic, supernatural beings, or other supernatural powers to deliberately attempt to harm or destroy another person. The individual who practices sorcery is known as a sorcerer.

SORORAL POLYGYNY: The marriage of one man to two or more sisters at one time.

SORORATE: The marriage of a man to the sister of his deceased wife.

SPECIALISTS: Members of a culture who perform a task which is not performed by most members of that culture. The products of this task, or the performance of this task itself, may be sold or traded to other members of the culture for goods and services.

SPEECH COMMUNITY: A local group whose members communicate with each other through at least one language and by means of a mutually understood set of rules for the conduct and interpretation of speech.

STATE: A political community headed by a king or dictator.

STEM FAMILY HOUSEHOLD: A small extended family household consisting of three generations of related individuals, including only one marital group in each of two adjacent generations.

STRATEGY, GAME OF: A game in which the outcome is determined by rational choices among possible courses of action.

STRATIFICATION: An arrangement of layers or strata, one on top of the other in a hierarchical manner. In the social sciences the hierarchical order is created by noticeable differences in attributes of different groups of people.

SUBSISTENCE TECHNOLOGY: An activity which people perform to exploit their physical environment in order to gain a livelihood.

SUDANESE KINSHIP TERMINOLOGY: Each category of cousin is referred to by a distinct term.

SUPERIOR GOD: A supernatural being who controls all phases of one or more, but not all, human activities.

SUPERNATURAL BEINGS: Beings or spirits which belong to the realm of the supernatural. They are believed to be real (by members of the culture); they have personal identities, and they often have names.

TEMPERATE FORESTS: Forests which are characterized by broadleaf and coniferous trees that obtain their growth from plentiful rain.

TOWNS OR CITIES: Settlement pattern in which the members of a culture reside in permanent homesteads or houses which are close to each other. The population of a town or city is over 5000 persons. In some cultures there are cities with outlying satellite towns.

TRADE LANGUAGE: See PIDGIN.

TROPICAL FORESTS: Both rain forests and semideciduous forests are classified as tropical forests. Rain forests have heavy daily rainfall which results in dense vegetation. Semideciduous forests have a dry season in which many trees lose their leaves.

TROUBLE CASES: Conflicts or disputes between individual members of the same or of different local groups which create ruptures in intra-political community relationships.

UNRESTRICTED DESCENT GROUP: A descent group whose membership is based upon a rule of multilineal descent.

UXORILOCAL: Marital residence in which the couple establishes their household in a local group where the woman's parental home is located, but not the man's parental home.

VILLAGES, COMPACT: *See* HAMLETS or COMPACT VILLAGES.

VIRILOCAL: Marital residence in which the couple establishes their household in a local group in which the man's parental home is located, but not the woman's parental home.

WAR, CAUSES OF: The causes of war—that is, the reasons that military organizations go to war—include subjugation and tribute, land, plunder, trophies and honors, revenge, and defense.

WARFARE: Armed combat between political communities. The frequency of warfare can be classified as either "continual," "frequent," "infrequent," or "never." *See also* EXTERNAL WAR and INTERNAL WAR.

WARRIORS, NONPROFESSIONAL: Military personnel who have not had intensive training in the art of war.

WARRIORS, PROFESSIONAL: Military personnel who devote a substantial part of their time during their early adulthood to intensive training, which may involve not only practice in the use of weapons but also practice in performing maneuvers. They may be members of age-grades, military societies, or standing armies.

WITCHCRAFT: Used synonymously with the term SORCERY in this book.

REFERENCES

REFERENCES

Adams, Richard N., 1960, "An Inquiry into the Nature of the Family," in *Essays in the Science of Culture*, ed. G. E. Dole and R. L. Carneiro. New York: Thomas Y. Crowell Company, pp. 30–49.

Appell, G. N., 1967, "Observational Procedures for Identifying Kindreds: Social Isolates among the Rungus of Borneo," *Southwestern Journal of Anthropology* 23:192–207.

Baily, F. G., 1969, *Stratagems and Spoils: A Social Anthropology of Politics.* New York: Schocken Books, Inc.

Bartholomew, George A., Jr., and Joseph B. Birdsell, 1953, "Ecology and the Proto-hominids," *American Anthropologist* 55:481–498.

Barry, Herbert, III, 1957, "Relationships between Child Training and the Pictorial Arts," *The Journal of Abnormal and Social Psychology* 54:380–383.

Beals, Alan R. (with George and Louise Spindler), 1967, *Culture in Process.* New York: Holt, Rinehart and Winston (2d ed., 1973).

Befu, Harumi, and Leonard Plotnicov, 1962, "Types of Corporate Unilineal Descent Groups," *American Anthropologist* 64:313–327.

Bell, Norman W., and Ezra F. Vogel, 1960, "Introductory Essay," in *A Modern Introduction to the Family.* New York: The Free Press, pp. 1–33.

Boas, Franz, 1955, *Primitive Art.* New York: Dover Publications, Inc. Originally published 1927.

Bohannan, Paul, 1963, *Social Anthropology.* New York: Holt, Rinehart and Winston.

Brown, Judith, 1963, "A Cross-Cultural Study of Female Initiation Rites," *American Anthropologist* 65:837–853.

Buchler, Ira R., and Henry A. Selby, 1968, *Kinship and Social Organization: An Introduction to Theory and Method.* New York: The Macmillan Company.

Burling, Robbins, 1973, *English in Black and White.* New York: Holt, Rinehart and Winston.

Campbell, Donald T., and Robert A. LeVine, 1961, "A Proposal for Cooperative Cross-Cultural Research on Ethnocentrism," *Journal of Conflict Resolution* 5:82–108.

Carneiro, Robert L., 1970, "A Theory of the Origin of the State," *Science* 169 (3947):733–738.

Carrasco, Pedro, 1963, "The Locality Referent in Residence Terms," *American Anthropologist* 65:133–134.

Chagnon, Napoleon A., 1966, "Yąnomanö Warfare, Social Organization and Marriage Alliances." Ph.D. dissertation, The University of Michigan.

———, 1968, *Yąnomamö: The Fierce People.* New York: Holt, Rinehart and Winston (2d ed: 1977).

Chapple, Eliot, and C. S. Coon, 1942, *Principles of Anthropology.* New York: Holt, Rinehart and Winston.

Churchill, Winston S., 1956–1958, *A History of the English Speaking Peoples.* 4 vols. New York: Dodd, Mead & Company.

Crowley, Daniel J., 1966, *I Could Talk Old-Story Good: Creativity in Bahamian Folklore.* Folklore Studies No. 17. Berkeley and Los Angeles: University of California Press.

Divale, William T., 1974a, "Migration, External Warfare, and Matrilocal Residence," *Behavior Science Research* 9:75–133.

———, 1974b, "The Causes of Matrilocal Residence: A Cross-Ethnohistorical Survey." Ph.D. dissertation, SUNY at Buffalo.

Edgerton, Robert B., and L. L. Langness, 1974, *Methods and Styles in the Study of Culture.* San Francisco: Chandler and Sharp Publishers.

Ember, Melvin, 1963, "The Relationship Between Economic and Political Development in Nonindustrialized Societies," *Ethnology* 2:228–248.

Erickson, Pamela, and Stephen Beckerman, 1975, "Population Determinants in the Andaman Islands," *Mankind* 10:105–107.

Firth, Raymond, 1958, *Human Types: An Introduction to Social Anthropology.* New York: Mentor Book.

Fischer, John L., 1961, "Art Styles as Cultural Cognitive Maps," *American Anthropologist* 63:79–93.

Fogelson, Raymond D., 1975, "An Analysis of Cherokee Sorcery and Witchcraft," in *Four Centuries of Southern Indians,* ed. Charles Hudson. Athens: The University of Georgia Press, pp. 113–131.

Fortes, Meyer, 1958, "Introduction," in *The Developmental Cycle in Domestic Groups,* ed. Jack Goody. Cambridge Papers in Social Anthropology No. 1. Cambridge: Cambridge University Press, pp. 1–14.

———, and E. E. Evans-Pritchard, 1940, "Introduction," *African Political Systems,* ed. Fortes and Evans-Pritchard. London: Oxford University Press, pp. 1–23.

Fox, Robin, 1967, *Kinship and Marriage.* Baltimore: Penguin Books, Inc.

Frazer, James G., 1911, *The Golden Bough: A Study in Magic and Religion,* Vol. 1. London: Macmillan & Co., Ltd.

Freeman, J. D., 1961, "On the Concept of the Kindred," in *The Journal of the Royal Anthropological Institute of Great Britain and Ireland* 91:192–220.

Fried, Morton H., 1952, "Land Tenure, Geography and Ecology in the Contact of Cultures," *American Journal of Economics and Sociology* 11: 391–412.

———, 1967, *The Evolution of Political Society: An Essay in Political Anthropology.* New York: Random House, Inc.

Gamst, Frederick C., 1969, *The Qemant: A Pagan-Hebraic Peasantry of Ethiopia.* New York: Holt, Rinehart and Winston.

Goodenough, Ward H., 1970, *Description and Comparison in Cultural Anthropology.* Chicago: Aldine Publishing Company.

Gough, Kathleen, 1959, "The Nayars and the Definition of Marriage," *The Journal of the Royal Anthropological Institute of Great Britain and Ireland* 89:23–34.

Gould, Harold A., 1971, *Caste and Class: a Comparative View.* Reading, Mass.: Addison- Wesley Publishing Company, Module 11.

Griffiths, Donald F., n.d., Unpublished research on house form.

Gumperz, John J., 1969, "Communication in Multilingual Societies," in *Cognitive Anthropology,* ed. Stephen A. Tyler. New York: Holt, Rinehart and Winston, pp. 435–449.

———, 1972, "Introduction," in *Directions in Sociolinguistics: The Ethnography of Communication,* ed. J. J. Gumperz and D. Hymes. New York: Holt, Rinehart and Winston, pp. 1–25.

———, and Dell Hymes, eds., 1972. *Directions in Sociolinguistics: The Ethnography of Communication.* New York: Holt, Rinehart and Winston.

Harris, Marvin, 1975, *Culture, People, Nature: An Introduction to General Anthropology,* 2d ed. New York: Thomas Y. Crowell Company.

Hayes, Rose Oldfield, 1975, "An Ethnographic and Demographic Study of the Presqu'ile: The Adaptation of a Social Group in a Pluralistic Society." Unpublished doctoral dissertation, SUNY at Buffalo.

Hays, H. R., 1958, *From Ape to Angel: An Informal History of Social Anthropology.* New York: Capricorn Books.

Herskovits, Melville J., 1948, *Man and His Works: The Science of Cultural Anthropology.* New York: Alfred A. Knopf.

Hoebel, E. Adamson, 1954, *The Law of Primitive Man: A Study in Comparative Legal Dynamics.* Cambridge: Harvard University Press.

Holmes, Lowell D., 1971, *Anthropology: An Introduction,* 2d ed. New York: The Ronald Press Company.

Homans, George C., and David M. Schneider, 1955, *Marriage: Authority, and Final Causes: A Study of Unilateral Cross-Cousin Marriage.* New York: The Free Press.

Honigmann, John J., 1959, *The World of Man.* New York: Harper & Row, Publishers.

Hymes, Dell, 1972, "Models of the Interaction of Language and Social Life," in *Directions in Sociolinguistics: The Ethnography of Communication,* ed. J. J. Gumperz and D. Hymes. New York: Holt, Rinehart and Winston, pp. 35–71.

Kang, Gay Elizabeth, 1976a, "Conflicting Loyalties Theory: A Cross-Cultural Test," *Ethnology* 15:201–210.

———, 1976b, "Solidarity Theory: A Cross-Cultural Test of the Relationships among Exogamy, Cross-Allegiance, Peace, and Survival Value." Ph.D. dissertation, SUNY at Buffalo.

Kasdan, Leonard, 1970, "Introduction," in *Migration and Anthropology*, ed. Robert F. Spencer. Proceedings of the 1970 Annual Spring Meeeting of the American Ethnological Society. Seattle: University of Washington Press, pp. 1–6.

LaFlamme, Alan G., 1976, "An Annotated, Ethnographic Bibliography of the Bahama Islands," *Behavior Science Research* 11:57–66.

Lambert, William W., Leigh M. Triandis, and Margery Wolf, 1959, "Some Correlates of Beliefs in the Malevolence and Benevolence of Supernatural Beings: A Cross-Societal Study," *The Journal of Abnormal and Social Psychology* 58:162–169.

Lessa, William A., and Evon Z. Vogt, 1958, *Reader in Comparative Religion: An Anthropological Approach.* Evanston, Ill.: Row, Peterson & Company.

Lévi-Strauss, Claude, 1969, *The Elementary Structures of Kinship* (Les Structures elementaires de la parente), trans. of revised ed. by J. H. Bell, J. R. von Sturmer, R. Needham. Boston: Beacon Press. Originally published 1949.

Linton, Ralph, 1936, *The Study of Man: An Introduction.* New York: Appleton-Century-Crofts.

———, 1942, "Age and Sex Categories," *American Sociological Review* 7:589–603.

Malinowski, Bronislaw, 1930, "Parenthood—The Basis of Social Structure," in *The New Generation*, ed. V. F. Calverton and S. D. Schmalhausen. New York: The Citadel Press, Inc., pp. 113–168.

———, 1960, *A Scientific Theory of Culture and Other Essays.* New York: Oxford University Press.

Mandelbaum, David G., 1963, "A Design for an Anthropology Curriculum," in *The Teaching of Anthropology*, ed. D. G. Mandelbaum, G. W. Lasker, and E. M. Albert. American Anthropological Association Memoir 94:49–64.

———, Gabriel W. Lasker, and Ethel M. Albert, eds., 1963, *The Teaching of Anthropology.* American Anthropological Association Memoir 94.

Mead, Margaret, 1964, "Warfare Is Only an Invention—Not a Biological Necessity," in *War: Studies from Psychology, Sociology, Anthropology*, ed. L. Bramson and G. Goethals. New York: Basic Books, Inc., pp. 269–274.

———, and Rhoda Métraux, eds. 1953, *The Study of Culture at a Distance.* Chicago: The University of Chicago Press.

Mitchell, William E., 1963, "Theoretical Problems in the Concept of Kindred," *American Anthropologist* 65:343–354.

Moore, Harry E., 1964, "Slavery," in *A Dictionary of the Social Sciences*, ed. Julius Gould and William L. Kolb. New York: The Free Press, p. 642.

Morgan, Lewis H., 1871, *Systems of Consanquinity and Affinity of the Human Family.* Washington, D.C.: Smithsonian Institution Contributions to Knowledge.

———, 1962, *League of the Iroquois.* New York: Corinth Books. Originally published 1851.

Murdock, George P., 1934, *Our Primitive Contemporaries.* New York: The MacMillan Company.

———, 1944, "The Common Denominator of Cultures," In *The Science of Man in the World Crisis,* ed. Ralph Linton. New York: Columbia University Press, pp. 123–142.

———, 1949, *Social Structure.* New York: The Macmillan Company.

———, 1957, "World Ethnographic Sample," *American Anthropologist* 59:664–687.

———, 1967, "Ethnographic Atlas: A Summary," *Ethnology* 6:109–236.

———, *et al.*, 1961, *Outline of Cultural Materials.* New Haven: Human Relations Area Files Press.

Naroll, Raoul, 1956, "A Preliminary Index of Social Development," *American Anthropologist* 58:687–715.

———, 1964, "On Ethnic Unit Classification," *Current Anthropology* 5:283–312.

———, 1966, "Does Military Deterrence Deter?" *Trans-action* 3(2):14–20.

———, 1968, "Some Thoughts on Comparative Method in Cultural Anthropology," in *Methodology in Social Research*, ed. H. M. and A. B. Blalock. New York: McGraw-Hill, Inc., pp. 236–277.

Needham, Rodney, 1960, *Structure and Sentiment: A Test Case in Social Anthropology.* Chicago: The University of Chicago Press.

Noland, Soraya Q., 1976, "Ethnography of an Iranian Village." Ph.D. dissertation, SUNY at Buffalo.

Oliver, Symmes C., 1962, *Ecology and Cultural Continuity as Contributing Factors in the Social Organization of the Plains Indians.* University of California Publications in American Archaeology and Ethnology, vol. 48, no. 1. Berkeley and Los Angeles: University of California Press.

Otterbein, Charlotte Swanson, and Keith F. Otterbein, 1973. "Believers and Beaters: A Case Study of Supernatural Beliefs and Child Rearing in the Bahama Islands," *American Anthropologist* 75:1670–1681.

Otterbein, Keith F., 1963, "Marquesan Polyandry," *Marriage and Family Living* 25:155–159.

———, 1964, "A Comparison of the Land Tenure Systems of the Bahamas, Jamaica, and Barbados," *International Archives of Ethnography* 50:31–42.

———, 1965*a*, "Conflict and Communication: The Social Matrix of Obeah," *Kansas Journal of Sociology* 3:112–128.

———, 1965*b*, "Caribbean Family Organization: A Comparative Analysis," *American Anthropologist* 67:66–79.

———, 1966, *The Andros Islanders: A Study of Family Organization in the Bahamas.* Lawrence: University of Kansas Press.

———, 1967, "The Evolution of Zulu Warfare," in *Law and Warfare*, ed. Paul Bohannan. New York: Natural History Press, pp. 345–349.

———, 1968*a*, "Internal War: A Cross-Cultural Study," *American Anthropologist* 70:277–289.

———, 1968*b*, "Cross-Cultural Studies of Armed Combat," *Studies in International Conflict*, Research Monograph No. 1, Buffalo Studies 4(1):91–109.

———, 1969, "Basic Steps in Conducting a Cross-Cultural Study," *Behavioral Science Notes* 4:221–236.

———, 1970*a*, *The Evolution of War: A Cross-Cultural Study.* New Haven, Conn. Human Relations Area Files Press.

———, 1970*b*, "The Developmental Cycle of the Andros Household: A Diachronic Analysis," *American Anthropologist* 72:1412–1419.

———, 1972, "A Typology of Evolutionary Theories," *Behavior Science Notes* 7:237–242.

————, 1975, *Changing House Types in Long Bay Cays: The Evolution of Folk Housing in an Out Island Bahamian Community*. HRAFlex Book No. SW1–001. New Haven, Conn.: Human Relations Area Files Press.

————, n.d., "Changes in the Composition of the Andros Household: 1961–1975." Unpublished manuscript.

————, and Charlotte Swanson Otterbein, 1965, "An Eye for an Eye, a Tooth for a Tooth: A Cross-Cultural Study of Feuding," *American Anthropologist* 67:1470–1482.

Parsons, Talcott, and Robert F. Bales, 1955, *Family, Socialization and Interaction Process*. New York: The Free Press.

Polanyi, Karl, 1957, "The Economy as Instituted Process," in *Trade and Market in the Early Empires*, ed. K. Polanyi, C. M. Arensberg, and H. W. Pearson. New York: The Free Press, pp. 243–270.

Pospisil, Leopold, 1958, *Kapauku Papuans and their Law*, Yale University Publications in Anthropology 54.

————, 1963, *The Kapauku Papuans of West New Guinea*. New York: Holt, Rinehart and Winston, Inc.

Radcliffe-Brown, Alfred R., 1922, *The Andaman Islanders*. Cambridge: Cambridge University Press.

————, 1952, *Structure and Function in Primitive Society*. New York: The Free Press.

Rapoport, Amos, 1969, *House Form and Culture*. Englewood Cliffs, N.J.: Prentice-Hall, Inc.

Redfield, Robert, 1930, *Tepoztlán: A Mexican Village*. Chicago: University of Chicago Press.

————, 1952, "The Primitive World View," *Proceedings of the American Philosophical Society* 96(1):30–36.

Rivers, William H. R., 1924, *Social Organization*. New York: Alfred A. Knopf.

Roberts, John M., and Brian Sutton-Smith, 1962, "Child Training and Game Involvement," *Ethnology* 1:166–185.

————, Malcolm J. Arth, and Robert R. Bush, 1959, "Games in Culture," *American Anthropologist* 61:597–605.

Sahlins, Marshall D., 1960, "Evolution: Specific and General," in *Evolution and Culture*, ed. Marshall D. Sahlins and Elman R. Service. Ann Arbor: University of Michigan Press, pp. 12–44.

————, 1964, "Culture and Environment," in *Horizons of Anthropology*, ed. Sol Tax. Chicago: Aldine Publishing Company, pp. 132–147.

————, 1965, "On the Sociology of Primitive Exchange," in *The Relevance of Models for Social Anthropology*, ed. Michael Banton. A. S. A. Monographs 1, London: Tavistock, pp. 139–236.

Saucier, Jean-Francois, 1972, "Correlates of the Long Postpartum Taboo: A Cross-Cultural Study," *Current Anthropology* 13:238–249.

Schapera, Issac, 1956, *Government and Politics in Tribal Societies*. London: C. A. Watts & Co., Ltd.

Schusky, Ernest L., 1972, *Manual for Kinship Analysis,* 2d ed. New York: Holt, Rinehart and Winston.

Secoy, Frank R., 1953, "Changing Military Patterns on the Great Plains," *American Ethnological Society Monograph* 21.

Service, Elman R., 1962, *Primitive Social Organization: An Evolutionary Perspective.* New York: Random House, Inc.

Sipes, Richard G., 1973, "War, Sports and Aggression: An Empirical Test of Two Rival Theories," *American Anthropologist* 75:64–86.

Solien, Nancie L., 1960, "Household and Family in the Caribbean: Some Definitions and Concepts," *Social and Economic Studies* 9:101–106.

Southwick, Charles H., 1972, *Aggression among Nonhuman Primates.* Reading, Mass.: Addison-Wesley Publishing Company, Module 23.

Spiro, Melford E., 1968, "Causes, Functions, and Cross-Cousin Marriage: An Essay in Anthropological Explanation," in *Theory in Anthropology,* ed. Robert A. Manners and David Kaplan. Chicago: Aldine Publishing Company, pp. 105–115.

Stephens, William N., 1962, *The Oedipus Complex: Cross-Cultural Evidence.* New York: The Free Press.

Stevenson, Robert F., 1968, *Population and Political Systems in Tropical Africa.* New York: Columbia University Press.

Stocking, George W., Jr., 1966, "Franz Boas and the Culture Concept in Historical Perspective," *American Anthropologist* 68:867–882.

Swanson, Guy E., 1960, *The Birth of the Gods.* Ann Arbor: The University of Michigan Press.

Titiev, Mischa, 1943, "The Influence of Common Residence on the Unilateral Classification of Kindred," *American Anthropologist* 45:511–530.

Tumin, Melvin M., 1973, *Patterns of Society: Identities, Roles, Resources.* Boston: Little, Brown and Company.

Tylor, Edward B., 1879, "On the Game of Patolli in Ancient Mexico, and its Probable Asiatic Origin," *The Journal of the Royal Anthropological Institute of Great Britain and Ireland* 13:116–131. (Bobbs-Merrill Reprint A-392)

———, 1888, "On a Method of Investigating the Development of Institutions; Applied to Laws of Marriage and Descent," *The Journal of the Royal Anthropological Institute of Great Britain and Ireland* 18:245–270. (Bobbs-Merrill Reprint A-391)

———, 1958, *Primitive Culture.* New York: Harper Torchbooks. Originally published 1871.

van Gennep, Arnold, 1960, *The Rites of Passage.* Chicago: The University of Chicago Press. Originally published 1909.

van Velzen, H. U. E. Thoden, and W. van Wetering, 1960, "Residence, Power Groups and Intra–societal Aggression," *International Archives of Ethnography* 49:169–200.

Vayda, Andrew P., 1961, "Expansion and Warfare among Swidden Agriculturalists," *American Anthropologist* 63:346–358.

———, 1968, "Hypotheses about Functions of War," in *War: The Anthropology of Armed Conflict and Aggression,* ed. M. Fried, M. Harris, and R. Murphy. Garden City, N.Y.: Natural History Press, pp. 85–91.

————, 1970, "Maoris and Muskets in New Zealand: Disruption of a War System," *Political Science Quarterly* 85:560–584.

————, and Roy A. Rappaport, 1968, "Ecology: Cultural and Non-Cultural," in *Introduction to Cultural Anthropology*, ed. James Clifton. Boston: Houghton Mifflin Company, pp. 476–497.

Warner, W. Lloyd, Marchia Meeker, and Kenneth Eells, 1960, *Social Class in America: A Manual of Procedure for the Measurement of Social Status.* New York: Harper & Row, Publishers.

Webster's Unabridged Dictionary, 1973, *Webster's New Twentieth Century Dictionary of the English Language,* Unabridged, 2d ed. Cleveland and New York: The World Publishing Company.

Whiting, Beatrice B., 1950, *Paiute Sorcery.* Viking Fund Publications in Anthropology 15.

Whiting, John W. M., 1959, "Sorcery, Sin, and the Superego: A Cross-Cultural Study of Some Mechanisms of Social Control," in *Nebraska Symposium on Motivation: 1959*, ed. Marshall R. Jones. Lincoln: University of Nebraska Press, pp. 174–197.

————, 1964, "Effects of Climate on Certain Cultural Practices," in *Explorations in Cultural Anthropology*, ed. Ward H. Goodenough. New York: McGraw-Hill, Inc., pp. 511–544.

————, Richard Kluckhohn, and Albert Anthony, 1958, "The Function of Male Initiation Ceremonies at Puberty," in *Readings in Social Psychology*, 3rd ed., ed. E. E. Maccoby, T. M. Newcomb, and E. L. Hartley. New York: Holt, Rinehart and Winston, Inc., pp. 359–370.

Whiting, John W. M., and Barbara Ayres, 1968, "Inferences from the Shape of Dwellings," in *Settlement Archaeology*, ed. K. C. Chang. Palo Alto, Calif.: National Press Books, pp. 117–133.

Wolf, Eric R., 1966, *Peasants.* Englewood Cliffs, N.J.: Prentice-Hall, Inc.

Wright, Quincy, 1942, *A Study of War*, Vol. 1. Chicago: The University of Chicago Press.

Young, Frank W., 1965, *Initiation Ceremonies: A Cross-Cultural Study of Status Dramatization.* Indianapolis: The Bobbs-Merrill Company, Inc.

NAME AND TITLE INDEX

Adams, J., 99
Adams, R. N., 83, 89
African Political Systems (Fortes and Evans-Pritchard, 19
Andaman Islanders, The (Radcliffe-Brown), 6
Andros Islanders, The (Otterbein), 9, 13
Anthony, A., 176, 178, 186
Appell, G. N., 105
Arth, M. J., 180, 181
Ayers, B., 50

Baily, F. G., 19
Bales, R. F., 89
Barry, H., III, 190
Bartholomew, G. A., Jr., 44
"Basic Steps in Conducting a Cross-Cultural Study" (Otterbein), 210
Beals, A. R., 4
Beckerman, S., 45
Befu, H., 96
Birdsell, J. B., 44
Boas, F., 3, 4, 188–189, 190
Bohannan, P., 40, 68, 113, 122
Brown, J., 186
Buchler, I. R., 105
Burling, R., 25
Bush, R. R., 180, 181

Campbell, D. T., 123
Carneiro, R. L., 46
Carrasco, P., 78
Chagnon, N. A., 13, 23, 27, 31, 36, 43, 46, 49, 53, 57, 58, 63, 64, 81, 88, 103, 112, 117, 128, 132, 136, 140, 144–145, 148, 150, 160, 170, 175, 179, 183, 186, 188, 192
Chapple, E., 28, 40, 48, 164

Churchill, W. S., 33
Coon, C. S., 28, 40, 48, 164
Crowley, D., 27

Divale, W., 35

Edgerton, R. B., 8, 10
Eells, K., 69
Ember, M., 2, 3
Erickson, P., 45
Evans-Pritchard, E. E., 19, 131

Firth, R., 167
Fischer, J. L., 190
Fogelson, R. D., 174
Fortes, M., 19, 89, 131
Fox, R., 83
Frazer, J. G., 168
Freeman, J. D., 107
Fried, M. H., 35, 67, 136

Gamst, F. C., 13, 23, 31, 36, 44, 46, 49, 53, 54, 57, 59, 65, 66, 67, 70, 82, 88, 103–104, 107, 117, 128, 129, 133, 137, 141, 145–146, 150, 161–163, 165–166, 170–171, 175, 179, 188, 192
Golden Bough, The (Frazer), 168
Goodenough, W. H., 83, 95
Gough, K., 83
Gould, H. A., 68
Griffiths, D. F., 50
Gumperz, J. J., 24, 25

Haile Sellasie I, Emperor, 133, 151
Harris, M., 68
Hayes, R. Oldfield, 100
Hays, H. R., 190
Herskovits, M. J., 5

Hoebel, E. A., 19, 134, 135
Holmes. L. D., 19
Homans, G. C., 109
Honigmann, J. L., 164
Hymes, D., 24

Johannes IV, Emperor, 150

Kang, G. E., 110, 143
Kasdan, L., 32
Kluckhohn, R., 176, 178, 186

LaFlamme, A. G., 13
Lambert, W. W., 156
Langness, L. L., 8, 10
Law of Primitive Man, The (Hoebel), 19
League of the Iroquois (Morgan), 179
Lessa, W. A., 164
LeVine, R. A., 123
Lévi-Strauss, C., 109
Linton, R., 6, 47

Malinowski, B., 49, 83
Manual for Kinship Analysis (Schusky), 116
Mead, M., 20, 137
Meeker, M., 69
Menelik II, Emperor, 150
Métraux, R., 20
Mitchell, W. E., 105
Moore, H. E., 69
Morgan, L. H., 112, 179, 180, 182
Murdock, G. P., 6, 8, 18, 50, 76, 77, 78, 80, 85, 87, 89, 95, 112, 117

Naroll, R., 3, 7, 56, 126, 140
Needham, R., 109
Noland, S. Q., 111

Oliver, S. C., 34
Otterbein, C., 143, 156, 159, 210, 211
Otterbein, K., 2, 9, 13, 22, 26, 31, 33, 34, 36, 42, 46, 48, 49, 52, 53, 57, 58, 62, 63, 69, 70, 80, 85, 87, 93, 94, 98, 99, 102, 111, 116, 127, 128, 131, 132, 136, 138, 139, 140, 143, 144, 146, 148, 156, 159, 165, 167, 169, 174, 178, 187, 201, 202, 209, 210, 211
Our Primitive Contemporaries (Murdock), 19
Outline of Cultural Materials, 8

Parsons, T., 89
Plotnicov, L., 96
Polyanyi, K., 59
Pospisil, L., 105, 130, 135
Primitive Art (Boas), 188
Primitive Culture (Tylor), 157

Primitive Social Organization: An Evolutionary Perspective (Service), 61

Qemant, The: A Pagan-Hebraic Peasantry of Ethiopia (Gamst), 13

Radcliffe-Brown, A., 6, 112, 135
Rapoport, A., 50
Rappaport, R. A., 28
Redfield, R., 20, 155
Rites of Passage, The (van Gennep), 185
Rivers, W. H. R., 112
Roberts, J. M., 180, 181, 182

Sahlins, M. D., 28, 34, 59, 62
Saucier, J.-F., 177
Schapera, I., 127
Schneider, D. M., 109
Schusky, E. L., 116
Secoy, F. R., 35
Selby, H. A., 105
Service, E. R., 61, 78
Shaka, 131
Sipes, R. G., 180
Social Structure (Murdock), 76
Solien, N. L., 50
Southwick, C. H., 45
Spier, L., 117
Spiro, M. E., 109, 110
Stephens, W. N., 176, 178
Stevenson. R. F., 46
Stocking, G. W., Jr., 3
Study of Culture at a Distance, The (Mead and Métraux), 20
Sutton-Smith, B., 180, 181, 182
Swanson, G. E., 157–158

Triandis, L. M., 156
Tumin, M. M., 68
Tylor, E. B., 3, 76, 109, 110, 157, 179, 180

van Gennep, A., 185, 186
van Velsen, H. U. E. T., 142
van Wetering, W., 142
Vayda, A. P., 28, 33, 34, 45
Vogt, E. Z., 164

Warner, W. L., 69
Whiting, B. B., 50, 172
Whiting, J. W. M., 176, 177, 178, 186, 203
Wolf, E. R., 20
Wolf, M., 156
Wright, Q., 140

Yanomamö: The Fierce People (Chagnon), 13, 53
Young, F. W., 176, 184, 185, 186, 187

SUBJECT INDEX

Abyssinia, 128, 150–151
Abyssinians, 129
Agaw, 23, 27, 36, 129
Agriculture, 40, 41, 42, 44, 45
  slash-and-burn, 41, 43
Ambilineages, 96, 97–98, 100, 101, 104
Ambilocal residence, 77, 78, 79, 92
Amhara, 129, 161, 171
Analysis, 8–9, 14
Andaman Islanders, 6, 45
Andros Islanders, 2, 4, 5, 9, 10, 13, 22,
  144, 147, 150, 192; descent groups,
  102; division of labor, 48–49; economy, 62–63; history, 36; house form,
  52, 53; households, 94; kindreds, 106–
  107; kinship terminology, 116; language, 22, 26–27; magic and, 169–170;
  marital residence, 79, 80–81; marriage, 87, 111–112; people, 22; physical environment, 31; political system,
  127–128; population density, 46; post-
  partum sex taboo, 178; religious
  practitioners, 165; settlement pattern,
  58; settlement size, 57; sorcery and,
  174; stratification system, 69–70; subsistence technology, 42–43; supernatural beings and, 159–160; transition
  from childhood to adulthood, 187
Animal husbandry, 40–41, 42, 45
Animism, 157
Anthropological research, 8–12
Anthropology, concepts (basic), 2–7,
  12; cultural, 1, 2, 12
Apartments, 51, 52
Art, 188–192
Authorities (see Political leaders)
Avunculocal residence, 77, 79, 80, 91

Bahamas, 2, 9, 10, 13, 22, 27, 31, 52, 62,
  102, 127–128, 132, 136, 140, 209
  See also Andros Islanders
Bands, 61
Behavior, ideal versus real, 75–76, 80
Belief system, 4, 5–6
Bilateral cross-cousin marriage, 111
Bilingual cultures, 24, 26, 27
Bilingualism, 123
Bilocal residence, 77
Boreal forests, 29–30

Castes, 68, 69
Castration anxiety, 178
Ceremonial tasks, 7
Ceremonies, 164; initiation, 184–188
Chiefdoms, 61
Chiefs, 19, 61, 131, 132, 133, 134, 142,
  148, 172
Cities, 55, 56
Clans, 101, 103, 123, 127; Qemant, 104
Classes, 68, 69
Commonlocal residence, 78, 79, 80, 81,
  82, 83, 89
Communities, 6; peasant, 20, 67, 68, 70;
  political, 6–7, 18, 19, 20, 21, 22, 23,
  25–26, 49, 69, 122–151, 172; speech,
  24–26
Comparative research, 11–12
Comparison, controlled, 12, 208–209
Compounds, 51, 52, 53, 54
Concepts, basic, anthropological, 2–7,
  12
Concubinage, 88
Controlled comparison, 12, 208–209
Cosmopolitanism, 56
Cousin marriage, 108–112, 143

"Creale" languages, 25, 27
Cross-cousin marriage, 108–112; matrilateral, 108–110, 111, 112; patrilateral, 108, 109–110, 111, 112
Cross-cultural studies, 12, 35, 50, 110, 209
Crow kinship terminology, 114
Cultivation, shifting, 41, 42, 43
Cultural system, 4–5, 17, 33–34
Culture(s), 4, 6, 18–19, 21, 22, 24; bilingual, 24, 26, 27; comparison of, 197–203; components of, 122; concept of, 2–6; criteria of, 2, 18, 21, 22, 23; definitions of, 3; monolingual, 24, 26; multilingual, 24, 25, 26, 27; physical environment of, 27–32; primitive, 18–19, 22, 24, 33; summary analysis of (Table), 199–200
Culture change, 10, 11
Culture traits, 5–6, 10, 11, 12, 13, 14, 34; comparison of, 197–203; linkages between, 203–206

Data sheet, 13–14, 21, 35, 69
Dependent native peoples, 19–20, 67, 68
Descent, double, 101; multilineal, 96, 98, 99, 100, 102; rules of, 95–98
Descent groups, 95–104; Andros Islanders, 102; defined, 95; endogamous, 110; exogamous, 108; Qemant, 103–104; unrestricted, 96, 98–99, 100, 101, 102; Yanomamö Indians, 102–103
    See also Ambilineages; Clans; Lineages; Matrilineages; Moieties; Patrilineages; Phratries
Deserts, 28, 31, 49; polar, 30
Dialects, German-Dutch, 2–3
Dictators, 19, 131, 132, 134, 142, 148
Diffusion, 203
Diplomacy, 122, 123
Districts, 125, 127, 131
Divination, 164
Division of labor (see Labor, division of)
Domestic groups, 51, 52, 89, 90
Double descent, 101
Dry lands, 28
Dual organization, 103
Duolocal residence, 82, 83
Dwellings (see House form)

Economic system, 4, 5, 39
Economic tasks, 7
Economics, definition of, 121
Economy, 59–67; Andros Islanders, 62–63; Qemant, 65–67; Yanomamö Indians, 63–64
Ego, 104–106

Encapsulation, 19, 34
Endogamy, 110–111
Environment (see Physical environment)
Environmental possiblism, 27, 50
Eskimo kinship terminology, 113, 116, 117
Ethiopia, 128–129, 133, 137, 141, 148, 150–151
Ethnic groups, 21, 67, 70
Ethnographers, 9–10, 18, 19, 20, 21, 32, 35, 51, 75–76, 78, 79, 86, 93, 106
Ethnographic present, 19–20, 21, 35, 127
Ethnographic research, 12
Ethnographies, 9–14, 18, 20, 21–22, 23, 28, 30, 32, 35, 46, 57, 78, 79, 93, 111, 211; focused, 9, 10; general, 9–10
Ethnohistorical studies, 20
Ethnolineal descent rule, 100
Ethnology, 12
Evolution, specific, 34
Exogamy, 108–110, 143
Explorers, reports of, 20
Expressive roles, 89

Family, 76; nuclear, 11, 89, 90
Feudal system, 70
Feuding, 137, 141–146, 210; Yanomamö Indians, 144–145;
Field research, 8–12, 33
Fieldwork, 8, 10, 13, 18, 20, 22, 23, 27, 35
Filiation, 95–100
First cousin marriage (see Cousin marriage)
Fishing, 40, 42, 43
Fissioning, 144–145
Force, 134
Forests, boreal, 29–30; Mediterranean scrub, 29; rain, 28; semideciduous, 28; temperate, 29, 31; tropical, 28–29, 31
Fraternal interest groups, 142–143, 146
Fraternal polyandry, 85, 88

Gambling, 180
Games, 179–184, classification of, 180
Ganda, 19
Gathering, 40, 42, 45
Genealogy, Adams', 99–100
Generation property, 102
Geographic separation, 2, 3, 21, 22, 23
Gods, 156–163
Grasslands, 29, 31
Group marriage, 84
Groups, 21; descent, 95–104; domestic, 51, 52, 89, 90; ethnic, 21, 67, 70; fraternal interest, 142–143, 146; kinship,

86; local, 6, 8, 9, 11, 17, 18, 21, 22, 24, 39, 41, 51, 52, 54, 55, 57, 64, 65, 122–123, 125, 127, 131, 133, 135; marital, 83–90; polyandry-polygyny, 85

Hamlets, 55, 56
Hawaiian kinship terminology, 113
Headmen, 19, 131, 132, 134, 136, 142, 148, 172
Hekura, 170
History, 32–36; Andros Islanders, 36; Qemant, 36; Yanomamö Indians, 36
Homesteads, 53–54; dispersed, 55, 56, 58, 59
Horse, 5
Horticulture, 40, 41, 42, 43, 45, 55
House form, 39, 49–54; Andros Islanders, 52, 53; physical environment and, 49; Qemant, 53–54; Yanomamö Indians, 53
Households, 50–52, 77, 78; Andros Islanders, 94; defined, 50, 88; extended family, 91–92; fraternal joint family, 93; functions of, 89; independent nuclear family, 90, 94, 95; independent polygamous family, 91, 95; mother-child (female headed), 93; Qemant, 95; stem family, 92–93; types of, 88–95; Yanomamö Indians, 95
Hunting, 40, 42, 45
Hypotheses, 12, 205–206; testing of, 206–211

Ice caps, permanent, 30
Incest taboo, 112
Index of Status Characteristics, 69
Indians, American, 5, 34–35, 100, 114–115
    See also Iroquois Indians; Yanomamö Indians
Industrial revolution, 41, 68
Industrialism, 40–41, 42, 45
Informants, 8, 10, 20, 26, 75–76
Initiation rites, 184–188; Yanomamö Indians, 187–188
Instrumental roles, 89
Interviewing, 8, 75
Iroquois Indians, 179; kinship terminology, 114, 117

Jamaica, 209

Kindreds, 99, 102, 104; Andros Islanders, 106–107; Qemant, 107–108
Kings, 19, 52, 131, 132, 133, 134, 142, 148
Kinship, 76, 95, 121–122
Kinship groups, 86
Kinship terminology, 112–117; Andros

Islanders, 116; Qemant, 117; Yanomamö Indians, 117

Labor, division of, 39, 47–49, 88; Andros Islanders, 48–49; Qemant, 49; Yanomamö Indians, 49
Language, 17, 18, 21, 24–27; Andros Islanders, 22, 26–27; "Creole," 25, 27; pidgin, 25, 27; Qemant, 23, 27; trade, 25, 26, 27; Yanomamö Indians, 23, 27
Language distinctness, 2, 18, 22, 23
Law, 123, 134–137; civil, 134; criminal, 135; primitive, 134, 135; of private delicts, 134, 135, 136, 137; of public delicts, 135, 136, 137
Leaders (see Political leaders)
Legal system, 122, 133–137, 172
Levirate, 85–86
Life cycles, 155–156
Linkages, 203–206
    See also Ambilineages; Matrilineages; Patrilineages
Lineages, 100–101, 127
Linguistic continuums, 2–3
Linguistic distinctness (see Language distinctness)
Local groups, 6, 8, 9, 11, 17, 18, 21, 22, 24, 39, 41, 51, 52, 54, 55, 57, 64, 65, 122–123, 125–127, 131, 133, 135
Long Bay Cays, 9, 22, 42, 53, 57, 58, 62, 63, 69, 79, 80–81, 87, 102, 111
Long houses, 51, 52

Magic, 164, 166–171, 172, 174, 175; Andros Islanders and, 169–170; black, 159, 167, 171, 174; contagious, 168–171, 172; homeopathic, 168–171; Qemant and, 170–171; Yanomamö Indians and, 170
Manufacturing (see Industrialism)
Maori, 33
Marital groups, 83–90
Market exchange, 59, 60–61, 62, 65
Marquesan Islanders, 85
Marriage, 83–88, 188; absence of, 87; Andros Islanders, 87, 111–112; cousin, 108–112, 143; definition of, 83; group, 84; Qemant, 88, 112; Yanomamö Indians, 88, 112
Maternal dyad, 89
Mating system, 87–88
Matrilineages, 96, 97, 101, 109
Matrilocal residence, 35, 76, 77, 79, 80, 81, 82, 83, 91
Matri-patrilocal residence, 76, 77, 79, 80, 82
Medicine men, 164
Mediterranean scrub forests, 29

Menstrual taboos, 178
Migration, 32–36, 54
Military organizations, 137–141, 142, 146–151; Yanomamö Indians, 140–141
Missionaries, reports of, 20
Moieties, 101, 102, 103, 104
Money, general purpose, 60–61, 62; limited purpose, 60
Monogamy, 83–88, 89
Monolingual cultures, 24, 26
Monotheism, 159
Mountains, 30, 31
Multilineal descent, 96, 98, 99, 100, 102
Multilingual cultures, 24, 25, 26, 27

Nations, modern, 18, 20–21, 22, 67
Neolocal residence, 77, 78, 79, 80, 81, 89
New Guinea, 127
New Zealand, 33, 34
Nomadic settlement pattern, 54, 55, 56

Observation, 8, 10, 76
Oedipus complex, 177
Omaha kinship terminology, 115
Ostracism, 137

Parallel-cousin marriage, 108, 110–111
Paranoia, 178
Patrilineages, 96–97, 99, 101, 102–103, 109
Patrilocal residence, 35, 76–77, 79, 81, 82, 83, 91
Peasant communities, 20, 67, 68, 70
Penal sanctions, 134–135, 136, 137
People, 18–23; Andros Islanders, 22; Qemant, 23; Yanomamö Indians, 22–23
Phratries, 101, 123, 127
Physical environment, 27–32, 39, 40; Andros Islanders, 31; house form and, 49; Qemant, 31–32; types of, 28–30; Yanomamö Indians, 31
Pidgin language, 25, 27
Plow, 41
Polar deserts, 30
Polar lands, 30, 49
Political communities, 6–7, 18, 19, 20, 21, 22, 23, 25–26, 49, 69, 122–151, 172
Political leaders, 7, 19, 62, 122, 123, 125, 126, 129–135, 137, 142, 143, 148–149, 172; Andros Islanders, 132; Qemant, 133; Yanomamö Indians, 132
Political systems, 4, 5, 19, 121–129; Andros Islanders, 127–128; Qemant, 128–129; Yanomamö Indians, 128
Political tasks, 7
Polyandry, 83–87, 90; fraternal, 85, 88
Polyandry-polygyny group, 85
Polygamy, 84

Polygyny, 83–88, 90, 142; general, 87, 88, 176, 177; limited, 86, 87; sororal, 85
Polynesians, 33, 34
Polytheism, 159
Population density, 39, 44–46; Andros Islanders, 46; Qemant, 46; subsistence technology and, 44–45; Yanomamö Indians, 46
Post-partum sex taboo, 176–179, 186, 203; Andros Islanders, 178; Qemant, 179; Yanomamö Indians, 179
Power, economic, 121; political, 121
Priests, 163–166
Primitive cultures, 18–19, 22, 24, 33
Primitive states, 19, 20, 68
Property, generation, 102
Provinces, 125, 127, 131

Qemant, 2, 5, 13, 145–146; clans, 103–104; descent groups, 103–104; division of labor, 49; economy, 65–67; history, 36; house form, 53–54; households, 95; kindreds, 107–108; kinship terminology, 117; language, 23, 27; legal system, 137; magic and, 170–171; marital residence, 82; marriage, 88, 112; people, 23; physical environment, 31–32; political leaders, 133; political system, 128–129; population density, 46; post-partum sex taboo, 179; religious practitioners, 165–166; settlement pattern, 59; settlement size, 57–58; sorcery and, 175; stratification system, 70; subsistence technology, 44; supernatural beings and, 161–163

Race relations, 125
Rain forests, 28
Ramages (see Ambilineages)
Rank, 67
Reciprocity, 59–60, 61, 62; balanced, 60, 62, 63, 64; generalized, 60, 62, 63, 66
Recreational activities, 180
Redistribution, 59, 60, 61, 62, 66–67
Religion, 156–166
Religious practitioners, 163–166; Andros Islanders, 165; Qemant, 165–166; Yanomamö Indians, 165
Research, anthropological, 8–12; comparative, 11–12; ethnographic, 12; field, 8–12, 33
Residence, 76–83; ambilocal, 77, 78, 79, 92; Andros Islanders, 79, 80–81; avunculocal, 77, 79, 80, 91; bilocal, 77; commonlocal, 78, 79, 80, 81, 82, 83, 89; duolocal, 82, 83; marital, 76–83; matrilocal, 35, 76, 77, 79, 80, 81, 82, 83, 91; matri-patrilocal, 76, 77, 79, 80,

82; neolocal, 77, 78, 79, 80, 81, 89; patrilocal, 35, 76–77, 79, 81, 82, 83, 91; Qemant, 82; uxorilocal, 77–78, 79, 80, 81, 89; virilocal, 77, 78, 79, 80, 81, 82, 83, 89; Yanomamö Indians, 81–82
Restitutive sanctions, 134, 135, 137
Rites, initiation, 184–188; of intensification, 164
Rituals, 164
Roles, expressive, 89; instrumental, 89

Semideciduous forests, 28
Seminomadic settlement pattern, 54, 55, 56
Settlement pattern, 39, 54–56, 58–59; Andros Islanders, 58; Qemant, 59; Yanomamö Indians, 58–59
Settlement size, 39, 56–59; Andros Islanders, 57; Qemant, 57–58; Yanomamö Indians, 57
Sexual anxiety, 177, 178
Shamans, 163–166, 170, 172
Shifting cultivation, 41, 42, 43
Slash-and-burn agriculture, 41, 43
Slavery, 68–69
Social class (see Classes)
Social systems, 4, 5, 35
Socialization, 89
Societies, 4; rank, 67; stateless, 19; stratified, 67
Sociocultural system, 4
Sorcery, 164, 171–175, 178; Andros Islanders and, 174; Qemant and, 175; Yanomamö Indians and, 175
Sororal polygyny, 85
Sororate, 85, 86
Specialists, 47–49, 56; full-time, 48, 49, 158, 163, 165; part-time, 48, 49, 158, 163, 165
Specific evolution, 34
Speech communities, 24–26
Spell, magic, 167, 171
Spirits, 156–163, 172
States, 18, 19, 67, 131, 148; modern, 18, 20–21, 22; pre-industrial, 19; primitive, 19, 20, 68
Stratification, 67–70, 100; Andros Islanders, 69–70; Qemant, 70
Subcultures, 21, 26, 67, 68
Subsistence technology, 39, 40–44; Andros Islanders, 42–43; defined, 40; population density and, 44–45; Qemant, 44; Yanomamö Indians, 43–44
Subsystems, 4–6, 10, 17
Sudanese kinship terminology, 114
Supernatural beings, 156–163, 172, 174; Andros Islanders and, 159–160; Qemant and, 161–163; Yanomamö Indians and, 160–161

Surveys, cross-cultural, 12, 35, 50, 110, 209

Taboos, incest, 112; menstrual, 178; post-partum sex, 176–179
Tasks, ceremonial, 7; economic, 7; political, 7
Tattooing, 188, 192
Technology (see Subsistence technology)
Tegre, 129
Temperate forests, 29, 31
Tepoztlan, Mexico, 20
Towns, 55, 56
Trade, 123
Trade languages, 25, 26, 27
Tribes, 61, 110
Tropical forests, 28–29, 31
Trouble cases, 134–136, 143
Tundra, 30

Unrestricted descent group, 96, 98–99, 100, 101, 102
Urbanization, 56
Uxorilocal residence, 77–78, 79, 80, 81, 89

Villages, 55, 56, 57, 58
Virilocal residence, 77, 78, 79, 80, 81, 82, 83, 89

War, 122, 123, 137–151; causes of, 148–151; external, 138, 146; internal, 138, 146–147; migration and, 33–35; Yanomamö Indians and, 147–148, 150
Witchcraft, 173–174, 175
Witches, 173, 175
World view, 155–156

Yanomamö Indians, 2, 5, 10, 13, 136–137; art, 192; descent groups, 102–103; division of labor, 49; economy, 63–64; feuding, 144–145; history, 36; house form, 53; households, 95; initiation rites, 187–188; kinship terminology, 117; language, 23, 27; magic and, 170; marriage, 88, 112; military organizations, 140–141; people, 22–23; physical environment, 31; political leaders, 132; political system, 128; population density, 46; post-partum sex taboo, 179; religious practitioners, 165; residence, 81–82; settlement pattern, 58–59; settlement size, 57; sorcery and, 175; subsistence technology, 43–44; supernatural beings and, 160–161; warfare, 147–148, 150

Zulus, 131

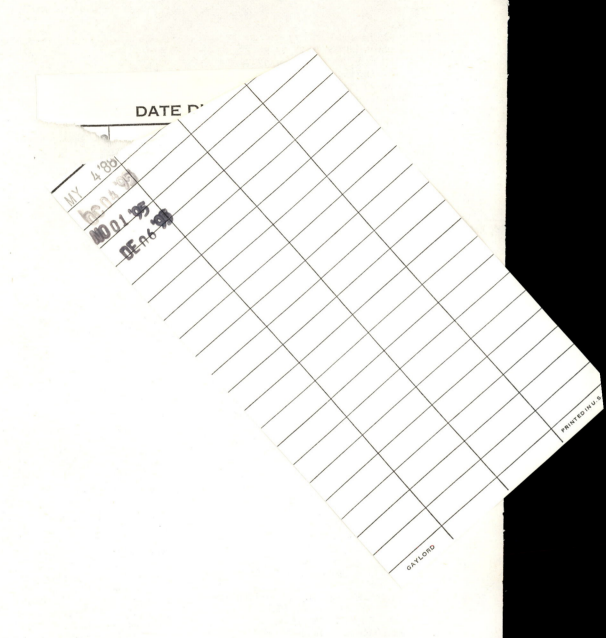